THIS IS BUSINESS ETHICS

THIS IS PHILOSOPHY
Series editor: Steven D. Hales

Reading philosophy can be like trying to ride a bucking bronco—you hold on for dear life while "transcendental deduction" twists you to one side, "causa sui" throws you to the other, and a 300-word, 300-year-old sentence comes down on you like an iron-shod hoof the size of a dinner plate. *This Is Philosophy* is the riding academy that solves these problems. Each book in the series is written by an expert who knows how to gently guide students into the subject regardless of the reader's ability or previous level of knowledge. Their reader-friendly prose is designed to help students find their way into the fascinating, challenging ideas that compose philosophy without simply sticking the hapless novice on the back of the bronco, as so many texts do. All the books in the series provide ample pedagogical aids, including links to free online primary sources. When students are ready to take the next step in their philosophical education, *This Is Philosophy* is right there with them to help them along the way.

This Is Philosophy: An Introduction
Steven D. Hales

This Is Philosophy of Mind: An Introduction
Pete Mandik

This Is Ethics: An Introduction
Jussi Suikkanen

This Is Political Philosophy: An Introduction
Alex Tuckness and Clark Wolf

This Is Business Ethics: An Introduction
Tobey Scharding

Forthcoming:

This is Early Modern Philosophy
Kurt Smith

This Is Environmental Ethics
Wendy Lee

This is Epistemology
Clayton Littlejohn and Adam Carter

This is Metaphysics
Kris McDaniel

This Is Bioethics: An Introduction
Udo Schuklenk

THIS IS BUSINESS ETHICS

AN INTRODUCTION

TOBEY SCHARDING

WILEY Blackwell

This edition first published 2018
© 2018 John Wiley & Sons, Inc.

The right of Tobey Scharding to be identified as the author of this work has been
asserted in accordance with law.

Registered Office
John Wiley & Sons, Inc., 111 River Street, Hoboken, NJ 07030, USA

Editorial Office
9600 Garsington Road, Oxford, OX4 2DQ, UK

For details of our global editorial offices, customer services, and more information
about Wiley products visit us at www.wiley.com.

Wiley also publishes its books in a variety of electronic formats and by print-on-
demand. Some content that appears in standard print versions of this book may not be
available in other formats.

Library of Congress Cataloging-in-Publication data applied for

Hardback ISBN: 9781119055051
Paperback ISBN: 9781119055044

Cover design by Wiley

Set in 10.5/13pt Minion by SPi Global, Pondicherry, India

Printed in the United States of America

10 9 8 7 6 5 4 3 2 1

BRIEF CONTENTS

Preface   xii

Part I   Problems in Business Ethics   1

1   Ethics: Doing the Right Thing   3
2   Business: Maximizing Profit   14
3   Classic Business Ethics Dilemmas: When Doing the
    Right Thing Does Not Maximize Profits   32

Part II   Tools to Solve Business Ethics Dilemmas   47

4   Ethical Theories   49
5   Theories of Corporate Personhood   77
6   Theories of Political Economy   92

Part III   Contemporary Case Studies   119

7   Business Ethics in Employment   121
8   Business Ethics in Advertising   149
9   Business Ethics in the Financial Sector   167
10   Business Ethics in the Environment   190
11   Business Ethics in Globalization   210

Part IV   The Future of Business Ethics   229

12   Predicting and Preventing Future Business Ethics Scandals   231

Index   247

CONTENTS

Preface   xii

Part I Problems in Business Ethics   1

1 Ethics: Doing the Right Thing   3
   Introduction to Ethics   3
      What are ethical questions   3
      How to answer ethical questions   4
   Introductory Case Studies   5
      Sam and the substandard notes   5
      Casey and the overly-demanding internship   6
      Tatiana and the fair distribution of chores   7
      Alex and the too-easy-to-cheat course   8
   Evaluating the Case Studies   9
      Non-ethical guidelines for thinking about the cases   9
      Ethical guidelines for thinking about the cases   11
      Limitations of ethical evaluation: the problem of controversy   12
   Reference   13

2 Business: Maximizing Profit   14
   Theory of the Firm   14
      Firm organization   15
      Why the firm exists at all   16
      Problems for firm organization   17
   Business Decision-Making: Shareholders and Cost-Benefit Analysis   17
      The Dominant Model   19
      Shareholder Theory   22
      Cost-benefit analysis   25

Contents   vii

Business in Society: Consumers, Employees, and Community   27
References and Further Reading   31

3   Classic Business Ethics Dilemmas: When Doing the
     Right Thing Does Not Maximize Profits   32
     Doing Right by Consumers: The Ford Pinto Case   33
     Doing Right by Employees: The Walmart Case   38
     Doing Right by the Community: The B.P. Case   40
     Doing Right by Shareholders: The Enron Case   42
     References and Further Reading   46
     Case Cited   46

Part II   Tools to Solve Business Ethics Dilemmas   47

4   Ethical Theories   49
     The Three Major Ethical Theories   51
        Utility-based ethics   52
        Kant's duty-based ethics   61
        Aristotle's virtue-based ethics   67
     Other Bases for Ethics   72
        Natural law theory   72
        Contract theory   73
        Ethics of care   74
        Feminist ethics   75
     References and Further Reading   76

5   Theories of Corporate Personhood   77
     Businesses as Ethical Persons   78
     Businesses as Bureaucracies   83
     Businesses as Collective Persons   87
     References and Further Reading   91

6   Theories of Political Economy   92
     Private Property   95
        The justification of private property   96
        Distributive justice   106
     The Division of Labor   112
        Smith's productivity-based defense of the division   112
        Marx's alienation-based criticism of the division   115
     References and Further Reading   118

Part III Contemporary Case Studies 119

7 Business Ethics in Employment 121
Employment at Will: The Bechtel Case 121
  Bechtel's corporate identity 122
  Facts of the case 122
  What happened 124
  Historical significance 124
  Ethical significance: conditions of employment 125
Executive Compensation: The A.I.G. Case 130
  A.I.G.'s corporate identity 131
  Facts of the case 131
  What happened 133
  Historical significance 133
  Ethical significance: executive compensation 134
Preventing Discrimination and Achieving Diversity:
The Google Case 136
  Google's corporate identity 137
  Facts of the case 138
  What happened 139
  Ethical significance: unconscious bias 141
Work-Life Balance: The Amazon Case 143
  Amazon's corporate identity 144
  Facts of the case 144
  What happened 145
  Historical significance 146
  Ethical significance: work-life balance 146
References and Further Reading 147
Case Cited 148

8 Business Ethics in Advertising 149
Manipulative Advertising: The Four Loko Case 149
  Phusion Projects' corporate identity 150
  Facts of the case 150
  What happened 151
  Historical significance 152
  Ethical significance: manipulative advertising 152
Targeted Advertising: The Facebook Case 155
  Facebook's corporate identity 156
  Facts of the case 156

What happened 157
Historical significance 157
Ethical significance: targeted advertising 158
The Dependence Effect: The Lipitor Case 158
Pfizer's corporate identity 159
Facts of the case 159
What happened 160
Historical significance 160
Ethical significance: the dependence effect 161
Discriminatory Advertising: The Abercrombie & Fitch Case 161
Abercrombie & Fitch's corporate identity 162
Facts of the case 163
What happened 163
Historical significance 164
Ethical significance: discriminatory advertising 164
References and Further Reading 165

9   Business Ethics in the Financial Sector 167
Predatory Lending: The Countrywide Financial Case 167
Countrywide Financial's corporate identity 168
Facts of the case 168
What happened 170
Historical significance 171
Ethical significance: predatory lending 171
Investment Risk: The Lehman Brothers Case 172
Lehman Brothers' corporate identity 173
Facts of the case 175
What happened 176
Historical significance 176
Ethical significance: investment risk 176
Short Selling: The Herbalife Case 178
Herbalife's corporate identity 179
Pershing Square Capital Management's corporate identity 179
Facts of the case 180
What happened 181
Historical significance 182
Ethical significance: short selling 182
Insider Trading: The Nomura Case 184
Nomura's corporate identity 184
Facts of the case 185

What happened   186
Historical significance   186
Ethical significance: insider trading   186
References and Further Reading   187

10   Business Ethics in the Environment   190
Water Supply: The Coca-Cola India Case   190
Coca-Cola India's corporate identity   191
Facts of the case   191
What happened   192
Historical significance   193
Ethical significance: tragedy of the commons   193
Indigenous Populations: The TransCanada Case   194
TransCanada's corporate identity   194
Facts of the case   195
What happened   196
Historical significance   196
Ethical significance: indigenous populations   197
Food Supply: The FieldScripts Case   198
Monsanto's corporate identity   199
Facts of the case   199
What happened   201
Historical significance   202
Ethical significance: data privacy and trust in business   202
Emissions: The VW Case   203
VW's corporate identity   204
Facts of the case   205
What happened   206
Historical significance   207
Ethical significance: emissions   207
References and Further Reading   208

11   Business Ethics in Globalization   210
Obtaining Raw Materials: The GlaxoSmithKline Case   210
GlaxoSmithKline's corporate identity   211
Facts of the case   211
What happened   213
Historical significance   214
Ethical significance: raw materials   214

Child Labor: The Victoria's Secret Case   214
   Victoria's Secret's corporate identity   215
   Facts of the case   215
   What happened   217
   Historical significance   217
   Ethical significance: child labor   218
Different Cultures: The Yahoo! Case   218
   Yahoo's corporate identity   219
   Facts of the case   219
   What happened   220
   Historical significance   221
   Ethical significance: repressive political regimes   221
Doing Business with Corrupt Regimes: The IKEA Case   222
   IKEA's corporate identity   222
   Facts of the case   223
   What happened   223
   Historical significance   224
   Ethical significance: bribery   224
   References and Further Reading   225

Part IV   The Future of Business Ethics   **229**

12   Predicting and Preventing Future Business Ethics Scandals   **231**
Resolving Conflicts in Ethics   232
   What kind of a person do you want to be   234
   What kind of world do you want to live in   238
Looking for and Understanding New Cases   240
   Patterns of wrongdoing   240
   Key values for business   244
Technology and the Future of Business Ethics   245

Index   **247**

PREFACE

A company learns that one of its products has a safety flaw, which makes it seriously dangerous to consumers. A large number of these products have already been manufactured, and it will be expensive for the company to repair the products. The company calculates that it would cost them more to repair the safety flaw than to compensate the people who will be injured by it. What should they do?

Another company operates in areas with weak labor markets, in which there are always many workers who are desperate to earn money. The company pays its employees very low wages, denies them employment benefits, such as paid sick leave and health insurance, and requires them to work very hard. Although the workers are miserable, the company's owners earn huge profits. What should they do?

A third company does business in an environmentally fragile part of the world. Part of its business has the potential to create a large amount of pollution if an accident occurs. In an attempt to lower costs, the company reduces its safety standards to protect against the potential pollution. An accident occurs and the pollution escapes, devastating the fragile environment around it. What should the company do?

A finance company is very optimistic about its business initiatives' potentials to earn high profits. It is so confident about the potential for profit that it credits those profits to its ledger right away: as soon as the business executives come up with their great ideas. This exposes the business owners to great risk if those profits fail to come through. But the executives are very confident about their ideas. What should they do?

In each of these cases, companies face decisions about what is *the right thing* to do. For some of the cases, you may have an idea about what the company should do. (Sometimes we think of these internal ideas as our *conscience* talking to us; ethicists also call these inner thoughts *intuitions*.)

But how do you know if your idea is the right one? What if one of your friends, or the CEO of the company, has a different idea about what is the right thing to do? The point of business ethics is to solve, or work on solving, dilemmas like these. Business ethics offers distinctive decision-making strategies to recommend what the business should do in problematic circumstances. These decision-making strategies also provide reasons that it is the *right* thing for the business to do what the decision-making strategy recommends.

Students come to business ethics from a variety of perspectives. Some are concerned about unethical practices in the business community. Some are philosophy majors who want to understand how to apply philosophy to concerns that arise in their daily life. Others are business students who want to learn how to run their businesses more ethically or avoid scandals. All of these are good reasons to study business ethics. Students bring different intuitions about right and wrong to their studies. Their diverse perspectives enhance everyone's experiences by allowing students to argue with one another (in a respectful and friendly way) about the various actions they think the businesses should take.

The curriculum included in this book is designed to navigate through students' diverse standpoints. The aim is for you to be able to use business ethics to do at least two things: (1) make recommendations about what it is ethical for businesses to do; and (2) convince others (or try to convince them) that your recommendations are the right ones. But there is work to be done before we can start recommending. In particular, we must first understand: (1) how ethics makes its recommendations about what is the right thing to do; and (2) how business make decisions as businesses. These topics are the subjects of our first two chapters. To complete Part I of the book, "Problems in Business Ethics," we examine four classic business ethics case studies. These case studies, included in Chapter 3, are the kinds of cases people will expect you to be familiar with when they know that you have taken a business ethics class. The case studies also help to set the stage for the 20 case studies that we will examine in Chapters 7–11.

Before getting there, though, we must lay some additional groundwork. We do this in Part II of the book, "Tools to Solve Business Ethics Dilemmas," including Chapters 4–6. In Chapter 4, we offer an overview of some of the most powerful decision-making strategies available in ethics. These decision-making strategies, known as ethical theories, will help you to figure out what is the ethical thing to do in any circumstance that you face. We cover three major ethical theories in Chapter 4, along with four other ethical theories that capture important ethical values (though they are not as widely used as the three major theories). In Chapter 5, we address some important theories of political economy. These theories draw out some especially difficult aspects of business ethics controversies, so that we can address them more adeptly. We also address several theories about business organization for the same reason: to isolate important concepts and problems in business that will help us to evaluate business ethical controversies. Theories of business organization are covered in Chapter 6.

Then, we move on to Part III, "Contemporary Case Studies," to five kinds of business ethics controversies, related to employment (Chapter 7), advertising (Chapter 8), finance (Chapter 9), the environment (Chapter 10), and globalization (Chapter 11). We examine four cases related to each topic. These cases are more cutting-edge than the foundational cases examined in Chapter 3. Many relate to some of the most prominent companies doing business in the first quarter of the twenty-first century. Many of them have occurred recently and are ongoing. Because they have not yet been resolved, they are not yet as classic as the case studies included in Chapter 3. So there is more work to do on these cases and an opportunity for you to play a role.

In our final chapter, Chapter 12 in Part IV, "Predicting and Preventing Business Ethics Scandals," we reflect on some of the best ways for you to get involved with business ethics in your own life and in the future.

Part I
PROBLEMS IN BUSINESS ETHICS

1

ETHICS
DOING THE RIGHT THING

Introduction to Ethics

Ethics is a discipline that answers certain kinds of questions. Unlike science, 1.1
which answers questions about what is true of the world—how fast does
light move? What does one atom of Beryllium weigh?—ethical questions
concern right and wrong, good and bad. We begin by addressing the kinds
of questions ethics asks and what makes people able—and required—to
answer ethical questions.

What are ethical questions?

Ethics asks what action it is right (or wrong) to take, what kind of person it 1.2
is right (or wrong) to be, and in what kind of a world it is right (or wrong)
to live. Although we could certainly try to answer those three questions
abstractly, often the particular circumstances in which we find ourselves
will raise the questions for us. For example, we might consider doing an
action but worry that the action is wrong (or feel that it is right, even though
others disagree). We might observe that a public figure, or a family member
or a friend, seems like a good (or a bad) person. We might feel, based on a
particular event, that our world is good or bad. Ethical questions can arise
in many different circumstances, even those that seem quite ordinary. We
will examine some ordinary circumstances in which ethical questions arise
later in this chapter.

This is Business Ethics: An Introduction, First Edition. Tobey Scharding.
© 2018 John Wiley & Sons, Inc. Published 2018 by John Wiley & Sons, Inc.

1.3   Often people's awareness that they face an ethical question starts with a vague sense that something seems amiss. These vague senses are *intuitions*: natural sentiments that inform us about what is right or wrong, good or bad. These intuitions are also called people's *consciences*.

1.4   If human beings have a natural sense of what is right and wrong, good and bad, it might seem like there is not much for a course in business ethics to do. To know what is ethical in a business context, all students need to do, perhaps, is immerse themselves in the business world: once they are there, their consciences will naturally guide them toward right and good behavior.

1.5   Indeed, students will often rely on their internal senses of right and wrong to recognize the ethical questions that confront them. But you can improve your ethical judgment by studying ethics. By reflecting on various case studies, you will learn to recognize the most important aspects of ethical challenges. The ethical theories we will study in Chapter 4, in turn, will highlight different kinds of ethical values, making them easier to recognize in the situations you confront. After we examine our first set of case studies later in this chapter, we will consider some characteristics that generally characterize ethical questions.

How to answer ethical questions?

1.6   Recognizing that an ethical questions is present is only one of the challenges associated with ethics. We also need to *answer* ethical questions. In order to figure out how to answer ethical questions, it is helpful to spend a little time thinking about what allows human beings to answer ethical questions in the first place.

1.7   The most important capacity that helps human beings to answer ethical questions is probably their consciences, as discussed above. A famous philosopher of ethics, Immanuel Kant, once said "Two things overwhelm the mind with constantly new and increasing admiration and awe the more frequently and intently they are reflected upon: the starry heavens above me and the moral law within me." For Kant, conscience was a "moral law within." Kant did not think that having a conscience was the end of ethics, however. He set out a detailed decision-making procedure to help people answer ethical questions. We will study his views about how to decide what is the right thing to do, what is the right kind of person to be, and in what kind of world it is right to live, in Chapter 4.

1.8   The second most important capacity is the human capacity to make choices: surveying a range of possible actions and deciding which action they will do. (This capacity might be even more important than consciences.

Whereas consciences give us a *sense* of what is right and wrong, being able to make choices is what allows us actually to *do* the right thing, not just have a sense of what it might be.) Another important capacity is the capacity to experience benefits and harms, to the extent that these capacities influence the way we answer questions about what to do, what kind of a person to be, and what kind of a world in which to live.

Of these capacities, though, it is probably people's consciences that most 1.9 hold them to meet ethical standards. Even when it is inconvenient, consciences point people toward the right thing to do and will not let them rest until they have met that standard.

Introductory Case Studies

Now that we have looked into what ethical questions are, and what makes 1.10 human beings able (and required) to answer ethical questions, it is time to start making some real ethical recommendations. College students face decisions about what to do every day, including:

- May I loan my classmate substandard notes?
- If I believe that my friend is being exploited in an unpaid internship, should I encourage my friend to quit?
- May I skip cleaning up the dorm when it is my turn, forcing my room- mates to pick up the slack?
- May I cheat in a course?

Some of these questions are easy to answer, others not so easy. We will consider cases involving each of these questions, in turn. Try to pay attention to *when* you see ethical questions arising and take note of *how* you recognize that they are ethical questions.

Sam and the substandard notes

Sam is leaving his introduction to geology class one morning after another 1.11 slack-off hour of not paying much attention and jotting down notes only haphazardly. It was actually a pretty interesting topic today, he thinks, but for some reason I just can't seem to get it together to take decent notes.

As he is passing through the door to the hallway, another student, Maria, 1.12 approaches him. Sam doesn't know Maria well but they have chatted a few times before or after class. "Hi Sam," Maria says. "Hey, Maria," Sam smiles.

"Would you mind lending me your notes for last week?" she asks. "I had to go home for a few days and I missed class."

1.13   Although Sam is happy to lend Maria his notes, he feels a bit conflicted as he knows that the notes are not very good. Should he tell her the truth? It would be embarrassing to do so. Sam figures that Maria has probably noticed his slack-off tendencies and is indifferent to them. She would rather borrow notes from someone she already knows rather than try to get better notes from someone she doesn't know as well. "Sure," Sam answers, handing over his notebook, "Here you go." Maria smiles happily and disappears with the notebook.

1.14   After scores are posted for the next examination, though, Maria is not so happy. She confronts Sam after class that day. "Your notes weren't very good," she complains. "I studied really thoroughly but half of the stuff on that test didn't even appear in your notes. The rest of it was barely covered and I think that you might have actually gotten some stuff wrong when you wrote it down." Sam, who also didn't do well on the exam, is indifferent to her concerns. "Hey, I guess you should have borrowed someone else's notes, then," he replies. "Let the borrower beware."

Sidebar Exercise

What do you think: should Sam have shared his sub-standard notes with Maria? What features of the situation seem most important, from an ethical perspective, to you? For example, you might consider whether Sam did anything ethically wrong in not warning Maria that his notes were poor quality. Is he responsible for her low score on the examination? Consider what you would have done in Sam's situation and how you would feel if someone did to you what Sam did to Maria.

Casey and the overly-demanding internship

1.15   Now, consider a case related to the second question. Casey's friend, Fred, was selected for an internship at a prestigious advertising firm in their city. Although the internship was unpaid, Fred was so excited to receive it: he felt that it was the first step toward the successful career in advertising he had always wanted.

As the internship has worn on, though, Fred's enthusiasm has waned. 1.16 "They always ask me to do the most menial things. Getting coffee. Making coffee. Making copies. Work that is almost custodial: emptying waste paper baskets, wiping down the kitchen. I don't feel that I am learning anything about advertising at all."

Initially, Casey was not that sympathetic to Fred's complaints. Having an 1.17 internship is an opportunity to learn all aspects of the business, she thought. Fred should be grateful for the opportunity to learn about the firm and learn about working in an office, even if he is not always doing the most glamorous things that you might see on a TV show. Over time, though, she has grown worried about the internship. Fred is working such long hours that she rarely sees him. When she does see him, he appears harried and unhappy. Casey wonders if there is someone that she should call about Fred's situation but then she realizes that she has no idea whom to call, even if she wanted to call someone.

Sidebar Exercise

What do you think: should Casey call someone? Whom should she call? What would you have done in this situation? If you were Fred, what would you want Casey to do? What features of the situation seem most important, from an ethical perspective, to you?

Tatiana and the fair distribution of chores

In the third case, we examine an issue between Tatiana and her roommates, 1.18 Erin and Paul. Tatiana has been working really hard recently. She has been taking a number of advanced classes in her economics major and has been working a part-time job as a receptionist to help pay the rent. Erin, by contrast, has taken the semester off and is being supported by her parents. Paul is taking a normal course load and relies on loans, rather than a part-time job, to pay his living expenses.

Ordinarily, the three roommates split the chores evenly. Each person 1.19 has a set of chores that they cover for one month and they switch every month. This month, Tatiana's responsibilities are cleaning the kitchen (once a week) and vacuuming (once every two weeks). Each time she plans to do one of the chores, though, something comes up and she finds herself too busy to complete her responsibilities. Although neither Erin nor Paul has said anything to her yet, Tatiana can tell that they are annoyed. She feigns indifference to their annoyance, however: if they are really bothered by the mess, she figures that they can clean it up themselves. They have enough time, after all. She will get back to her cleaning responsibilities once her classes and work responsibilities ease up a bit.

Sidebar Exercise

Is Tatiana's behavior ethically acceptable? What would you do in her circumstances? What would you do in Erin or Paul's circumstances?

Alex and the too-easy-to-cheat course

1.20   Finally, consider the question that Alex faced when he took a class in which it was all to easy to cheat. He decided to take the course, focusing on Sports Ethics, because he was interested in the topic. When he found out that most of his grade for the class would be determined by in-class electronic responses to the professor's questions, and he could simply give this device for making the responses to a friend, who would make the responses for him, Alex realized that he use the class time to do other things that he would like even better.

1.21   Alex decided to give his device to a friend, Tiffany, who was willing to enter responses for him. Everything was going well for a few weeks, until he received an email from the course professor. The email was addressed to all of the students in the class. It said:

> Dear Students, I have become aware that some of you have given your electronic devices to other students, who are entering answers on your behalf. I became aware of this because I was receiving hundreds of responses even though the lecture hall was half empty. As it is impossible for me to determine who was absent, who was entering scores on behalf of absent students, and who was present but entering only their own scores, I have decided to lower everyone's grade for the course by one letter. If students come forward and confess to skipping class or entering scores for other students, I will not lower your grade further. This may, however, allow me to recognize which students were not cheating, and give them the grades they have earned.

Depressed about the lowered grade, Alex contemplates whether he should come forward. Ultimately, he decides not to. In the first place, he does not want to get Tiffany in trouble. She was only being nice to him, after all. In the second place, he does not really trust the professor. It seems unethical for the professor to lower everyone's scores when not everyone cheated. Given that behavior, Alex does not trust the professor not to take further disciplinary action against him, even though the professor said that he would not take further disciplinary action.

Sidebar Exercise

Is Alex's decision not to come forward ethically acceptable? Is the professor's decision to punish everyone ethically acceptable? What would you do in Alex's circumstances, or the professor's circumstances? What would you do if you were one of the students in the course who did not cheat?

Evaluating the Case Studies

Now that we have presented the cases, and started thinking about them from an ethical perspective in a general sense, let us become more precise in our ethical thinking. First, let us try to figure out when we are using ethical guidelines, and when we are using other kinds of guidelines, to think about these cases. Second, let us consider how to use ethical guidelines to evaluate the cases. Finally, we discuss some of the limitations of ethical evaluation. Being aware of these limitations will help us to do our ethical evaluating more effectively. 1.22

Non-ethical guidelines for thinking about the cases

Return to Sam's case. In considering whether to loan his friend his shoddy notes, Sam could have consulted a variety of guidelines. Different guidelines might recommend that Sam do different things. Some of these guidelines are ethical—but not all of them. Sam could also have consulted his emotions, his community's etiquette, the law, or his religion. In order to figure out what guidance ethics can distinctively provide, then, let us separate ethics from these other kinds of guidance. 1.23

1.24   First, consider Sam's emotional response to the question that Maria presented to him. He felt embarrassed that his notes were poor quality and guilt when he loaned Marie the notes without telling her that they were inadequate. When Marie confronted him after the examination, though, Sam felt defensive and was inclined to rationalize Maria's poor performance as being her fault. In this sense, we can see how Sam's emotions help to guide his behavior. His embarrassment overcame his guilt, inclining him to conceal the truth from Marie; his defensiveness prevented him from accepting any responsibility for her poor performance on the test.

1.25   If Sam behaved unethically in loaning Maria the substandard notes, then, his emotions seem to have contributed to his unethical action. In some ways, his feeling of embarrassment is what motivated him to keep silent about his notes' inadequacy. Thus, it is clear that emotional guidance is not the same as ethical guidance (in the sense that Sam did not remain silent because he felt it was the right thing to do). This does not mean, though, that your emotions cannot help to guide you to act ethically. For example, think of Sam's feeling of guilt in lending Maria the shoddy notes. That feeling might have inspired him to act more ethically. So, we should pay attention to our emotions when trying to act ethically. We should not be *completely* guided by them, though.

1.26   The same is true of etiquette, or the social norms that guide behavior in whatever part of the world you happen to be acting. Such norms include relatively minor things like how much space people usually leave between themselves and another person with whom they are conversing. They also include potentially more significant things such as whether Marie can be expected to double-check that Sam's notes are complete or whether she will be inclined to trust that they are. In this case, Sam was confused about whether Marie would trust that his notes were complete or whether she would be suspicious. It can be difficult to figure out what social norms are involved in our decision making. (This problem will be discussed in greater detail in Chapter 4, with respect to the Kantian ethical theory.) One strategy for figuring out what social norm is in place is asking yourself: what would I expect in the other person's circumstances? It can be difficult to answer this question honestly, so it is probably better to err on the side of being overly cautious. When Sam was unsure whether Marie would know that he was a poor notetaker, it would have been most honest to tell her that he had some doubts about just how useful his notes would be to her.

1.27   Next, consider how the law might guide Sam. It is probably not illegal to lend someone shoddy notes without first revealing that they are incomplete. If Marie were inclined to, though, she might be able to bring a civil lawsuit against Sam, alleging wrongful damages. Even as Sam and Marie hashed it out in court, though, they would not resolve whether what Sam did was ethically wrong. The judge would decide, rather, whether Sam's actions caused Marie damages for which she was legally entitled to be compensated.

Similarly, consider an informal law like a student code of conduct. Most 1.28 student codes of conduct do not specify that students must disclose that their notes are faulty when loaning faulty notes to a classmate. If the code of conduct at Sam and Marie's school did have such a provision, though, Sam's action would be in violation of the code but not necessarily unethical.

Sam's failure to disclose the shoddy nature of his notes to Marie might 1.29 violate some of his religious obligations as well. Many religions have a prohibition against lying and Sam's action could violate that provision. Like the codes of conduct discussed about, though, most religions do not go into great detail about what is required of people in particular circumstances. Studying ethics can help us to address these particular details.

Ethical guidelines for thinking about the cases

Now that we have set out some other forms of guidance that Sam could 1.30 have considered in making his decision to lend Maria inadequate notes, let us think about this decision from an ethical perspective. Above, it was suggested that there seems to be something ethically wrong about Sam's action. Let us now try to be more precise about what (if anything) was ethically wrong about what Sam did. We shall begin by considering what aspects of his decision seem ethically significant.

Some of the things that seem ethically significant could include: 1.31

- Maria experienced harm.
- Sam was (to some extent) a cause of this harm.
- Sam was (in some sense) dishonest.
- Sam and Maria's friendship was damaged.
- Sam might have failed to live up to what Maria expected from him.

Sidebar Exercise

Is there anything else about the event that seems ethically significant? Try to say why the things that seem ethically significant to you seem ethically significant. What makes these things important, from an ethical point of view?

1.32   We can consider this problem from several different standpoints:

- Sam
- Maria
- an "impartial observer"
- all of society looking in
- an ethical hero, who always acts ethically.

In considering what, if anything, was wrong about what Sam did, we should evaluate his action from each of these standpoints. In Chapter 4, we will use this analysis of what seems ethically significant, and what standpoints seem ethically important, to decide what is the right thing to do using three different ethical theories.

Sidebar Exercise

Carry out the ethical consideration of Sam's actions from each of these standpoints. Do they evaluate Sam's action in the same way? If there are differences in their evaluations, which one should have priority?

Limitations of ethical evaluation: the problem of controversy

1.33 As you reflected on the case studies and completed the sidebar exercises, you might have come to (tentative) conclusions about who acted rightly or wrongly and what were the most important considerations in determining who acted rightly or wrongly. You might also have a sense that your ideas are correct. In discussing your ideas with a friend or classmate, however, you might be surprised to realize that other people have different views. They might even think that different considerations are more (or less) important than you think. These kinds of *controversies* in ethical evaluations are actually some of the most important parts of ethics, and they are something with which we will have to get comfortable.

1.34   At the beginning of this chapter, we contrasted ethics with science in order to get a better grasp of what ethics is. Contrasting ethics with science can also illuminate the problem of controversy. Whereas educated people generally agree about what is scientifically true, people can reasonably disagree about many ethical matters—even when they are well informed about the relevant issues. This is in part because of the diverse perspectives that people bring to bear on ethical questions. As noted above, people's responses to ethical questions draw upon their intuitions: internal ideas they have about right and wrong. People develop their intuitions over many years based on the different experiences they have had, the various people who have influenced them, books they have read, and so on. In short, people's intuitions can be very different from one another and it is complicated to parse out the reasons for the differences. Because intuitions inform the ethical evaluations people will reach, then controversies are an unavoidable part of ethics. We cannot expect to reach consensus on most of the ethical issues we will discuss in this book.

This should not be reason for discouragement, however. Whereas con- 1.35
sensus is an important part of science, we can do ethics very well without needing to reach consensus. In fact, the lack of consensus can even make our ethical evaluations stronger. People's different perspectives enhance ethical deliberation in the sense there are many uncertainties in ethics. Discussing your ethical ideas with someone who has different intuitions can help you both to see where there might be a weakness in your ethical reasoning and to work to correct it.

Reference

Kant, Immanuel. 1788. *Critique of Practical Reason*, trans. Philip McPherson Rudisill. http://kantwesley.com/Kant/CritiqueOfPracticalReason.pdf

2

BUSINESS
MAXIMIZING PROFIT

2.1 Now that we have covered some foundational issues about ethical thinking, our next step is to understand how businesses function. Understanding how businesses function, in turn, will allow us to figure out what role ethical thinking can play in business decision making. We will be doing that in detail in Part III of this book (Chapters 7–11). In this second chapter, our topic is business organization. We need to understand both what makes a business a business and what role business plays in society. We begin by setting forth the *theory of the firm*, including the corporation's organization and the centrality of the so-called *profit motive* to that organization. Next, we examine how business decisions affect many people throughout society: shareholders, suppliers, employees, customers, and the community at large.

Theory of the Firm

2.2 Many of the business ethics controversies that we will examine in this book arise, at least in part, because the size and complexity of businesses make it difficult for any one person to monitor what is going on in every corner of the business at every moment. Before delving into business ethics controversies, then, it is worth understanding why many businesses are so big in the first place. These understandings belong to what economists call the *theory of the firm*. The theory of the firm explains why the firm, or business, is organized as it is and for what purpose it exists.

Firm organization

First, let us understand how the firm is organized. At its most basic, the 2.3 firm is organized into two distinct parts: the people who own the business and the people who run, or manage, the business. Firms are owned by *shareholders*. Business owners are called shareholders because they *hold*, or own, *shares*, or parts, of the business. The shareholders invest money in the firm but do not manage the firm. They typically invest money in the firm because they believe they will earn a *return* on their investment: when the firm earns a profit, they will receive a part of that profit. Thus, shareholders generally want firms to earn as much profit as possible. Shareholders in publicly traded corporations can be called *stockholders* if they own the company's *stock*, or publicly traded shares of the business. Stocks are traded—bought and sold—in *stock exchanges* like the New York Stock Exchange (NYSE) on Wall Street in New York City.

Firms are managed by executives. Executives usually do not own much 2.4 of the business. Another way of saying that executives do not own many *shares* of the business is that executives typically have little *equity* in the corporation. Equity is yet another word for what the shareholders own. We can also say that shareholders own *capital* in the business. Executive management consists of the firm's chief executive officer (CEO), along with other executives who assist the CEO, such as the chief financial officer (CFO) or the chief operations officer (COO). The number and kinds of other executives vary from firm to firm. Every firm, though, is run by a CEO.

The CEO typically provides the firm's vision. He or she hires teams of 2.5 employees to carry out this vision, with the ultimate aim of producing profit for the shareholders who have invested funds to create the business. The CFO oversees the firm's financial performance. The COO is responsible for daily operations, such as advertising and staffing. Both the CFO and the COO report directly to the CEO.

The CEO, in turn, reports to the firm's board of directors, who are elected 2.6 by the shareholders to oversee executive management. One of the main activities of the board of directors is to ensure that executive management is pursuing the shareholder's wishes to maximize shareholder profits. (This is where the *profit motive* comes from.) The CEO sometimes serves as the chairperson of the board of directors.

Why the firm exists at all

2.7 Next, let us investigate why the firm exists on a large scale with many permanent employees, rather than on a smaller scale with temporary employees who are hired to do specific work and then move on. According to an early (1937) theory of the firm offered by economist Ronald Coase, it seems as if it would be less expensive for the CEO to hire independent contractors on a job-by-job basis rather than employing full-time workers. With such independent contractors, the CEO would simply pay the contractor for whatever work was to be performed; the business would not be responsible for paying people when their work was not directly needed. Such an arrangement would also keep the size of the firm fairly small, as few permanent employees would be needed.

2.8 Coase observes, though, that contractors are actually much more expensive than permanent employees. If the CEO relies on contractors, he or she must continually engage in expensive activities: locating appropriate contractors, determining that they are appropriate, negotiating their salaries with them, haggling over their share of the firm's profits, overseeing their activities to ensure that they perform the work correctly, preventing them from disclosing the company's trade secrets, and so on. Thus, Coase concludes that it will typically be more efficient for the CEO to form a firm with a large team of permanent employees.

2.9 Moreover, without the employment hierarchy created by corporate organization, the CEO would have to find an independent contractor whenever he or she needed any task completed, even a very small one like purchasing a new pen. If the CEO could always count on suitable labor being available, he or she might not need to maintain a large, permanent staff. In conditions of greater uncertainty, however, the firm's stability can prove to be a major boon. The labor is always available. Indeed, Coase associates the firm very closely with the conditions of uncertainty in which business takes place: "it seems improbable that a firm would emerge without the existence of uncertainty."

Sidebar Exercise

What do you consider to be the better way of organizing firms: hiring a large staff of permanent employees or hiring independent contractors to perform specific tasks as they are needed? What ethical questions are associated with this choice?

Problems for firm organization

Even when the firm is in place as a stably organized, hierarchical organiza- 2.10
tion, though, problems still remain. Perhaps most seriously, the firm must
find ways to assure that all employees perform their jobs properly, pursuing
the firm's interests. Difficulties arise at every level of employment, beginning with the CEO. Like other employees, CEOs may be inclined to put
their own interests ahead of the firm's. As economist Oliver E. Williamson
(1964) highlights, CEOs are naturally inclined to seek maximal salaries,
security, and prestige for themselves. These inclinations can conflict with
their responsibilities to perform well for the firm, such as by earning maximal profits. Of course, CEOs must achieve some profits to satisfy shareholders. After a minimal sufficient level has been reached, however, CEOs
appear to have wide discretion to pursue their own interests. The problem
for shareholders in monitoring CEOs is that CEOs tend to know far more
about the businesses than shareholders do. Thus, it is difficult for them to
guarantee that the CEO's activities always pursue firm interests above the
CEO's personal interests.

Lower-ranking employees can also be inclined to pursue their personal 2.11
interests over the firm's. Here, though, the firm's organization can help to
mitigate the problem: by providing a way to centralize monitoring activity. Shapiro and Stiglitz (1984) show that paying employees a slightly
higher wage than they could command based on the productivity of their
work alone helps to secure compliance with the firm's profit-seeking
activities. Paying employees a slightly higher wage than they are really
"worth" to the market gives them an incentive to do what they need to do
to preserve their jobs, such as pursuing the firm's interests over their own.
The slightly-higher-than-merited wages that the firm pays to secure its
interests are sometimes called wage *rents*. Williamson, Wachter and Harris
(1975) add that the possibility of being promoted in virtue of good works
offers additional incentives to employees to perform well.

Business Decision-Making: Shareholders
and Cost-Benefit Analysis

We have seen that businesses have complicated organizations, in which 2.12
many different people most be motivated to put their own interests aside
and pursue the firm's interests (typically, as discussed above, maximal profits for the firm's shareholders). In this section, we see how businesses

attempt to simplify their decisions in order to assure that maximal profits are pursued. We will discuss three theories of business decision making: (1) the *Dominant Model* (DM); (2) the *Shareholder Theory* (ShareT); and (3) *cost-benefit analysis* (CBA).

2.13   Let us begin by defining our terms. In ethics, we will always be discussing controversial decisions, as discussed above: in the sense that people will disagree about what is the right thing to do. So, when discussing ethical matters it is especially important to ensure that the aspects of the discussion about which people can agree are clearly stated. One important thing about which people can agree are the definitions of the terms that they are discussing. By explicitly defining these terms at the start of the discussion, everyone participating in the discussion can make sure that they are using the words in the same way. If they need to diverge from that common understanding for some reason, discussion participants can say clearly when they are diverging. This helps to organize the discussion and pinpoint exactly where disagreements arise.

2.14   People affected by the business's decisions include shareholders, employees, suppliers, customers, and the community in which the business is located. We defined shareholder in the last section. The shareholders of the firm are the firm's owners. They provide the money, or capital, that the firm needs to get started and to conduct business once it is established. In a fitness club, for example, the shareholders might own the exercise equipment. The value of their share of the company increases when the company makes a profit and decreases when it loses money. Their ownership is different from that of a *sole proprietor*, who both owns and runs a business, in that the shareholders do not direct day-to-day business activities; the firm's board of directors and executive management handle those responsibilities. Shareholders do, however, elect the board of directors.

2.15   The employees are people who work for the firm and are paid salaries in exchange for their work. Unlike the shareholders, who earn money only when the firm produces a profit, employees receive their salaries regardless of how much profit the firm earns or even whether it earns a profit. Because they are subject to a hierarchy of power, such that each reports to a boss, who ultimately reports to the board of directors, which responds to shareholders, however, employees also experience pressure to make the firm produce a profit.

2.16   The suppliers of a firm sell the firm its raw products. They continually negotiate with the firm about the price the firm pays for the materials out of which it manufactures its finished products. Both sides typically seek an agreement that most benefits them.

The firm's customers buy its products. They are interested in paying 2.17 low prices and receiving high quality goods. They do not directly haggle with the business over prices and quality. Their choices to buy or not to buy the business's products, though, give the business information about what price they should charge and what quality of goods they should provide.

The community refers to the other people living where the firm does its 2.18 business, who may be affected by the firm's activities. For example, they may be benefited if the firm creates jobs or pays tax revenue; they may be harmed if the firm pollutes the local environment.

The Dominant Model

The *Dominant Model* (DM) is a business decision-making strategy 2.19 invented by R. Edward Freeman, an American business ethicist. The DM is not the actual decision-making strategy that any particular firm uses. Rather, it is a simplified model of corporate decision-making that seeks to explain how many firms decide what to do. The DM assumes that there is a conflict of interest among the parties discussed above. For example, customers want inexpensive products, which conflicts with the shareholders' interest in earning maximal profits. Employees have interests in high salaries and suppliers have interests in high prices for their supplies, which also conflict with the shareholders' desires for maximal profits.

Because of these conflicts, the DM infers that it is impossible to serve 2.20 all of the interests of all of the people who are affected by business decisions. Therefore, it does not attempt to serve all of the interests. Rather, it privileges the shareholders' interests and makes decisions that will benefit the shareholders. That is, it chooses to maximize profits even when the profit-maximizing strategy damages the interests of some people whom the strategy affects.

The DM privileges the shareholders' interests for at least two reasons. As 2.21 noted above, the conflict of interests among people affected by business decisions hinders the business decision-maker's ability to serve all interests. Second, the shareholders own the business and, as such, ultimately control the business from a legal standpoint.

Sidebar Exercise

Following the DM might not mean the business people do not care about interests other than those of the shareholders. Rather, they might regard the shareholder's authority as the most important in conflicts. Do you agree with this way of resolving conflicts? Is it justified to regard obligations to meet fiduciary responsibility as more important than obligations to meet other kinds of legal and moral responsibilities? Why or why not?

2.22   Freeman is unhappy with this decision-making strategy, which he believes neglect certain concerns. For example, he notes that, for the DM.

> If customers are unhappy, if accounting rules have been compromised, if product quality is bad, if environmental disaster looms, even if competitive forces threaten, the only interesting questions are whether and how these forces for change affect shareholder value, measured by the price of stock every day.

Unlike the DM decision-making process, Freeman considers all of these questions to be interesting. Even if the value of the company's stock is very high, he thinks it is problematic if the company's customers are dissatisfied. Or if its products are not well made. Or if its business activities harm the environment. Or if it manipulates its accounting to make its profits appear higher than they actually are. Freeman thinks that taking an interest in these questions is part of "basic ethics." That means that all of these questions are part of a normal range of ethical concern. He believes that the business should, from an ethical perspective, consider all of these questions. Decision-makers can evaluate the ethics of any business decision—who is benefited, whether rights are respected, what kind of people we become in making certain decisions—so business concerns cannot be isolated from concerns about ethics.

2.23   Moreover, Freeman notes that the DM might even encourage the business to break the law. He notes that certain laws require companies to consider the interests of customers, employees, and local communities, even when those interests undermine the business's profit-making activities. Five such laws are:

1. The Consumer Product Safety Act
2. The National Labor Relations Act

3. The Equal Pay Act of 1963
4. Title VII of the Civil Rights Act of 1964
5. The Clean Air Act and the Clean Water Act

The Consumer Product Safety Act sets safety standards for the products that businesses produce, serving consumers' interests in purchasing quality merchandise. To the extent that safer products are more expensive for the business to produce, the Consumer Product Safety Act harms shareholders' interest in earning maximal profits. The National Labor Relations Act protects employees' abilities to join unions, thereby serving their interest in trying to obtain higher salaries and better working conditions. Paying employees higher salaries and providing better working conditions for them can, again, undermine profit maximization.

The Equal Pay Act of 1963 prohibits businesses from discriminating 2.24 against female employees. Although it can be unpleasant to think about it, requiring businesses to pay women the same salaries as men, when they perform the same work, does undermine the business's ability to maximize profits. After all, if the business can pay women less money for performing the same work as men, it can increase its profits by hiring more women. Title VII of the Civil Rights Act of 1964 prohibits businesses from discriminating against employees and customers based on their race, ethnicity, or religion. To the extent that such discrimination could help businesses to maximize profits, Title VII further conflicts with profit maximization while serving employees' and customers' interests. Finally, the Clean Air Act and Clean Water Act set standards for the maximum permissible pollution, serving communities' interests in being free from pollution. It undermines profit-maximizing activities because cleaning up pollution is generally more expensive for the company than releasing their pollution into the community.

Sidebar Exercise

Philosophical Skills: Raising an Objection

As discussed above, ethics always involves controversial matters, about which people disagree. One of the ways that philosophy contributes to the debate is by trying to figure out what is problematic about various positions and where they might go wrong. Noting a weakness in someone's ethical view is called raising an objection to that view.

In his discussion of the DM, what objections does Freeman raise to the DM? Do you agree with his objections? Why or why not? What other objections would you raise against the DM?

How might someone who supports the DM defend the DM against Freeman's objections? How might someone who supports the DM defend the DM against your objections?

Shareholder Theory

2.25 In a famous paper in 1970 called, "The Social Responsibility of Business Is to Increase its Profits," American economist Milton Friedman described another business decision-making model. It is similar to, but importantly different from, the DM. Friedman did not give his decision-making model a name like Freeman did but we can name it for him. In philosophy, it is often helpful to give a philosophical view a short name so that you can refer to it easily. So, we can call Milton Friedman's business decision-making model the "Shareholder Theory" (ShareT).

2.26   Friedman introduces his theory by criticizing the idea that business has "social" responsibilities above and beyond its responsibilities to earn profit. Friedman does not say exactly what he means by "social responsibilities." Remember how we carefully specified what all of our terms meant earlier in this chapter? Well, we can see here how it is a problem when you do not specify what you mean, because people could mean different things by the same term. One person might mean that businesses should put social needs, like reducing unemployment, before their profit-maximizing activities. Another person might mean that businesses should undertake charitable activities only when they can do so at the same time as producing profits.

2.27   In fact, it is part of Friedman's argument for the claim that business does not have social responsibilities that the people who say that business *does* have social responsibilities cannot seem to spell out what exactly they mean:

> The discussions of the "social responsibilities of business" are notable for their analytical looseness and lack of rigor. What does it mean to say that "business" has responsibilities? Only people can have responsibilities. A corporation is an artificial person and in this sense may have artificial

responsibilities, but "business" as a whole cannot be said to have responsibilities, even in this vague sense.

So, in order to continue with Friedman's argument for his ShareT business decision-making strategy, let us stipulate what we will understand by business's social responsibilities. "Business's social responsibilities" will mean ethical responsibilities to a business' employees, suppliers, customers, and community. These responsibilities are different from what the business needs to do to earn profits for its shareholders. They sometimes, but need not always, undermine the business's profit-maximizing activities.

Here is the crux of Friedman's argument against that view. Only people 2.28 have responsibilities. Why is that? Well, for some of the reasons we discussed in the last chapter about ethical decision-making. People have consciences and can make choices, perceive things as benefiting and harming themselves, and so forth. It is these abilities, especially having consciences and being able to make choices that agree with those consciences, that give people responsibilities.

Then Friedman says something strange: "A corporation is an artificial 2.29 person." A corporation is "artificial" in that it is something made by human beings, like an artifact (hence the word) or a computer program. It is a "person" in that it has some of the characteristics of a person. In particular, a business can do certain things and make choices. Like a human being, a corporation is (or can be) responsible for the choices it makes. Because it is artificial, though, corporations can only "do" and "choose" as people program them to. Corporations do not have powers on their own (in the way, for example, that people have consciences "on their own," without having to be programmed, or educated, to have consciences). Therefore, we cannot automatically assign business *social* responsibilities. Ultimately, it is up to the people who create the corporations: the shareholders. Shareholders either program their business to accept social responsibilities or do not program the business to accept these responsibilities.

The next step in understanding Friedman's argument is to figure out 2.30 whether we think that shareholders should program social responsibilities into their businesses or not. Friedman thinks that they should not. He considers a few examples of businesses acting for social rather than business objectives:

1. Not raising prices so as to prevent inflation.
2. Reducing pollution more than is required by law.
3. Hiring chronically unemployed people rather than better qualified workers so as to reduce income inequality.

Friedman opposes these possibilities because they require business people to spend the firm's money on social initiatives with which other people in the firm might not agree. If not raising prices lowers profits, Friedman claims that the business is spending shareholders' money. If reducing pollution more than is required by law raises prices, the business is spending customers' money, for Friedman. If hiring chronically unemployed people lowers the wages that the business pays to its other employees, the business is spending employees' money. In any of these cases, Friedman thinks that the right thing is for the business to pursue maximal profits and allow each person to decide how to spend his or her own money.

2.31   Key to understanding Friedman's argument, in this sense, is the idea that choosing to act ethically is a personal decision, not one that is forced on you. Unlike the law or religion, which requires people to act in lawful or holy ways, ethics is up to you. This is not to say that, on Friedman's view, people do not have any ethical obligations. Actually, they do. He notes, for example, that businesspeople are also people, independent of their work. As people, they have innumerable responsibilities: to their families, to themselves, to their communities. Because these are ethical responsibilities, Friedman believes that the must be pursued on people's own time and at their own expense. It is up to the person to hold him- or herself to ethical standards. Ethics should not be forced on someone: people are capable of making up their minds for themselves.

2.32   At work, by contrast, the corporate executive is the employee of the shareholders. As an employee, the executive "has direct responsibility to his employers." In particular, according to Friedman, the executive is obligated to pursue maximal profits for the shareholders. That is the reason that they invested their money in the business and the executive is bound to do as they wish. Friedman does note that shareholders want the executive to pursue profits legally and, indeed, ethically. As long as the company obeys the law and does not violate ethical norms, though, the business's purpose is to pursue profits for the shareholders, for Friedman.

2.33   In this sense, ShareT is similar to the DM in that it privileges the shareholders' interests. It differs from the DM, though, in that it explicitly conforms to the laws of the society, including obeying the five laws that Edward Freeman discusses. It also explicitly conforms to the society's ethical customs. Although it is not totally clear what it means to conform to society's ethical customs, it seems like a plausible interpretation to say that ShareT takes an interest in the ethical problems specified, above, by Edward

Freeman—the unhappiness of customers, breaching accounting rules, producing poor quality products, threatening environmental disaster—in which the DM took no interest.

Sidebar Exercise

What are some weaknesses of ShareT? How might you object to it? How could Milton Friedman respond?

Cost-benefit analysis

The final business decision-making model we will discuss is called cost-benefit analysis (CBA). CBA is a basic tool of business decision-making. CBA examines the costs (in dollars) and benefits (in dollars) of every decision and recommends whatever action will produce the greatest overall benefits (in dollars).   2.34

CBA is the name of the technical strategy that is used to serve shareholder interests in maximizing profits. It could be used by either the DM or by ShareT.   2.35

It is worth spending some time on how CBA reaches its recommendations, in particular, as we will be using CBA in subsequent chapters to understand business decisions. Typically, the following steps are followed: 2.36

1. First, the decision-maker makes a list of all possible decisions.
2. Then, the decision-maker specifies how costs and benefits will be measured (typically, in dollars).
3. Next, the decision-maker assesses all costs and benefits of all possible decisions.
4. As part of this assessment, the decision-maker decides on a *discount rate* for future costs and benefits (say, costs and benefits a year from now are valued at 80 percent of the costs and benefits that occur immediately). Note that the discount rate can be zero, such that future costs and benefits are valued at 100 percent of today's costs and benefits. Usually, though, decision-makers discount future costs and benefits either because they are less certain or simply because they are further away.

5. *Sensitivity analysis* is subsequently performed on the assessment of
    costs and benefits to evaluate, overall, how confident decision-makers
    are about their costs-and-benefits calculations.
6. Finally, the costs and benefits for each alternative decision are assessed,
    discounted, and analyzed. The alternative with the most benefits, or the
    fewest costs, is selected and implemented.

It is clear that both the DM and ShareT could use CBA. In the case of DM, the
costs of breaking various laws and ethical norms would be assessed. If the
costs of violating the law—say, a fine—were less than the benefits of breaking
that law, then the DM would advise the business to break the law. In the case
of ShareT, decision-makers simply assume that shareholders wish to conform
to the law and do not consider any alternatives that involve breaking the law.

2.37   Certain problems arise in the use of CBA, which will be explored in later
chapters. In the first place, CBA typically uses a financial measure of costs
and benefits, like dollars. Not all things that can be lost or gained have a precise dollar value, however. Consider the value of human life, or the value of
the environment. One of the costs of a particular business decision might be
that a certain number of people will die. In order to include these costs in
CBA, though, a dollar value must be assigned to human life. This strikes
many people as ethically wrong. Similarly, if environmental degradation is a
possible cost of a decision, a value must be assigned to the environment. It is
not easy to asses how much money the environment is worth; moreover,
some people believe that the value of the environment is more than (merely)
monetary. Having more than monetary value means that there might be no
price for which human beings are willing to give up our environment.

Sidebar Exercise

Philosophical Skills: Doing Cost-Benefit Analysis

Consider a decision of what to major in using CBA. Assess the costs
and benefits of three to five different majors: Business, Philosophy,
Physics, English, or what you like. Decide on your discount rate and
perform sensitivity analysis on your results. Which major is selected?
Do you agree with this result? What are some possible problems with
using CBA to choose a college major?

Business in Society: Consumers, Employees, and Community

Although each of these three decision models does a good job at simplify- 2.38
ing business decisions, some people think that the DM, ShareT, and CBA
simplify too much. They leave out information that is important to the
business's decision about what it should do. In fact, you might even think
that the simplifications introduced by the first three decision models may
create problems greater than the one they solve.

We looked at R. Edward Freeman's discussion, and criticism, of the 2.39
DM above. Freeman raised two objections to the DM: (1) it conflicts
with various laws; and (2) it conflicts with basic ethics. That is, in making shareholders' interest in maximizing profits the basis for all business
decision-making, Freeman pointed out that the business would decide
to act illegally or unethically whenever doing so would maximize shareholders' profits.

Sidebar Exercise

Are ShareT and CBA also vulnerable to Freeman's objections? How
could someone who favors ShareT as a decision-making model try
to defend ShareT against Freeman's objections? How could someone
defend CBA?

Freeman does more than criticize the DM, though. He also offers his 2.40
own view, which is intended to avoid the problems with the DM. In examining his view, which he calls Stakeholder Theory (StakeT), we will see if it
avoids the problems associated with ShareT and CBA as well.

Freeman begins by objecting to one of the most basic elements of the 2.41
DM: the idea that the people affected by a business decision—shareholders, employees, consumers, the community at large—necessarily experience conflicts in the realization of their interests. He thinks that businesses
should find ways jointly to satisfy the various interests of people affected
by the decisions they make. Freeman points out that these people's interests are interdependent: so there should be ways of satisfying the interests
jointly.

Sidebar

What does it mean for interests to be interdependent? Think about two tennis players engaged in a game of tennis. Even though they compete with one another, they share certain interests. For example, both want the other to play tennis with them and both want the other person to follow the rules of the game. Each depends on the other to be able to play at all. Thus, each person's interest depends on the other person's interest. It is in this sense that the tennis players' interests are interdependent.

2.42   Here, we are presented with a stark difference between the two decision-making strategies. It must either be the case (1) that the interests inevitably conflict or (2) that the interests are interdependent and may be jointly satisfied. Both (1) and (2) cannot be true at the same time. To see which one is correct, consider ways in which the interests of shareholders, employees, consumers, and the community at large do seem to conflict with one another. Some of these were discussed above: the higher employee wages, the lower are profits; the higher the profits, the more expensive (or lower quality) the merchandise available to consumers.

2.43   Not all of the interests of the shareholders, employees, consumers, and community conflict, however. Freeman has a point: all parties have an interest in the sustainability of the business. The shareholders want the employees to stay employed; the suppliers want customers to continue purchasing goods; the employees want the company to stay in business (i.e., to remain profitable).

2.44   Freeman builds on all of these shared interests and argues that, "businesses, and the executives who manage them, actually do and should create value for customers, suppliers, employees, communities, and financiers (or shareholders)." Thus, he recommends a different model for businesses, such that not only shareholders benefit. Rather, executives seek to assure that the interests of all parties receive attention.

2.45   Indeed, according to the strict model that Freeman recommends, the executives should strive to maximize value for all parties who are affected by every business decision. Note here that "value" could include more than financial value. Freeman notes that stakeholders' interests depend on one another: no one's can be fulfilled without help from the others.

Worksheet Exercise

Philosophical Skills: Constructing an Argument

One of the best ways to see if there are any problems in an argument is to try to represent the argument logically: as a deductive argument. A deductive argument consists of premises and a conclusion. Premises are sentences that state the philosopher's beliefs about the world. For example, Friedman claims that "Businesses are artificial persons." Premises should be uncontroversial, in that most people should agree with your premises. The conclusion, though, can be more controversial. That is what the philosopher is trying to convince you to believe when he or she offers an argument. In a deductive argument, when the premises are true, the conclusion must be true as well. The conclusion must be true as a matter of logic. Here is an example of a famous deductive argument:

Premise 1 (P1):Socrates is a person.
Premise 2 (P2):All people are mortal.
Conclusion (C):Socrates is mortal.

You may know that Socrates was a famous philosopher in Ancient Greece. He is used in this example of a deductive argument to emphasize how basic and important this argumentative form is. In the same way that Socrates' ideas are the basis of most of philosophy, deductive arguments are the basis of most philosophical arguments. Of course, the conclusion here is not very controversial. But the point of this example is just to understand how deductive arguments work. If the premises are true, then the conclusion must, logically speaking, also be true. That is because these premises fit together like puzzle pieces. Replacing the nouns with variables, the premises say: "S is a p and all p are M. Therefore, it must be the case that S is M."

Now, let us try to reconstruct Friedman's claims in the form of a deductive argument. We can start with Friedman's conclusion:

C: Business does not have social responsibilities.

This is a controversial conclusion. Many people disagree with it. So, we should try to use premises that are more widely accepted. The goal here is to offer a number of premises, with which people will agree, and then show that they lead logically to a controversial conclusion. So, some of the premises that Friedman rely on to motivate his conclusion might include:

P1:People have social responsibilities.
P2:Businesses are artificial people.
P3:Artificial people have artificial responsibilities.
P4:Artificial responsibilities are different from social responsibilities.

Do you see how these premises can fit together logically to lead to the conclusion that business does not have social responsibilities?

Most philosophical arguments, including this one, are much more controversial than the first one we looked at concerning Socrates. Most philosophical arguments are also less convincing than that argument. In fact, one of the reasons we write philosophical arguments as deductive arguments is to try to understand what the weaknesses in the argument are. So, what weaknesses do you see here? For example, do you disagree with any of the premises? Which ones? Why?

Now that we have analyzed Milton Friedman's argument together, try constructing R. Edward Freeman's argument about StakeT on your own. First, decide what Freeman's conclusion is. Then, try to think of premises that can be logically linked such that Freeman's conclusion must be true. Remember, the premises should be as uncontroversial as possible!

After you have constructed Freeman's argument, analyze it to see if you can find any weaknesses. For example, do any of the premises strike you as being problematic? Be sure not to construct the argument with an eye to undermining it, such as by basing it on premises that are obviously false. You will find the most value in analyzing arguments if you first construct them as well as possible. Only then will you be able to see where the arguments' true weaknesses lie.

References and Further Reading

Berle, Adolf and Gardiner Means. 1964. *The Modern Corporation and Private Property*. London: Macmillan.

Coase, R.H. 1937. "The Nature of the Firm." *Economics*, 4: 386–405.

Freeman, R. Edward. 2007. "Managing for Stakeholders." (January). http://ssrn.com/abstract=1186402

Friedman, Milton. 1970. "The Social Responsibility of Business Is to Increase its Profits." *The New York Times Magazine*, September 13.

Shapiro, Carl and Joseph E. Stiglitz, 1984. "Equilibrium Unemployment as a Worker Discipline Device," *The American Economic Review*, 74(3): 433–444.

Shiller, Robert. 2012. *Finance and the Good Society*. Princeton, NJ: Princeton University Press.

Simon, Herbert A. 1959. "Theories of Decision Making in Economics." *American Economic Review*, 49: 56–65.

Williamson, Oliver E. 1964.*The Economics of Discretionary Behavior*. Englewood Cliffs, NJ: Prentice-Hall.

Williamson, Oliver, Michael Wachter, and Jeffrey E. Harris. 1975. "Understanding the Employment Relation: The Analysis of Idiosyncratic Exchange," *Bell Journal of Economics*, 6(1): 250–278.

3

CLASSIC BUSINESS ETHICS DILEMMAS
WHEN DOING THE RIGHT THING DOES NOT MAXIMIZE PROFITS

3.1 Now that we have discussed what ethics does, and what business does, in the first two chapters, we can begin exploring the business ethics controversies that arise when the goal of profit maximization clashes with the goal of doing the right thing. We will explore these conflicts through four of the most central cases in the business ethics canon: (1) the Ford Pinto; (2) Walmart; (3) B.P.; and (4) Enron.

3.2   In the Pinto case, Ford executives decided whether to fix a dangerous flaw in a popular car (doing right by their consumers) when paying off consumers injured by the flaw would be less expensive (maximizing profits). In the Walmart case, the business decided whether to pay employees a living wage (doing right by their employees) while requiring backbreaking, degrading work (maximizing profits). The B.P. case covers the 2010 oil spill in the Gulf of Mexico, in which the company decided whether to protect the environment (doing right by the community) when it was cheaper not to (maximizing profits). In the Enron case, the business risked its ability to continue as a business (doing right by the shareholders) when it decided whether to engage in accounting improprieties (for the sake of maximizing profits).

3.3   These cases develop the view of business and ethics set forth in the first two chapters and serve as paradigms for the 20 cases that will be covered in Part III (Chapters 7–11).

This is Business Ethics: An Introduction, First Edition. Tobey Scharding.
© 2018 John Wiley & Sons, Inc. Published 2018 by John Wiley & Sons, Inc.

Doing Right by Consumers: The Ford Pinto Case

The Pinto was just the kind of car that would be popular with young people: 3.4 cute, small, fun to drive, inexpensive. Manufactured by the Ford Motor Company from 1971–1980, it was designed to please the consumer. And it did just this, until a serious defect was revealed in the fuel tank engineering. When rear-ended, even at low speeds, the car's gas tank could rupture. If the fuel leaked, if there was a spark, the car could explode: killing or maiming the car's occupants.

Design flaws sometimes occur in manufacturing. A flawed product is 3.5 not necessarily unethical. What elevated the Pinto fuel tank flaw from an engineering error to a full-blown business ethics scandal was the way the company responded to the problem. One issue with Ford's response is what the company decided to do: after learning of the defect, it allegedly decided to sell the cars anyway. Another issue is the reason why Ford made its decision: allegedly, because it was cheaper to sell the defective vehicles than to fix them. That is, it was cheaper *even when* the "cost" of human life was assessed and included in the company's cost-benefit analysis. Putting profits before human lives is the root of the ethical scandal in the Ford Pinto case.

Sidebar Exercise

Think back to the cases of college ethics in Chapter 1, where we analyzed what information we would need to know in order to determine whether an action was ethically right or wrong. What do we need to know in this case in order to evaluate whether what Ford did was ethically wrong?

This textbook is going to introduce some information about the Pinto 3.6 case. But one important piece of information about this case is that we do not know all of the details about Ford's business decision-making. The company has refused to reveal many relevant details about the case to the public. Refusing to share information could suggest that the information incriminates Ford—but it need not. The company may decline to reveal all of the facts about the case because some of those facts would reveal its *trade secrets*, compromising Ford's ability to compete with other car manufacturers.

3.7   Let us begin, though, with what we do know. The most natural starting point is the "Pinto Product Objectives," which we can think of as the business model for the Ford Pinto. This list was created by a Ford manager, Lee Iacocca. Iacocca was so closely involved with the Pinto's design that the vehicle is sometimes called "Lee's Car."

1. The Ford Pinto is a "true" subcompact in terms of both its size and its weight. The Ford Pinto weighs less than 2,000 pounds.
2. The Ford Pinto is low cost in terms of initial price, gas usage, and reliability. It costs less than 2,000 dollars.
3. The Ford Pinto is a superior product in terms of comfort, features, handling, and performance. It is a fun car to drive and a fun car in which to ride.

The first thing that many people note about this business model is that there is no mention of "safety." Iacocca was well known for believing that "safety doesn't sell." His main concerns were moving Pintos off of the lots and increasing revenue for the Ford corporation. This list reflects those concerns.

Sidebar Exercise

Is it ethically wrong that the Pinto business model does not include safety as an objective? Think about your own preference in cars. What is most important to you? How important is safety? How unsafe a car would you be willing to buy if it had the other features that are important to you?

3.8   On the topic of safety, we should try to put ourselves into the position of Ford executives in the 1970s. Nowadays, car consumers are used to having a variety of well-functioning and (relatively) safe cars to choose from, at various price ranges. Cars in the 1970s were much less reliable, however. Have you ever seen a car at the edge of the highway with its hood open and smoke pouring out? We hardly ever see this now but overheating and other problems used to be common experiences for drivers. In the 1970s, the government did not regulate the car industry as closely as it does today and safety requirements were much laxer. In fact, it was during the same time that the Pinto scandal was playing out that safety regulations were being standardized for the first time. So things that seem obvious to us about car safety might not have appeared so clear to Ford executives.

We should not make too much of this point, however. Yes, there are 3.9 significant differences in the automobile industry between the 1970s and the 2010s. Yes, customers have variable preferences: some prefer safer cars, others prefer cars with better performance, others prefer cars with a "cute" or "sexy" appearance. Even taking these two points into account, though, most people would presumably reject a car that was seriously unsafe.

And that was precisely the problem with the Ford Pinto. It was seriously 3.10 unsafe. The fuel system's precarious location next to the bumper meant that the gas tank could rupture when the car was rear-ended, even at speeds as low as 20 miles per hour. If the tank ruptured and there was a fuel leak, the car could ignite: killing or injuring the inhabitants. Everyone could die as a result of a routine, minor accident, the kind that happens every day.

And, indeed, such routine, minor accidents—producing horrifying 3.11 deaths—occurred throughout the 1970s. One of the most infamous incidents occurred in 1978, when a 1973 Pinto carrying three teenage girls was struck from behind and ignited. The young driver and her passengers were all incinerated. One of the experts who testified at the trial, Byron Bloch, called the fuel tank design a "catastrophic blunder." Drawing on his expertise in automobile engineering and industrial design, Bloch testified that, "Ford made an extremely irresponsible decision when they placed such a weak tank in such a ridiculous location in such a soft rear end. It's almost designed to blow up—premeditated." Bloch testified that it would have been safer to place the fuel tank in front of the rear axle, where it would be less likely to rupture if the car were rear-ended.

In a 1977 article, "Pinto Madness," published in *Mother Jones* magazine, 3.12 an unnamed Ford engineer addressed the issue of the gas tank design and placement. That engineer admitted that the gas tank was flawed from a safety perspective but emphasized that it had other merits. In particular, he emphasized that the Pinto tank created more trunk space in the car, which was an area in which the Pinto sought to be competitive.

In the face of mounting deaths, though, concerns about trunk space 3.13 appear frivolous. Hundreds of people had died or been injured in fiery crashes by the late 1970s. At this time, Ford had access to several strategies for making the cars safer. First, it could have reinforced the rear axle, improved the bumper, and provided additional support for the tank. Making these changes would have cost $15 per vehicle. They would have made the fuel tank able to withstand a 34–38 mile-per-hour rear-impact crash.

3.14   In addition to the axle reinforcement, bumper improvement, and tank support, Ford could have added a bladder at a cost of about $5 per vehicle. Making these changes—at a cost of $20 total per vehicle—would have allowed the fuel tank to withstand a 40–45 miles-per-hour rear impact. If the tank had been located over the rear axle and surrounded with a protective barrier, at a cost of approximately $10 per vehicle, it would have been safe in a rear impact at 50 miles per hour or more.

3.15   Why did Ford decide not to make any of these changes? As with any decision, it is difficult to figure out, from the outside, why other people decided to act as they did. We can ask them, and take their word for it. Alternatively, we can construct a theory about why we believe that they acted as they did and try to argue for that theory. In the case of the Pinto disaster, both strategies have been attempted. When Lee Iacocca was asked about the design choices, he explained that he did not know that the design would have the deadly consequences that it ended up having.

3.16   When looking more broadly at how the Ford Motor Company tended to make decisions during this time, however, another possibility emerges. This possibility is offered in the *Mother Jones* article. In the 1950s and 1960s, a person who had an important influence on the Ford Motor Company was Robert McNamara. McNamara was the first person who was not a member of the Ford family to serve as the president of that company. He subsequently served as Secretary of Defense in the Kennedy administration. Trained as an accountant, McNamara was a strong proponent of cost-benefit analysis (CBA), the decision-making strategy discussed in Chapter 2. Based on McNamara's influence on the Ford Company, many people have inferred that the company decided to keep selling the Pinto, rather than performing one of the other actions, listed above, because continuing to sell the defective car was favored by CBA.

3.17   As noted above, CBA has obvious value in business decision-making. In particular, it is highly effective at maximizing the bottom line. Problems with the decision-making strategy arise, though, when it is applied to decisions concerning human life. The most serious of these problems is that analysts must place a dollar value on human life. For Ford, that value was $200,000. A non-fatal burn was valued at $67,000. (Adjusted for inflation, that is over $1 million per life and around $400,000 for a non-fatal burn in contemporary dollars.)

3.18   A memo that Ford created using CBA to assess whether the car industry as a whole should use a safer gas tank has been made public. In that memo,

Ford estimates the human "cost" of the riskier tank, industry-wide, per year, at 180 lives and 180 burns. Industry-wide, 12.5 million vehicles that caused these kinds of injuries (cars and "light trucks") were sold. That means that, industry-wide, the costs of burn deaths and injuries is projected to be $49.5 million but the cost of selling safer cars (assuming that the safer car costs $11 more to manufacture) is $137 million.

These industry-wide costs and benefits, though, do not settle the ques- 3.19
tion of what Ford ought to do from a CBA standpoint. To figure that out, we will have to make some assumptions. First, we can plausibly estimate that the Pinto had a sales volume of 300,000 vehicles per year. (This figure is based on a 2003 article by Robert Sherefkin in *Automotive News*, in which the author notes that Pinto sales in 1971 were 328,275 in the United States.). According to Ford Vice President Herbert L. Misch, there were 12 fatalities in all Pinto accidents in 1975 that involved fires. We know from the memo that Ford assumes that burn deaths and injuries are the same number. So, assume that Ford is deciding whether to install the safety devices discussed above (costing $10, $15, or $20) for the next operating year (say, 1976). It anticipates 12 deaths and 12 burns per year.

Estimated CBA: 3.20

- ($200,000 per death × 12 projected deaths) + ($67,000 per burn × 120 projected burns) = approximately *$3 million* per year.
- $15.00 × 300,000 Pintos per year (estimated) = *$4.5 million* to make the car safe at 34–38 mile-per-hour rear-impact collisions.
- $20.00 × 300,000 Pintos per year (estimated) = *$6 million* to make the car safe at 40–45 mile-per-hour rear-impact collisions.
- $10.00 × 300,000 Pintos per year (estimated) = *$3 million* to make the car safe at 50 mile-per-hour rear-impact collisions.

Because the bottom line is the same to fix the car as to pay for injuries, these figures do not make a compelling case for either alternative (in terms of CBA). Combined with Ford's $200 million investment in Pinto produc-tion with the defective cars, though, we can grasp how the bottom line might have influenced Ford to keep the defective cars in place. We do not have the information about costs of retooling Pinto assembly lines and improving the car's design. It does seem plausible, though, that these costs would have been greater than compensating survivors and the families of the deceased. Ford's decision to keep selling the unmodified Pintos sug-gests that, in this case, the bottom line trumped concerns about loss of human life.

Sidebar Exercise

What would the DM recommend that Ford do in this case? What would ShareT recommend? How about StakeT? Raise an objection against each decision-making strategy's recommendation. Then, consider how someone who supported the decision-making theory would respond to your objection.

Doing Right by Employees: The Walmart Case

3.21   In the Pinto case, we examined a conflict between shareholders and customers. In the Walmart case, we will look at a conflict between shareholders and employees. Walmart is one of the biggest companies in the world. In 2014, it had more than $250 billion in revenue (in the U.S. alone), more than 10,000 stores around the world, and two million employees worldwide. It was founded by Sam Walton in 1962. Walton's aim was to sell products at the lowest possible prices. He thought of his stores as serving consumers' interests. Although earning little profit on each item sold, Walmart sold more products than any of its competitors. In this sense, its business model served shareholders' interests as well. This can be seen in the immense wealth of Walmart's owners. Sam Walton was the richest person in the United States from 1982–88. Since his death in 1992, Walton family members have maintained ownership of more than 50 percent of Walmart stock. A 2011 *Forbes* magazine article profiled the Waltons as the richest family in the world, with a combined net worth of $93 billion.

3.22   The interests that may have seemed to have received short shrift in the Walmart business model are those of employees. In addition to paying employees very low wages, often without benefits like health care and retirement savings, Walmart has been accused of wage-and-hour violations, race- and gender-based discrimination, and maintaining a stressful, oppressive workplace. These claims were set forth in a series of employee interviews included in the 2005 documentary, *Walmart: The High Cost of Low Price*. We will examine each of the claims in turn.

3.23   According to the documentary, full-time Walmart employees (who work 28 hours/week) earn less than $12,000/year. Many employees can't afford to live on their own. One worker reported that "I can't afford to pay $75 a month for the medical coverage but because I earn such low income I am eligible for Medicaid." The documentary reported that Walmart's low wages and inadequate benefits cost taxpayers $1.5 billion via government-provided welfare, food stamps, and Medicaid.

Workers also claim that store managers violate the Fair Labor Standards 3.24 Act (FLSA), which requires employers to pay non-managerial employees one-and-a-half times their regular wage for any hours more than 40 per week. Walmart managers, however, are required not only to keep their expenses low but actually to lower expenses every month. Many managers say that the only way to do this is through payroll. Thus, they say: "No overtime whatsoever." Because most workers are desperate to keep their jobs, if there are two hours of work left to do but a worker has only half-an-hour left on his or her shift, the worker must do the remaining work unpaid.

Other workers allege race- and gender-based discrimination. At one 3.25 store, there was only one female worker, who claimed that she was made to clean the bathroom in addition to her sales responsibilities. At another store, an African-American woman applied for an assistant manager training program. A manager told her, "There's no place for people like you in management." The woman retorted, "What do you mean: that I'm black or that I'm a woman?" The manager replied, "Well, two out of two isn't bad." At a third store, African-American employees found nooses hanging in an employee break area. Nooses, which recall the era of lynching in the Southern United States after the Civil War, are a frequent means by which racist employees harass their African-American co-workers.

In addition to these workplace violations, the documentary shows that 3.26 Walmart has actively discouraged union participation. Unions allow employees to join forces and bargain collectively, which can allow them to be more successful in their negotiations with corporate management. One of the issues about which unions often negotiate are the workplace violations discussed above. As portrayed in the 2005 documentary, Walmart is one of the most aggressively anti-union companies in the United States.

More recently, Walmart workers have made renewed efforts to unionize, 3.27 or otherwise organize, their fellow employees. OUR Walmart ("Organization United for Respect at Walmart) was formed in 2011 by a Walmart employee, Cindy Murray. By 2012, it had gained over 4,000 members. OUR Walmart members say they do not seek legal recognition as a union or collective bargaining rights. OUR Walmart members say they simply want to make Walmart a better place to work and shop.

3.28   OUR Walmart held protests at about 1,000 stores on the Friday after Thanksgiving (the busiest day of the year for retailers, also known as "Black Friday") in 2012, seeking (1) full-time jobs with predictable schedules rather than part-time work with hours that can change every three weeks; (2) wages that can provide their families with a decent life; and (3) respect. Despite the organization's success in attracting attention to the Black Friday strikes, less than one-tenth of 1 percent of the company's U.S. workforce participated.

3.29   Walmart has always been opposed to unions. David Tovar, a Walmart spokesman, says the company is proud of the jobs it offers, that its benefits are affordable and comprehensive, and that there are plenty of opportunities for associates to advance: "The suggestion that the issues OUR Walmart is raising are widespread or representative of any sizable number of associates is ludicrous." The issue continues to develop.

Sidebar Exercise

What would the DM recommend that Walmart do in this case? What would ShareT recommend? How about StakeT? Raise an objection against each decision-making strategy's recommendation. Then, consider how someone who supported the decision-making theory would respond to your objection.

Doing Right by the Community: The B.P. Case

3.30   The next case study involves a conflict between shareholders and communities concerning environmental protection. The corporation under examination here is British Petroleum (B.P.). The ethical controversy occurred in April 2010, when an oil rig, the Deepwater Horizon, exploded and sank in the Gulf of Mexico. Eleven people were killed in the wreck; hundreds more were injured. The explosion also damaged an oil well, the Macondo Prospect, owned by B.P., which gushed oil into the Gulf of Mexico for almost three months, discharging at least 134 million barrels of oil. The Macondo was a deep-sea well, designed to drill oil from 23 million-year-old sediment located 13,000 feet below the bottom of the sea. Underwater oil drilling is always risky. The frigid waters and intense pressures of deep-sea wells increase those risks. One of the Deepwater Horizon workers who was killed had described the Macondo to his wife as "the well from hell." Tragically, B.P.'s cost-cutting business activities appeared to have contributed to the well's rupture.

Sidebar Exercise

Think back again to the cases of college ethics in Chapter 1, where we analyzed what information we would need to know in order to determine whether an action was ethically right or wrong. What do we need to know in this case in order to evaluate whether what B.P. did was ethically wrong?

The well gushed oil, natural gas, and toxic sludge for almost three 3.31 months, discharging at least 134 million barrels into the Gulf of Mexico. This was the largest oil spill in history, and one of the most damaging. The most seriously affected areas were along the Louisiana shoreline and Florida panhandle. The oil damaged marine and wetlands habitats, along with beaches used for tourism. It contaminated estuaries from which human food is fished.

The U.S. government investigated the spill. One former B.P. executive, 3.32 Kevin Lacy, testified that he had quit B.P. shortly before the Macondo disaster because he felt that B.P.'s cost-saving strategies compromised its safety. Lacy contributed to a study of the well following the damage that rated the well's complexity on a five-point scale. Lacy and his co-authors found that the Macondo rated more than three on this scale.

Ultimately, the government cited weaknesses in the construction of the 3.33 well, especially shoddy cement, as causes of the rupture. In its report on the Macondo disaster, the U.S. Chemical Safety Board blamed flaws in a cement barrier designed to protect the well from high pressure below the sea floor for the disaster. The inadvertent release of this pressure led to the blowout, which precipitated the explosion, fire, and oil spill.

The government also criticized B.P. for providing inadequate safety 3.34 monitoring and security for the well. B.P. was forced to pay high penalties and submit to safety and ethics monitoring by the Environmental Protection Agency. Three months after the spill, it had lost over a third of its market value, worth about $70 billion.

3.35   Following the spill, *Harvard Business Review* reported that the company failed to acknowledge the extent of the damage for which it was responsible. For example, CEO Tony Hayward called the spill "relatively tiny" in the context of a "very big ocean." Moreover, the company failed to take the most rapid means of cleaning up the mess, resulting in further damages.

Sidebar Exercise

What would the DM recommend that B.P. do in constructing the Macondo Prospect oil well in terms of materials, safety monitoring, and security? What would ShareT recommend? How about StakeT? Raise an objection against each decision-making strategy's recommendation. Then, consider how someone who supported the decision-making theory would respond to your objection.

Doing Right by Shareholders: The Enron Case

3.36   Our final paradigm case study involves a conflict between the firm's business activities and the firm itself. It focuses on the (now defunct) Enron Corporation, whose extensive use of aggressive business practices to accelerate earnings led to overinflated claims about profits. Eventually, the exaggerated profit claims led to the bankruptcy of the company.

Sidebar Exercise

Think back again to the cases of college ethics in Chapter 1, where we analyzed what information we would need to know in order to determine whether an action was ethically right or wrong. What do we need to know in this case in order to evaluate whether what Enron did was ethically wrong?

3.37   Some key events to be examined include: the employment practice of rank-and-yank, the firm's use of mark-to-market accounting, and the firm's creation of Special Purpose Entities (SPEs). Key players are CEO Ken Lay,

Chief Operating Officer (COO) Jeff Skilling, and Chief Financial Officer (CFO) Andrew Fastow.

Let us begin by setting out Enron's corporate identity. The business was 3.38 founded in 1985 by Ken Lay as an American energy firm. Using aggressive tactics, the company grew rapidly, becoming the most successful energy company in the world by the late 1990s. Part of the fast growth also had to do with political events in the 1990s such as the deregulation of energy. Prior to deregulation, the federal government had controlled the cost of energy in order to make it affordable for low-income Americans. After the government stopped regulating the price of energy, Enron could sell energy at higher prices. Jeff Skilling, a Harvard Business School protégé, was brought in as COO, with Andrew Fastow completing the triumvirate as CFO. Ken Lay was a consummate entrepreneur and identified strongly with his company. Similar to French King Louis XIV's famous proclamation that "L'état, c'est moi" ("I am the state"), Lay was known for claiming that: "I am Enron."

Sidebar Exercise

How could StakeT, ShareT, and the DM evaluate Lay's claim?

One of the ways that Lay ensured adherence to his vision for the firm 3.39 was through an employment practice colloquially known as *rank-and-yank*. In this practice, employees were graded each year from 1–5 based on their performance during the foregoing year (that's the *rank* part). The bottom 15 percent were terminated, regardless of how good their performance was (the *yank*). Lay conceived of this practice as direct feedback from him about how each employee was contributing to the company's objectives.

Another way that Lay advanced his vision of the firm was through his 3.40 requirement that the firm use *mark-to-market accounting*. Mark-to-market accounting is a form of record-keeping in which a price is assigned to a product before the profits are actually realized, based on the product's current *market value*. This can be useful in registering products that are difficult to price, such as real estate or other assets whose value can vary. It can be dangerous, though, in the sense that it makes the company responsible for profits that are not yet secured.

Sidebar Exercise

Is mark-to-market accounting dishonest? Is dishonesty unethical? How do StakeT, ShareT, and the DM evaluate the decision to use mark-to-market accounting?

3.41   Lay and Skilling preferred mark-to-market over other kinds of accounting because mark-to-market allowed them to record potential profits on the day the deal was signed. This accorded with their belief that the person who had the idea for a new product was entitled to all of the profits associated with that product. According to the 2005 documentary, *Enron: The Smartest Guys in the Room*, Skilling believed that the idea was everything and you should be able to book the profits right away; otherwise, the profits would be gained by some "lesser man" for the ideas of a "greater man." Using mark-to-market placed Enron in a potentially precarious position, though, if the company realized less profit from its initiatives than it anticipated. The practice also left the firm's accounting open to manipulation—in the sense that accountants might have to try to produce the missing profits from some other source.

Sidebar Exercise

Does Ken lay have a good character? Does Jeff Skilling have a good character? Why or why not? Can StakeT, ShareT, and the DM capture this aspect of the case?

3.42   Problems of this nature occurred in two of their business transactions: involving the Dabhol Power Station and Blockbuster. The Dabhol Power Station was constructed in the early 1990s in the state of Maharashtra in India, after Skilling observed that the rapidly developing nation was in need of greater energy production in order to power its development. The problem was that at the time the power station was built, the local population was unable to afford the power it was to provide. For a while, Enron collected 4.67 rupees for each unit of power from the state of Maharashtra;

because Maharashtra collected only 1.89 rupees from its customers for the same amount of power, though, the situation was unsustainable. Enron ended up realizing almost nothing from the $3 billion project.

The Blockbuster deal of the early 2000s, in turn, was intended to deliver 3.43 Blockbuster's video content on demand to consumers at home via streaming on Enron's fiber-optics network. In retrospect, the idea seems quite prescient. Netflix and other companies later went on to significant success in delivering on-demand video content. The Enron-Blockbuster deal broke down, though, when the parties were unable to reach agreement about key issues.

One final business venture was the creation of *special purpose entities* 3.44 (SPEs), or shell companies that a business creates to serve narrow purposes that differ from the business's main purpose. Like mark-to-market accounting, SPEs have legitimate business uses but are open to manipulation. In the late 1990s, Enron used a series of SPEs to hide the debt created by failed deals like Dabhol Power Station and Blockbuster—which were marked in Enron's ledger as profitable.

Enron's downfall began in March, 2001, when a journalist, Bethany 3.45 McLean published an article, "Is Enron Overpriced?" in *Fortune* magazine. She questioned how Enron could maintain its high stock value, which was then 55 times its earnings. The company rapidly declined as information about its corrupt accounting practices were made public. Lay sold hundreds of millions of dollars worth of Enron shares 15–30 minutes before the information that Enron was collapsing went public on November 28, 2001. Enron's other stockholders—including employees who had their pensions in Enron stock—lost everything.

Sidebar Exercise

What would the DM recommend that Enron do in this case? What would ShareT recommend? How about StakeT? Raise an objection against each decision-making strategy's recommendation. Then, consider how someone who supported the decision-making theory would respond to your objection. Can your objections be adequately addressed? Or do they suggest more serious problems with the decision-making strategies?

References and Further Reading

Anon. 2015. "Five Years after BP Spill, Drillers Push into Riskier Depths." *The Chicago Tribune* (Apr. 20).

Bajaj, Vikas. 2010. "India's Woes Reflected in Bid to Restart Old Plant." *The New York Times* (Mar. 22). http://www.nytimes.com/2010/03/23/business/global/23enron.html

Birsch, Douglas and John H. Fielder. 1994.*The Ford Pinto Case: A Study in Applied Ethics*. Albany, NY: State University of New York Press.

Dowie, Mark. 1977. "Pinto Madness." *Mother Jones*. http://www.motherjones.com/politics/1977/09/pinto-madness

Fisher, Daniel. 2002. "Shell Game." *Forbes* (Jan. 7). http://www.forbes.com/forbes/2002/0107/052.html

Leggett, Christopher. 1999. "The Ford Pinto Case: The Valuation of Life as It Applies to the Negligence-Efficiency Argument." *Law and Valuation*. http://users.wfu.edu/palmitar/Law&Valuation/Papers/1999/Leggett-pinto.html

McLean, Bethany, et al. 2005. *Enron: The Smartest Guys in the Room*. Magnolia Pictures.

Nader, Ralph. 1965. *Unsafe at Any Speed*. New York: Grossman Publishers.

Sherefkin, Robert. 2003. "Lee Iacocca's Pinto: A Fiery Failure." *Automotive News*. http://www.autonews.com/article/20030616/SUB/306160770/lee-iacoccas-pinto:-a-fiery-failure

Squeo, Anne Marie and Bruce Orwall. 2001. "Enron and Blockbuster Terminate Partnership for Video-on-Demand." *The Wall Street Journal* (Mar. 12). http://www.wsj.com/articles/SB984181374790463655

U.S. Chemical Safety Board. 2014. "Macondo Investigation Report." http://www.csb.gov/macondo-blowout-and-explosion/

Walmart: The High Cost of Low Price. Brave New Films (2005).

Winston, Andrew. 2010. "Five Lessons from the BP Oil Spill." *Harvard Business Review*, (June 3). https://hbr.org/2010/06/the-bp-oil-spill-top-5-lessons.html

Wojdyla, Ben. 2011. "The Top Automotive Engineering Failures: The Ford Pinto Fuel Tanks." *Popular Mechanics*. http://www.popularmechanics.com/cars/a6700/top-automotive-engineering-failures-ford-pinto-fuel-tanks/

Case Cited

Grimshaw vs. Ford Motor Company, Court of Appeal of California, Fourth Appellate District, Division Two, 119 Cal. App. 3d 757; 1981 Cal. App. LEXIS 1859; 174 Cal. Rptr. 348; CCH Prod. Liab. Rep. P8999, May 29, 1981.

Part II

TOOLS TO SOLVE BUSINESS ETHICS DILEMMAS

4

ETHICAL THEORIES

We have now seen the foundations of ethical thinking and of business 4.1
decision-making. We have looked at some of the decision-making strategies which businesses use to strive to maximize their profits. We have also seen a challenge to those business decision-making strategies in Edward Freeman's Stakeholder Theory (StakeT). As discussed in Chapter 2, StakeT argues that profit maximization should not be the only thing that businesses consider when deciding what to do. StakeT offered an alternative rationale for making business decisions: decision makers should examine the interests of each of the parties who are affected by their decisions. They should seek to act in a way that maximizes the value of *all* of these interests, not just those of shareholders.

Freeman's solution to the problem he presents is intriguing. But it is not 4.2
the end of our story about improving business decision-making. In fact, it is only the beginning. Whereas CBA's standard for decision-making is profit maximization, and StakeT's standard for decision-making is (what we might call) stakeholder-interest maximization, ethical theories showcase other values as determining what a decision-maker should do. Most importantly, they *set standards* for decision-making: offering strategies by which decision-makers can evaluate whether their decisions are ethically right or wrong.

These standards take the form of certain *ethical values*, or guidelines 4.3
for what is (ultimately) important in life. Ethical values inform people about what actions they should take, what kind of people they should be, and in what kind of world they should seek to live. In this chapter, we

This is Business Ethics: An Introduction, First Edition. Tobey Scharding.
© 2018 John Wiley & Sons, Inc. Published 2018 by John Wiley & Sons, Inc.

will examine several ethical theories, which will set different standards (highlighting distinctive ethical values) for making ethical decisions. The values relate to some of the characteristics of human beings that we discussed in Chapter 1, which make people capable of acting ethically in the first place: people's abilities to make choices, to experience benefits and harms, to be moved by their consciences. The various ethical theories will offer decision-making strategies for securing their distinctive ethical values. In this sense, ethical theory A pursues value A and ethical theory B pursues value B. The problem for us is that theory A may neglect value B and vice versa—but value A and value B might both be worth pursuing.

4.4   In the Preface to this book, we examined some of the differences between ethics and science in order better to understand what ethics is. The same strategy is useful here, so as to understand more clearly what ethical theories are. Both scientific and ethical theories explain phenomena in the world. Scientific theories explain why certain *events* occur: why people become ill when exposed to germs, what happens when you mix an acid and a base, why the planets in our solar system orbit around the sun. Ethical theories, by contrast, explain why some actions are *right* and others are *wrong*: why Ford should have chosen a different gas-tank design, why Enron should have avoided mark-to-market accounting. But whereas scientific theories can be tested using experiments, which affirm or falsify the theories, ethical theories are more difficult to confirm or falsify.

4.5   We test ethical theories by applying them to particular cases, such as the Ford, Walmart, B.P., and Enron cases explored in Chapter 3. As the ethical theories evaluate the cases, they offer guidance about what would be the right thing to do in the decisions the businesses faced. As we will see, these evaluations *also* provide feedback about the theories themselves: whether they evaluate decisions easily or only with great effort, whether their evaluations agree or disagree with our intuitions about right and wrong. In this sense, the evaluations can be used to assess the theories themselves—and try to decide which ethical theories are best for evaluating case studies. Because people tend to have differing intuitions about right and wrong, though, as discussed above, these evaluations and assessments are both likely to be controversial. Business ethicists will probably not reach consensus about ethical theories (or ethical evaluations of case studies) in the way that scientists will reach consensus about scientific theories.

4.6   In this chapter, we will focus on three ethical theories, associated with the philosophers Aristotle, Bentham, Mill, and Kant. (Bentham and Mill develop two versions of a single ethical theory.) Each of these decision-making strategies highlights distinctive ethical values. Aristotle focuses on *virtue*, Bentham and Mill focus on *utility*, and Kant focuses on *duty*. We do not have a single decision-making strategy that encompasses all of these ethically important concerns.

Not only do we lack a single decision-making strategy that includes three 4.7 key ethical values, there might be other relevant concerns that are neglected by the three major ethical theories. After presenting the main views, we investigate some of these other concerns, as set forth in natural law theory, contract theory, care ethics, and feminism. Because it is possible that no single theory will include all of the ethical values that are relevant to particular cases, we may sometimes have to choose between them. Sometimes the ethical theories recommend different actions from one another, moreover, and we must decide which of these actions we prefer, all things considered. So we will discuss the strengths of each decision-making strategy and then some potential problems with each of the strategies.

The Three Major Ethical Theories

We begin with utility: Bentham, Mill, and a third interpretation. Then, we 4.8 discuss Kant's duty-based view. Finally, we consider Aristotle's virtue-based view. Each of these ethical theories offers a deep and wide-ranging perspective on what is the right thing to do, what kind of person you should strive to be, in what kind of world it is right to live, and many other topics. In introducing these ethical theories for the purpose of understanding ethical issues in business and ethically evaluating business ethics cases, our coverage of the deeper and more wide-ranging topics will, of necessity, be somewhat limited. We will focus, instead, on how to use the theories in an applied sense: to investigate particular problems in specific circumstances.

Our narrow and applied focus does not imply, though, that the deeper and 4.9 more wide-ranging aspects of the ethical theories are unimportant. The material covered in this volume will allow students to understand the ethical aspects of business decision-making and use ethical theories to evaluate questions about what is the right thing to do in business. A more thorough appreciation of the ethical theories, though, would help you to apply the ethical theories even more effectively. As such, students are encouraged to explore the references to this chapter (including Bentham's, Mill's, Kant's, and Aristotle's original writings and some of the major scholars who have written about their views) along with the ethics textbook in this series, *This Is Ethics*.

4.10   One more caveat before we begin. Each of the ethical theories offers its own standard for ethical decision-making, which differs from that of cost-benefit analysis (CBA), discussed above. There are two aspects of the CBA decision-making procedure, though, that we will continue using when applying our ethical theories. In CBA we began by (1) making a list of all possible decisions. Then, we performed CBA on all of these possible decisions. In doing our ethical evaluations, we will also begin by considering the possible decisions that a business could make. Instead of performing CBA, though, we will perform utilitarian, Kantian, or virtue-ethics evaluations of each possible decision. One other aspect of the CBA procedure could also be useful in our ethical evaluations: step (5), sensitivity analysis. In the same way that CBA decision-makers want to assess how confident they are of CBA's recommendations, ethical decision-makers should consider how confident we are of our utilitarian, Kantian, and virtue-ethics recommendations. In this sense, even as we examine different decision-making rationales from CBA, we can retain some of CBA's strengths as a decision-making procedure.

Utility-based ethics

4.11   *Bentham's utilitarianism*   According to Jeremy Bentham, the right thing to do is whatever will create the most *utility* overall. This is because Bentham thinks that utility is the best thing possible. What is so great about utility? Well, look at the definition of the term. Utility refers to anything that is useful. So utility helps you to accomplish your goals, whatever those happen to be. Bentham thought that all people have one ultimate goal: to be happy. For this reason, his view is typically called *hedonic* utilitarianism, as he understands utility in terms of happiness. According to Bentham, then, the right thing to do is whatever produces the greatest happiness.

Sidebar

Is it controversial that everyone's ultimate goal is happiness? You might agree with this claim but other people have not. That means that the claim *is* controversial: people have different interpretations. The fact that a claim is controversial, though, does not mean that everyone is right or that you can believe whatever you want—anything goes. Rather, it just means that the issue has not been settled yet. Many issues are very difficult to resolve!

The first thing that is important to note about utilitarianism is that the 4.12
happiness or utility it seeks is the happiness of all of the people who are
affected by a decision, not just the person making the decision. Bentham
thought that what people value most is happiness. So, when they are trying
to do the *right* thing, what they should try to do is maximize overall happiness. They should not just try to maximize their own happiness because
their happiness is not the most valuable thing. Happiness *itself* has most
value. Overall happiness, then, is what should be maximized.

This idea about happiness has an important consequence. The right 4.13
decision to make, for Bentham, could cause decision-makers to be less
happy than they would have been if they had decided to do something else.
But the decision is still right if it makes other people happy: so long as there
is more happiness if you add up all together the happiness that everyone is
experiencing.

This idea of "adding happiness" is the next important thing to note about 4.14
Bentham's utilitarianism. When using utilitarianism to decide what to do,
you don't just guess what decision you think will produce the greatest overall happiness. Rather, Bentham offers a specific procedure, or decision-
making strategy, to use. This decision-making strategy is called the *hedonic
calculus*. That calculus is different from the math class you take. It just
means "calculation." The hedonic calculus gives you a way to add up all of
the happiness that will be caused by your decision, allowing you to decide—
by *calculating*—what is the right thing to do.

There are several steps to using the hedonic calculus to make a decision. 4.15
As mentioned above, we begin by listing all of the actions that could be
taken when facing a decision. How many actions? Well, at least two. There
may be hundreds of other actions that you could possibly take, at least in
theory. But you should include only the actions that are in practice possible:
things you might likely do. As in CBA, try to aim for three to five possible
actions on which to perform the hedonic calculus.

Next, consider all of the people who will be affected by each of the 4.16
actions. In Sam's decision about whether to loan Maria sub-standard notes,
which we looked at in Chapter 1, for example, both Sam and Maria would
be affected by Sam's decision. So each of them get one "vote" in the hedonic
calculus.

The next step is to consider how happy each person who is affected by 4.17
your decision will be as a result of your decision. This is a hard step. You have
to assign their amount of happiness a number. That, of course, is not the way
we are used to thinking about happiness. In order to make Bentham's hedonic
calculus work, though, decision-makers must *quantify* happiness: they must

translate the amount of happiness that each person affected by their decision feels, as a result of their decision, into a number.

4.18   One way of quantifying happiness is using a scale of 0–10 with 10 being the happiest and 0 being not at all happy. Bentham does not give the scale himself so you have to use the scale that seems the best to you. And you have to use your judgment—both in choosing which scale to use and in assigning the numbers. The fact that you are using judgment means that your assignment of numbers will be controversial. People could disagree with you about just how happy or unhappy they are as a result of a particular action.

Sidebar Exercise

Consider these questions about the controversial nature of those numbers. Is there any way to assign numbers for the hedonic calculus in a way that is less controversial? Is there any way to assign numbers for the hedonic calculus in a way that is uncontroversial? And, finally: Is the controversial status of the numeric values that decision-makers assign to happiness in the hedonic calculus a serious problem for utilitarianism, or only a minor problem?

4.19   Bentham does give some guidance, though, about how to estimate the number you assign to each person who is affected by the decision. He notes that there are different ways that happiness can be quantified. So, for each person affected by the decision, you have to consider each of the possible ways of quantifying their happiness. Bentham says there are seven ways to quantify happiness:

1. the *intensity* of the happiness;
2. the *duration* of the happiness;
3. the *certainty* of the happiness;
4. the *remoteness* of the happiness;
5. the *repeatability* of the happiness;
6. the *purity* of the happiness;
7. the *extent* of the happiness.

4.20   The intensity of the happiness means: how powerful is your feeling? Are you all smiles, bouncing up and down, unable to contain your glee (maybe a "10") or more mildly happy (a "5")? The duration of the happiness refers to how long the happiness lasts. Happiness that lasts for a longer time is more valuable on Bentham's calculus. That is because happiness that lasts longer is *more happiness* and, in Bentham's view, the amount of happiness is the most important thing, ethically speaking. As such, longer-lasting happiness receives a higher numeric value. The certainty of the happiness, in turn, refers to how confident you, the decision-maker, are that the happiness will actually result from your action. Remember that in utilitarianism we are evaluating actions based on their consequences: how much happiness will be *produced* by the action. The decision-maker may be more or less confident that the happiness will, in fact, result.

Decision-makers must also evaluate the remoteness of the happiness: is 4.21 this feeling produced immediately upon acting or does it take some time for the feeling to emerge? Usually we experience the feeling right away but sometimes—say, after a very difficult and stressful examination—we do not feel happy until we have had a chance to relax and recover. Bentham also instructs decision-makers to consider the purity of their happiness: whether it is a straightforward happiness or whether it is mixed with other feelings, such as guilt or envy. Finally, decision-makers consider the extent of the happiness, or what number of people experience the particular kind of happiness calculated by the previous six factors.

Phew! That is a lot of factors. In order to figure out how these quantifi- 4.22 cations can maximize overall happiness, it can be helpful to use a spreadsheet table, like Table 4.1. Let us test out our hedonic calculus by posing a simple ethical question. A college student, Fred, is in need of money to buy some beverages for a party this weekend. His possible actions are: put the beverages on his credit card and pay it back later, lie to his parents that he needs more money for books so that they will provide the money, and skip the party. The parties affected by the decision include Fred, Fred's friends, and Fred's parents. Let's say that Fred has ten friends who will be affected by the decision.

Try filling in Table 4.1 to figure out how much utility Fred would create 4.23 by using his credit card to purchase beverages for the weekend party. First, estimate what quantity of happiness Fred, Fred's friends, and Fred's parents experience for each of the first six categories: intensity through purity. Then, sum those numbers. Multiply the sum by the "extent" of the happiness: by one for Fred, by ten for Fred's friends, and by two for Fred's parents. Next, add the three numbers in the "extent" row. This sum is the total happiness created by the action.

Table 4.1   Action 1: Use credit card

	Fred	Fred's friends	Fred's parents
Intensity			
Duration	+		
Certainty	+		
Remoteness	+		
Repeatability	+		
Purity	+		
Sum:			
Extent	× 1	× 10	× 2
TOTAL:			

4.24   Next, perform the same calculations for each of the other two possible actions:

Action 2: Lie to parents
Action 3: Skip party

Whichever possible action has the highest numerical value is the one that utilitarianism recommends.

4.25   Sounds easy enough. But which of the three actions actually creates the most happiness overall? Paying for the beverages with a credit card would create happiness now but unhappiness later (when the credit card bill is due). Lying to his parents would create a lot of happiness, if no one found out. Fred's parents might even be happy about it because they would think that he was more studious than he actually is. Skipping the party might seem to create the least amount of happiness.

4.26   Now, this may seem like a complicated way of making a decision. But remember: ethics is hard. It is hard to answer these questions but it is very important to get the answers right. So it is worth it to put some time and effort into answering the questions well.

4.27   What you have just done—using an ethical theory, utilitarianism, to analyze a question about what to do—is one of the key methods of doing philosophy. But it is not the end of the philosophical process. As noted above, opinions about what to do are controversial. People disagree with them. Understanding those disagreements is the next important philosophical method to cover. We can call this method: raising an objection. Raising an objection to the ethical evaluation that we have just done will help us to understand what about the evaluation is controversial. It will also help us to see possible weaknesses in the evaluation. Considering these aspects of our evaluations will help us to improve our abilities both to figure out what is the right thing to do and to discuss our (controversial) conclusions with others.

One philosopher who was active very soon after Bentham published his 4.28 account was John Stuart Mill. Mill was both very influenced by, and very critical of, Bentham's ideas. You might even call Mill a philosophical *frenemy* of Bentham. Mill was also a utilitarian. He worried, though, that on Bentham's account, utilitarianism made some very immoral recommendations about what is the right thing to do. For example, Mill thought that honesty and justice were more important, ethically speaking, than a physical feeling of pleasure, and that the utilitarian calculus should recognize this importance. In the example we examined above, though, it looked like the action that would create the most happiness overall was the one in which Fred lied to his parents to gain some extra money for the party beverages.

Sidebar Exercise

Responding to an objection. How could Bentham respond to Mill's objections? In particular, would Bentham's utilitarian calculus recognize the importance of honesty and justice? Why or why not?

Mill's utilitarianism   On Mill's version of utilitarianism, the aim is not as 4.29 simple as happiness maximization. We might call Mill a *non-hedonic* utilitarian, in the sense that he thinks that something other than mere (physical) happiness is the most valuable thing, ethically speaking. On Mill's account, decision-makers must ensure that their decisions protect certain extremely valuable ethical ideals. As a utilitarian, Mill does think that these ideals create utility. It is just a more important kind of utility than, for example, the happiness Fred experiences from partying with his ten friends. To distinguish these more-valuable and less-valuable kinds of utility, Mill uses the concepts of *higher pleasures* and *lower pleasures*. Higher pleasures always trump lower pleasures: they must always count for more, quantitatively, in Mill's utilitarian calculus.

So how do we know what are these higher and lower pleasures? Mill 4.30 provides a list. The higher pleasures are pleasures of the intellect and noble feelings. These include things like reading a book and doing volunteer work. Lower pleasures are pleasures of the body and animal feelings. People experience lower pleasures when they do things like eat a hamburger or get a massage.

4.31 Now, you might say: hamburgers are pretty tasty. I like massages. But reading? Volunteering? Those things are work, not pleasurable at all. These are valid concerns. And we do not need to accept uncritically Mill's lists of the higher and lower pleasures. In fact, though, he thinks that if we have experience of both the higher and lower pleasures, and we reflect on our experiences, we will agree with him.

4.32 Here is what Mill has in mind. A hamburger tastes good and a massage feels nice. But they do not involve the elevated pleasures of reading a provocative book: which inspires us to consider an interesting topic in a new or insightful way. Similarly, volunteering may be hard work but it uplifts us. We *know* that we are doing something morally good and we also *feel* good about it.

4.33 Mill thinks that any person who has experience of both the higher pleasures and the lower pleasures will support the priority that he has given to higher pleasures. Now, it is true that someone who has only experienced the lower pleasures, such as a child, might prefer lower pleasures over the higher pleasures. Mill thinks that people like this are not good judges of which kind of pleasure is more valuable, however. To be able to judge which is better, higher pleasures or lower pleasures, he thinks that judges must have experienced both kinds of pleasures. Only then will they be able to give an opinion on the matter that others must take seriously.

Sidebar Exercise

What action does Mill's account of higher and lower pleasures advise for Fred's decision about whether to lie to his parents to obtain money for socialization? Although Mill criticizes Bentham's account, he does not offer a revised form of the utilitarian calculus to make his recommendations. So let us attempt to do it for him.

1. Decide what are the pleasures involved for each person affected by each of Fred's possible decisions: Action 1 (Credit Card), Action 2 (Lie to Parents), and Action 3 (Skip Party).

2. Decide which of these pleasures are higher and lower using Mill's criteria. A chart to help you think about this has been offered in Table 4.2. We can call it the "Higher-and-Lower-Pleasure Calculus."
3. Calculate which action best furthers the higher pleasures.

Is the recommended action the same as in the hedonic calculus?

Table 4.2 Higher and lower pleasures

	Fred	Fred's friends	Fred's parents
Higher pleasures			
Lower pleasures			

Sidebar Exercise

Raising objections. Does Mill's version of utilitarianism avoid the problems he raised with Bentham's utilitarianism? What objections could you raise to Mill's form of utilitarianism? How might he respond?

Other interpretations: rule utilitarianism There is another strategy for 4.34 people who think that maximizing happiness should be the ultimate end of ethics but are dissatisfied with Bentham's apparent tolerance for lying and injustice that maximizes happiness. That decision-making strategy is know as *rule utilitarianism*. When we are discussing rule utilitarianism, we contrast it with *act utilitarianism*. (By contrast, when we speak of Bentham's utilitarianism, we typically contrast it with Mill's utilitarianism.)

In act utilitarianism, decision-makers evaluate what action would maxi- 4.35 mize utility overall: considering just the action at the moment the decision is made and nothing about how the action relates to *other* actions. So, when we performed the hedonistic calculus and higher-and-lower-pleasures calculus on Fred's decision, we considered only his possible actions at that moment. Our ethical evaluations, though we did not realize it at the time, were act utilitarian.

4.36   When you perform a rule utilitarian evaluation, by contrast, you think about the action as being an instance of a *general rule*. Rule utilitarianism asks: which rule, generally followed, would produce the greatest amount of happiness? It instructs decision-makers to act in accordance with whatever rule would maximize happiness if it were generally followed. Rules, on our understanding, explain which *actions* lead to which *ends*, or outcomes. So, for the "Credit Card" action, the rule might be: To address the problem that I lack money for weekend entertainment, I charge the entertainment to my credit card. For the "Lie to Parents" action, the rule might be: To address the problem that I lack money for weekend entertainment, I tell my parents that I need to buy schoolbooks so they will give me some money. For the "Skip Party" action, the rule might be: To address the problem that I lack money for weekend entertainment, I skip the weekend entertainment. If everyone followed one of these rules whenever they lacked money for weekend entertainment, which rule would produce the greatest happiness, overall?

4.37   The first thing that you might want to ask about this decision-making strategy is: why should it matter what everyone else does? The answer to this question is somewhat profound. Rule utilitarianism is a powerful ethical decision-making strategy because it draws on the idea of people following ethical *norms*. Norms are unwritten rules that help to guide people as they decide what to do. For example, there is an ethical norm that people, generally speaking, tell the truth. You do not have to question whether every person who says anything to you is lying—because people generally tell the truth. Similarly, if a friend asks you to do them a favor that does not create a large burden for you, they expect you to do it. People generally assist others when they can.

4.38   What rule utilitarianism investigates, then, is: what would be the most beneficial ethical norms to have in society. That is, its standard for right actions. It is a deep and difficult standard. Rule utilitarianism demands far more of decision-makers than act utilitarianism's standard of what would create the most utility in the particular situation in which the decision is made. Because ethical norms are very important in shaping how people act, however, rule utilitarianism is potentially more powerful—and more interesting—than act utilitarianism.

4.39   The second thing you might want to ask is: are we talking about Bentham's hedonic utilitarianism or Mill's higher-and-lower-pleasures utilitarianism? The answer here is that you can use whichever form seems more promising to you, based on your consideration of the two views.

Let us begin by doing a short exploration of how to answer Fred's ques- 4.40
tion about what to do using Benthamite rule utilitarianism. We can do the
calculation for "Action 3: Skip Party" together. First, we need our rule: To
address the problem that I lack money for weekend entertainment, I skip
the weekend entertainment. Next, we consider what would happen if everyone followed this rule. Obviously, people would engage in less weekend
entertainment. What are some possibly upsides and downsides of this rule
being a general ethical norm in society?

Sidebar Exercise

Try considering the question of what Fred should do using rule utilitarianism of the Millian variety. What does Millian rule utilitarianism
recommend that Fred should do?

Sidebar Exercise

Raising objections. Does rule utilitarianism avoid any of the problems
we noted with act utilitarianism? What objections could you raise to
rule utilitarianism? How might a rule utilitarian respond? Of the various kinds of rule utilitarianism we have examined, which seems the
most useful for answering ethical questions?

Kant's duty-based ethics

We might want to have a better account of what exactly is unethical about 4.41
lying and other intuitively wrongful actions. For such an account, we can
turn to an ethical theory associated with the philosopher Immanuel Kant.
Whereas Bentham and Mill base their views on utility, Kant believes that
the most important ethical value is *duty*. For Kant, the standard for ethical
action is not maximizing happiness but, rather, acting in accordance with
one's duties. Like utilitarianism, the Kantian standard has some intuitive
appeal: it is easy to see why Kant thinks that it is right to fulfill one's duties.
A duty, after all, is something we are required to do—thus, it seems obvious
that we should do our duties.

4.42   It is not so obvious, though, what *are* people's particular duties. In the case discussed above, for example, Fred might be confused whether his duty is to get beverages for his friends, to refrain from lying to his parents, or to skip the party. Although duties are hard to determine in particular circumstances, Kant thought that there is one basic duty that is straightforward to understand. That is the duty to act in accordance with rules. This duty is so important that Kant calls it the *categorical imperative*. The name of this duty means that the basic duty to follow rules is an absolute (i.e., categorical) command (i.e., imperative)—no exceptions!

4.43   The rules in accordance with which one must act are similar to the ones we discussed above with respect to rule utilitarianism. They are the ethical norms that underwrite society. Kant felt that ethical norms make society possible in the first place. We could not have society if we did not have a system of ethical norms that help people to get along with one another and use their intellects to figure out what to do. So, it is very important to follow these rules. It might even be *irrational* not to follow the rules—because society would not be possible without them. In focusing on the norms that underlie actions, rather than individual actions, Kantian ethics has something in common with rule utilitarianism. As will become clear, though, Kant's view is very different from rule utilitarianism in almost every other respect.

4.44   Let us briefly survey those differences before investigating how to use Kantian ethics. The most important difference between Kantian ethics and utilitarianism is the standard the viewpoints offer for right actions. For utilitarianism, the right thing to do is whatever maximizes utility. For Kant, the right thing to do is conform to the categorical imperative: the ethical norms that make social interactions possible. Unlike utilitarians, who base their ethical theory on people's capacities to experience benefits and harms, Kant holds that the distinguishing ethical characteristic is people's abilities to choose what they do (or, as Kant would say, people's *rational capacities*). Kant's strategy for ethical decision-making does not, then, consider what will create the most happiness. Rather, he requires that people's actions meet certain rational standards. This means that more than one action in a particular circumstance can be ethical, according to Kant's decision-making strategy. Utilitarianism picks out what is the best thing to do and says that this is the (only!) ethical thing to do. Kantian ethics, by contrast, requires that people's actions conform to the categorical imperative—which many possible actions could do. Kantian ethics doesn't say which of those possible actions people must do. That choice is up to the decision maker.

Kant also does not require that people try to maximize duty fulfillment: remaining always on the lookout for additional duties to perform in the way that utilitarians must always seek additional sources of utility. In this sense, the categorical imperative is a somewhat less demanding ethical theory than utilitarianism.

Now that we have clarified some of Kantian ethics' differences from util- 4.45 itarianism, the next step is to figure out how to apply Kantian ethics to questions about what to do, such as the one Fred faces (or the ones Ford, Walmart, B.P., and Enron faced in Chapter 3). As noted above, the basis of Kantian ethics is the categorical imperative, or the idea that people should act in accordance with ethical norms. Because the categorical imperative is very general, it can be difficult to apply to particular circumstances. To guide individual actions in particular circumstances, then, Kantian ethics offers several tests by which decision makers can determine whether their actions meet Kantian standards. These tests are known as *formulas*. They are similar to mathematical formulas in the sense that they use variables and can be applied to specific questions. In this book, we focus on two of Kant's formulas: the *formula of universal law* (FUL) and the *formula of humanity* (FH). We define these formulas below, after setting out some key background information in the next paragraph.

That key background information is how to formulate a possible action 4.46 so that we can test whether it is ethical, according to the Kantian standard. This is the first step in using Kant's tests. The form in which we are to evaluate an action is called the action's *maxim*. A maxim is a general rule, similar to what we evaluated in our discussion of rule utilitarianism. As in our rule utilitarian evaluations, general rules describe *actions* that are to be performed in order to gain certain *ends* (or outcomes). Kant scholar Christine Korsgaard offers a useful form for the maxim, which we adapt to our purposes here. The maxim includes both the action itself (call this "*A*" for action) and the end ("*E*") that it seeks. So a maxim is written as:

In order to *E*, I *A*.

In this sentence, *E* and *A* are like the variables you use in math problems. We can fill in *E* and *A* with particular ends and actions. In the example discussed above, for example, E_1 = Address the problem that I lack money for weekend entertainment. One possible action is A_1 = Tell my parents that I need money to buy schoolbooks so they will give me some money. Call this maxim M_1: In order to address the problem that I lack money for weekend entertainment, I tell my parents that I need to buy schoolbooks so they will give me some money.

4.47   As noted above, the Kantian decision-making strategy tests whether (the maxim underwriting) an action meets certain rational standards. Now that we have a maxim to test, we can use Kant's ideas to evaluate whether it would be ethical to lie to your parents to get some money to socialize with friends. We begin with the first test, FUL. FUL inquires whether it is possible for everyone to gain the end specified by the maxim by performing the action specified by the maxim: that is, if it is possible for the maxim to be an ethical norm or (in Kant's phrasing) to be a *universal law* for society. If a person can only gain the end specified by the maxim when other people act differently, then it is *not* possible for the maxim to be a universal law. In that case, the maxim fails the test. Failing the FUL test indicates that people who wish to perform the action specified by the maxim to reach the end specified by the maxim are making themselves *exceptions* to a moral standard that they think that people generally should uphold—just not them in this particular circumstance.

4.48   Take M_1, above. What if this maxim were a universal law? Being a "universal law," in Kant's sense, means that this would be a norm of behavior: something that you expect from other people. Currently, there is a norm of truth-telling. When someone tells you something, whatever it is, you have a natural expectation that what they say will be the truth. Think about these universal laws, or norms, in the following way:

> **UL**: People tend to tell the truth.

So, when people's children tell them that they need money for schoolbooks, the parents believe them.

4.49   Now, consider what would happen if M_1 were a universal law.

> **M_1 as UL**: Children tend to tell their parents that they need money for schoolbooks when they are trying to get money for weekend entertainment.

> **A_1**: I ask my parents for money for schoolbooks.

When this A_1 is performed with M_1 as a universal law, it will fail to be effective. The parents will recognize that the child's aim in requesting money for schoolbooks is to secure money for socialization—and they will, recognizing the deception, fail to provide the requested funds. This failure of M_1 upon universalization shows that, in so acting, actors try to benefit from a norm by making themselves exceptions to that rule, so that they can extract benefit for themselves.

Another standard is set by the "formula of humanity" (FH). The formula 4.50 of humanity asks whether the maxim shows respect for the humanity of all of the people who are affected by the maxim. Kant understands humanity in terms of the distinctive mental and physical characteristics of human beings. They include the characteristics of human beings that make them able to answer ethical questions, as discussed above. Most important among these, for Kant, is people's rational decision-making abilities: the intellectual functions by which people decide what is the right thing to do and choose to act in that manner. Kant specifies that respecting a person's humanity involves treating humanity as an *end in itself* rather than as a *mere means* to something else. Treating something as a mere means is that we use it as a tool to serve our own ends. For example, food is a means of gaining energy. It is a mere tool in the sense that we simply use it in order to secure our own ends. We literally consume food. FH notes that it is unethical to treat people as though they exist merely to serve us. Rather, in treating them ethically, we are to respect that they have ends of their own. We are also to respect the abilities by which they pursue their ends.

It is worthwhile spending a moment on this point, to make sure that 4.51 Kant's intent is clear. FH does not prohibit us from using people as means to what we want. When a barista prepares a drink you have requested, he or she serves as a means to fulfilling your desires. Crucially, though, the barista is not a *mere* means. Baristas are paid for their work and you might add a tip to the tip jar to thank your barista for a job well done. If the barista were your unpaid slave, by contrast, you would use her as a mere means in the way that Kantian ethics prohibits.

Now, to apply FH to Fred's question. When using FH to evaluate a pos- 4.52 sible action, it is helpful to make a list of all the people who are affected by the maxim, so as to consider whether in so acting the actor would show respect for humanity. In this way, FH involves some of the same kind of work that we did in evaluating the decision using utilitarianism. This work is called analysis: breaking a problem down into smaller parts so it is easier to solve.

In M_1, the following people are affected: Fred, Fred's friends, and Fred's 4.53 parents. Fred is acting to serve his own end. He is also acting to serve (what he assumes to be) his friends' ends: socializing with each other and with Fred. But what about Fred's parents? In lying to them to get some money to serve his ends, Fred appear to be using them as a means to his end: they provide the cash that he needs. As discussed above, it is not ethically prohibited to use someone as a means. If a friend volunteers to lend Fred some money, for example, the friend is a means to his end of purchasing beverages for the party. The friend is not a *mere* means, though, in the sense that Fred respects the friend as someone to whom he will owe money and someone he is obliged to pay back. But Fred's parents' humanity includes their abilities to decide what to do with their money. In lying to his parents, then, Fred treats their humanity as a mere means to his end. He does not respect their abilities to make up their minds for themselves about what to do with their money. Rather, he manipulates that ability to serve his own ends.

Sidebar Exercise

Consider the following case, discussed by business ethicist Norman Bowie. General Motors had a practice of demanding that its suppliers reduce their prices after contracts had already been negotiated. Bowie asks: does this practice meet the standard of FUL?

According to Bowie's analysis, the practice fails FUL's standard. If everyone knew that contracts could be broken, then no one would sign contracts in the first place. Bowie notes, though, that businesses often break contracts with their suppliers. Business people still make contracts with one another. How would you explain this discrepancy?

4.54   Kant's strategy for solving ethical dilemmas is very promising. Like Bentham's and Mill's theories, though, it has its problems. In the first place, using FUL and FH to answer business ethics problems may seem to involve a lot of subjective judgment. For example, different people will formulate maxims to be tested in different ways. The way the maxim is formulated might seem to determine whether the maxim passes Kant's tests, even when the maxims describe the very same actions. Consider maxim M_1, above, for example. Fred might have formulated that maxim as: in order to address the problem that I lack money for weekend entertainment, I ask my parents to give me some money. This maxim, unlike M_1, appears universalizable.

Sidebar Exercise

How would Kant respond to this objection?

Second, FH's evaluations might seem to depend on how you define 4.55
"humanity" and different people do this differently. We discussed a variety
of human characteristics in Chapter 1: having a conscience, being able to
experience benefits and harms, being able to make choices. As noted above,
there are many controversies in thinking about ethics. The point of using
ethical theories to address ethical problems, though, is supposed to be to
reduce controversies. But if the very theory means different things to different people, this seems to defeat the purpose in certain respects.

Sidebar Exercise

How would Kant respond to this objection?

Remember how, after completing your utilitarian calculations, you 4.56
might have felt that utilitarianism is *too* hard to use? Although that's still a
mark against it, we can now see that the hard-to-use problem is not decisive
against utilitarianism. It is difficult to use Kantian ethics as well. Like many
activities that are worth doing, it appears that ethical evaluations will be
challenging for us to complete.

Aristotle's virtue-based ethics

One philosopher who might offer a more intuitive (i.e., easier to use) view 4.57
of ethics is the ancient Greek philosopher, Aristotle. We shall turn to his
view next, to understand both what insights it brings to answering questions
about ethics in business as well as the distinctive problems it encounters.

Aristotle was writing before Kant, Bentham, and Mill—and deeply influ- 4.58
enced all of them. As a way of introducing his view, we will first explain how
it differs from, and resembles, those of his successors. Unlike Bentham and
Mill, who think that the most important thing was happiness, and Kant,
whose primary concern is duty, Aristotle focuses on *virtue*. His ethical

theory seeks to assure both that people act virtuously and that they are always striving to be more virtuous. In this sense, his view is more like Bentham's and Mill's than like Kant's: he requires that people continually try to reach the best possible solution to dilemmas. As noted in the previous section, FUL and FH, by contrast, require only that actions meet certain rational standards.

4.59   Aristotle's view resembles Kant's more than Bentham or Mill's, though, in that he is concerned about the *process* by which an individual decides what to do. For Kant, actions are ethical if they meet certain rational standards: the maxim underlying the action is universalizable and does not treat humanity as a mere means. Bentham and Mill, by contrast, focus on the end result of that process of deciding-what-to-do: how much happiness the action creates. Aristotle does not require particular end results but, rather, that people model their actions on those of virtuous people and strive always to become more virtuous.

4.60   Unlike either Kantian ethics or utilitarianism, Aristotle does not directly address the question: what action should I do? Rather, he is concerned with what virtue is and what it means to be a virtuous person. He thinks that once people succeed in becoming virtuous, they will simply do virtuous things. This is why Aristotle's ethical view is often called *virtue ethics*.

4.61   Now, let us turn to Aristotle's view itself. We begin by investigating how people can become virtuous. There are three main ways that people can become virtuous, for Aristotle. The first is by engaging in continual reflections on the nature of virtue. Following this strategy, a person is always trying to cultivate a more virtuous character: by what they do, which authors they read, with whom they associate. The second is by choosing a virtuous role model, on whose behavior the person can pattern their own. Aristotle had a special name for the virtuous person, one whose actions all other actions should be based: the *phronimos*. Contemporary people using Aristotle's ideas to answer ethical questions can choose a particular ethical role model, someone like Martin Luther King, Jr. or Aung San Suu Kyi, whom they regard as being, or having been, very ethical.

4.62   The third way is by attempting to cultivate specific virtues. How do you know what are the specific virtues? Well, one way is by taking Aristotle's word for it. In his ethical writing, Aristotle lists a number of personal characteristics that he considers virtuous. These include: courage, temperance, magnanimity, patience, friendliness, and truthfulness. You can cultivate these virtues by trying to demonstrate them in your actions. For example, you might decide to focus on a different virtue every week. In the week that you focused on patience, then, you might try to be patient whenever you had an opportunity to. You could also try to notice and appreciate when other people took the time to be patient, even when it was inconvenient for them.

Sidebar Exercise

What are some other ways in which you can try to cultivate particular virtues?

Another way of knowing what are the virtues is following a strategy that 4.63 Aristotle recommends. Aristotle felt that every virtue was a *middle point* between two vices. This view is sometime called Aristotle's *doctrine of the mean*. So, courage is the middle point, or mean, between recklessness and cowardice. Friendliness is the mean between brown-nosing and being standoffish. This quality of being in the middle of two extremes reflects another one of Aristotle's ideas about the virtuous person. Virtuous people are able to use their judgment to determine the appropriate way to act: neither too much of one thing, nor too much of another.

Aristotle's doctrine of the mean is a helpful strategy for figuring out what 4.64 the virtues are. We should not make too much of this strategy, however. It is not a hard-and-fast rule, like utilitarianism's insistence that we must always maximize utility or Kant's demand that people always follow the categorical imperative. The doctrine-of-the-mean strategy is more like a rule of thumb. It is helpful in guiding people toward the virtues. It does not, however, simply pop out a virtue when you apply two vices. There will never be computational software that tells you what is the virtuous thing to do: no virtue ethics *app*. What is virtuous differs from circumstance to circumstance. Virtuous people, though, are very good at examining their circumstances to determine what is the virtuous thing to do in them.

Sidebar Exercise

Based on your study of ethics so far, do you agree that there will never be an ethics app? Why or why not?

Sidebar Exercise

Consider Fred's decision from the standpoint of virtue ethics. What virtues do each of his possible actions show? Which action is the most virtuous, in your view? What would a virtuous person do in Fred's circumstances?

4.65   Some business ethicists have examined Aristotelian ethics to determine what the virtues are that they think he would have specified for business decision-making. There were, of course, businesses in Aristotle's time. These businesses were nothing like the large corporations on which business ethics questions focus, however. So it is impossible to say, for sure, what virtues Aristotle himself would have recommended for business. Still, it is interesting and helpful to think about how Aristotelian scholars, who are interested in business ethics, interpret his view.

4.66   One such scholar, Robert Solomon, argues that there are six main business virtues: community, excellence, role identity, integrity, judgment, and holism. The virtue of community helps business people to see that their interests in the business are closely aligned with the business itself. For example, if the business fails, they will be out of a job. If they own the business's stock, they will lose all of the money they have invested. This virtue is based on Aristotle's idea that "to live the good life one must live in a great city."

4.67   Excellence means that virtuous business people must do more than simply follow the rules. They must always aim proactively to be better and more virtuous business people. Role identity acknowledges that people play different roles in their life and different roles have different virtues. Personal characteristics that are a virtue in one role might not be virtuous in other roles. Business people are also private citizens who have personal obligations to their families, friends, and associations. It might not be virtuous to use their business roles to fulfill these obligations, however.

Sidebar Exercise

Compare Aristotle's claim about role identity with Milton Friedman's claim that businesses should not act for social objectives (though individual people may act for social objectives). Do you think that Friedman would agree with Aristotle's claim about role identity? Why or why not?

Integrity is the virtue that helps to unite these disparate obligations. 4.68 Upholding the virtue of integrity helps business people to ensure that they meet ethical standards in all of their activities. They can never exempt themselves from ethical standards that they would recognize in other parts of their life or to which they hold other people. Judgment is the virtue that allows business people to look at all aspects of the situations about which they must make decisions, always striving to act in ways that respond to all of the concerns that they face. Holism, finally, draws on both integrity and judgment to summarize the ways in which virtuous business people make decisions. They consider all aspects of the situation. Their decisions are informed by all aspects of who they are. They always strive to make the very best decisions, all things considered.

Sidebar Exercise

Pick two virtues and discuss the extent to which Ford's decision to continue selling the flawed Pinto did, or did not, reflect these virtues.

Sidebar Exercise

Analyze Solomon's six virtues using Aristotle's doctrine-of-the-mean strategy for determining what the virtues are. What are the two extremes on either end of each of Solomon's six virtues? Do you see any of these vices in the actions of the businesses we examined in Chapter 3?

Sidebar Exercise

How does virtue ethics compare to Kantianism and utilitarianism as a strategy for making ethical decisions in business? Think about one reason to prefer Kantianism to virtue ethics and one reason to prefer virtue ethics to Kantianism. Then, think of one reason to prefer utilitarianism to virtue ethics and one reason to prefer virtue ethics to utilitarianism.

Other Bases for Ethics

4.69   We have looked at ethical ideals concerning happiness, duty, and virtue. We saw that these ethical ideals did not always recommend the same course of action. Each one, though, highlights something ethically important in a decision.

4.70   In closing this chapter, we might ask: but aren't there other ethically significant ideals? Indeed, there are. Business ethicists have written about a number of additional ethical theories, each of which spotlights a distinctive ideal. None of these other ethical theories have been as influential as the three on which we have focused, however. Moreover, none of them offers as clear a decision-making procedure as the three on which we have focused. For these reasons, we will not examine any of the other theories in great depth.

4.71   It is important, though, to touch on some other important ethical theories, for at least two reasons. First, looking at the other ethical theories helps to bring out the idea that ethical decision-making is complicated and there may be many significant features of the situations decision-makers face. Second, it is important to realize that these three ethical theories are not all there is to ethics. Ethics is a very rich discipline, which offers many ideals to consider and many ways to make decisions. Part of becoming good at ethical decision-making is being aware of all of these complexities. In this final section, we will cover four additional ethical ideas: (1) natural law theory; (2) contract theory; (3) ethics of care; and (4) feminist ethics. You can think of this section as offering a jumping-off point for considering what other values may be important to include in ethical deliberation. Although our treatment of these theories in this book is abbreviated, there is much additional information available. Consult this chapter's reference and further reading list for other readings about these ethical theories.

Natural law theory

4.72   Natural law theory specifies that right actions are based on human beings' natural purposes. One important natural law theorist, Aquinas, thought that natural purposes include: preserving life and health, seeking knowledge, and cultivating cooperative social relationships. Whenever there is a choice between serving human beings' natural purposes and not serving those purposes, natural law theory advises decision-makers to serve human purposes. Natural law theory draws upon the human capacity to experience benefits and burdens. Like Mill's utilitarianism, it focuses on distinctively human benefits and burdens. Like Kantian ethics, it highlights the importance of humanity to ethics.

To get an idea of how to apply natural law ideas to ethical issues in business, consider the Ford Pinto case. That business ethics dilemma pitted the desire for profits against human lives. Because preserving life is a more natural human purpose than pursuing profits, natural law theory would recommend that Ford take steps to preserve human life. 4.73

Sidebar Exercise

What other insights can natural law theory offer to the Pinto case? Does the Pinto case engage questions about pursuing knowledge and maintaining human relationships? How do these considerations help us to decide what would be the right thing to do in this case?

When using natural law theory to reflect on ethical issues in business, you can start by considering these four human purposes. How does the possible business action affect the natural human purpose of preserving life and health? Does the business action contribute to seeking knowledge or interfere with this natural human purpose? Does it help people to form and nurture social cooperation or hinder social relationships? Although these answers do not provide determinate guidelines in the manner of utilitarianism, Kantian ethics, and virtue ethics, they can add to our reflections of ethical matters in business. 4.74

Contract theory

Contract theory claims that the right thing to do is what everyone who is affected by the decision can agree to. Contract theory is based on the idea of writing a contract, which is an agreement between one or more parties. The key thing about contract theory, as an ethical theory, is that people have to be able to agree to an action from the position of anyone who is affected by the action—not just their own position. Contract theory thus involves a *hypothetical* agreement, rather than an actual one. Its standard for right 4.75

action is that everyone who is affected by the action must be able to agree, in principle, to that action. Contract theory is based on the human ability to make choices. It resembles Kantian ethics in its focus on respecting the choices that people could rationally make.

4.76   To explore applying contract theory to a business ethics case, try considering Walmart's decision to pay its employees low wages. In order to ethically evaluate that decision using contract theory, you must consider whether everyone affected by the decision could consent to the decision, including the Walmart executives, the Walmart workers, and Walmart customers (who might pay higher prices). If the executive would not agree to the pay rate from the perspective of the employee, then it would be unethical to impose that pay rate on workers.

Sidebar Exercise

Are Walmart's low wages ethical according to contract theory? Why or why not?

Ethics of care

4.77 Third, ethics of care offers the insight that people have special obligations to close friends, family members, and others we care for. These relationships are the bases of ethics and enjoy special priority when making decisions about what to do. In this focus, the ethics of care specifically counters utilitarianism and Kantian ethics, which insist that ethical decision-making should be dispassionate. In using utilitarian ethics, decision-makers are supposed to think merely of maximizing overall happiness, not of their own happiness or the happiness of those for whom they care. According to Kantian ethics, the ethically important thing is whether actions meet rational standards and respect humanity, not how they influence people's relationships. Ethics of care draws upon the human capacity to experience benefits and harms but in a rather different way from utilitarianism and natural law theory.

4.78   Consider the B.P. case. In evaluating B.P.'s decision to use cheap cement to build the risky, deep-sea Macondo well, ethics of care would direct B.P. to consider how this well would affect people's relationships with one another. Some important relationships that were destroyed by this decision are those between workers who lost their lives and their family members. Other relationships less seriously disrupted include tourists whose family vacations on the Gulf of Mexico became impossible due to pollution. Ethics of care would note that it is ethically important to support, rather than disrupt, those relationships.

Sidebar Exercise

Based on these considerations, would the ethics of care advise B.P. to take more safety precautions when constructing its Macondo Prospect well? Why or why not?

Feminist ethics

Feminist ethics is focused on advancing women's interests and correcting   4.79
injustices inflicted on women through social oppression. Feminist ethics is not only concerned with women's interests, though. Feminists focus on all victims of oppression. They claim that it is especially important to avoid oppression and to treat all human beings as equals. These goals— eliminating oppression and treating all people as equals—enjoy special priority in ethical decision-making, for feminists. Care ethics is sometimes taken to be a special version of feminist ethics, in the sense that it highlights characteristics that have typically been associated with women and have been undervalued by society. Feminist ethics draws upon the human capacity to experience benefits and harms, along with the capacity to make choices.

In the Enron case, feminist ethics would focus on how the Enron execu-   4.80
tives' selfish decisions impact women in the company as well as lower-income workers. It could criticize Enron executives' stereotypically male and macho behavior.

Sidebar Exercise

How would feminist ethics evaluate the Enron case? Do you agree with this evaluation? Why or why not?

Sidebar Exercise

First, evaluate each of the four foundational college student case studies using all seven of the ethical theories. Next, evaluate each of the four foundational business ethics cases using all seven of the ethical theories. Do some of the ethical theories seem better able to handle some of the cases than others? Why? Do any of the ethical theories appeal to you more than the others? Why?

References and Further Reading

Aristotle. 350 B.C.E. *Nicomachean Ethics*, trans. W.D. Ross. http://classics.mit.edu/ Aristotle/nicomachaen.html

Bentham, Jeremy. 1781. *An Introduction to the Principles of Morals and Legislation.* http://www.utilitarianism.com/jeremy-bentham/index.html

Bowie, Norman E. 1999 *Business Ethics: A Kantian Perspective*. Oxford: Blackwell.

Crimmins, James E. 2017. "Jeremy Bentham." In *Stanford Encyclopedia of Philosophy*. https://plato.stanford.edu/archives/spr2017/entries/bentham/

D'Agostino, Fred, Gerald Gaus, and John Thrasher. 2017. "Contemporary Approaches to the Social Contract." In *Stanford Encyclopedia of Philosophy*. https://plato.stanford.edu/entries/contractarianism-contemporary/

Gilligan, C. 1982. *In a Different Voice: Psychological Theory and Women's Development*, Cambridge, MA: Harvard University Press.

Kant, Immanuel. 1785. *Groundwork for the Metaphysics of Morals*, trans. Thomas Kingsmill Abbott. http://www.gutenberg.org/cache/epub/5682/pg5682.html

Korsgaard, Christine M. 1996. *Creating the Kingdom of Ends*. Cambridge: Cambridge University Press.

Mill, John Stuart. 1863. *Utilitarianism*. http://www.utilitarianism.com/mill1.htm.

Murphy, Mark. 2011. "The Natural Law Tradition in Ethics." In *Stanford Encyclopedia of Philosophy*. https://plato.stanford.edu/entries/natural-law-ethics/

Scanlon, Thomas. 1998. *What We Owe to Each Other*. Cambridge, MA: Harvard University Press.

Solomon, Robert C. 1992. "Corporate Roles, Personal Virtues: An Aristotelian Approach to Business Ethics." *Business Ethics Quarterly*, 2(3): 317–339.

Tong, Rosemarie and Nancy Williams. 2016. "Feminist Ethics." In *Stanford Encyclopedia of Philosophy*. https://plato.stanford.edu/entries/feminism-ethics/

Velasquez, Manuel, et al. 1989. "Calculating Consequences: The Utilitarian Approach to Ethics." *Issues in Ethics*, 2(1). http://www.scu.edu/ethics/practicing/decision/calculating.html

5

THEORIES OF CORPORATE PERSONHOOD

The ethical theories we covered in Chapter 4 are powerful tools for evaluating   5.1
business ethics controversies. They offer *insight* into the ethical values that
business people regularly encounter in the decisions they face along with
strategies for integrating those values into ordinary business decision-making.
As we will see in our applied cases (Chapters 8–11), the ethical theories and
very useful for addressing ethical problems in business.

Before beginning those applications, though, we must consider a chal-   5.2
lenge to the possibility of using ethical theories to evaluate business actions.
Thus far, we have been assuming that business actions can be ethically
evaluated in the same way that individual people's actions can be evaluated.
That is, we used utilitarianism, Kantian ethics, virtue ethics, and other ethical theories, to evaluate *both* Fred's question about how he should pay for
weekend entertainment *and* Ford's, Walmart's, B.P.'s, and Enron's questions
about how they should address business problems. Businesses, though,
have clear differences from human beings. Ethical theories were created for
human beings to evaluate their own actions, based on characteristics that
human beings possess: the capacity to make choices, experience benefits
and harms, and have a conscience. To what extent do businesses share
these characteristics? Do businesses' differences from human beings
undermine our ability to evaluate business activities using ethical theories?
In this chapter, we explore these questions centered on the issue of *corporate personhood*. Is the corporation a person? If it is *not* a person, then what
kind of thing is the corporation?

This is Business Ethics: An Introduction, First Edition. Tobey Scharding.
© 2018 John Wiley & Sons, Inc. Published 2018 by John Wiley & Sons, Inc.

5.3   We will examine three possible responses to these questions: (1) that the corporation is a moral person; (2) that the corporation is *not* a moral person; and (3) that it does not much matter whether the corporation is a moral person or not. Many theorists have written about these issues; students may consult the references and further reading list for articles to explore the full range of writings on these topics. In this chapter, we focus on three particular viewpoints so as to understand their arguments most precisely: (1) Peter French's view that businesses should be organized such that they can act as a single agent, or a "person"; (2) Robert Jackall's counterpoint that businesses are so complicated and involve so many different people that there is no way they can act as a single agent; and (3) Matthew Altman's compromise view that business ethicists must use ethical theories that can hold corporate agents morally responsible.

Businesses as Ethical Persons

5.4 Peter French, a twentieth-century American philosopher, wants to hold businesses morally responsible for the things that they do. This means that the *business itself* is responsible for wrongdoing: not just the people who work there. So, in the Ford Pinto case, French's ideas would offer grounds for holding the Ford Motor Company responsible for the decision to sell defective Pintos. That does not necessarily mean that Lee Iacocca, Robert McNamara, and the Pinto engineers would not be morally responsible for their role in the fatalities, according to his view. French's point is just that the corporation itself should be held responsible.

5.5   Now, it might seem strange to want to hold a corporation responsible for something that was done by the people who work there. As Milton Friedman argued in Chapter 2, businesses cannot have social (or moral) responsibilities: only people have moral responsibilities. French agrees with Friedman's claim that people have moral responsibilities. He challenges the claim that businesses do not have moral responsibilities, though, and argues that corporations are persons, too. He thinks they are "members of the moral community" with the same rights, duties, and privileges as other moral persons, like Martin Luther King, Jr. and Aung San Suu Kyi. This theory has several parts. First, we will explore his *fiction* and *legal aggregate* theories of corporate personhood. Next, we will investigate his account of intentionality and its role in personhood. Finally, we will explore three kinds of personhood.

The legal aggregate (LA) theory of corporate personhood is French's 5.6
interlocutor account: an account introduced only for the purposes of criticizing. In this, it resembles the dominant model (DM) account of business
decision-making by which Edward Freeman paved the way for his stakeholder theory. The LA theory has the same role in French's argument as the
DM has in Freeman's argument. French introduces the LA theory in order
to criticize it, creating intellectual space in which he can introduce his own
account of corporate personhood, the fiction theory.

According to the LA theory of corporate personhood, corporations are 5.7
like umbrellas for *biological* persons, or human beings. They are umbrellas
because they can include a lot of people: in the same way that many people
can stand under a single umbrella. Standing under a single umbrella does
not change the fact that the people under the umbrella are individual
human beings. In the same way, the morally significant thing about a corporation is the people inside the corporation, *not* the corporation inside of
which they are all working. If a group of thieves robs a bank while standing
under an umbrella, the thieves—not the umbrella—are held morally
responsible. Similarly, if workers in the corporation do something morally
wrong while working in the corporation, they will be held morally responsible, according to the LA theory of corporate personhood.

French objects to this conception of corporate personhood. He claims 5.8
that the LA model fails to distinguish between corporations and mobs. The
mobs that French has in mind are large groups of unruly people, such as
those referenced by the term *mob justice* or *flash mob*. Mob justice is unlike
the regular justice that the court system effects when it tries a person
accused of a crime, finds the person innocent or guilty, and punishes the
person if guilty. In mob justice, a large group of people takes revenge on a
perceived wrongdoer by physically harming that person, such as hanging
them in a public square. Flash mobs, by contrast, occur when a large number of people assemble publicly to perform a random or unexpected act.
These two instances of mobs seem quite unlike corporations. We can see,
then, why French would object to a theory that made corporations seem
like mobs.

So how exactly are mobs like corporations under the LA theory? Mobs 5.9
are like corporations, according the LA theory, in that both involve large
groups of people acting in coordinated ways. The LA theory evaluates
them in the same way: both are umbrellas for the people acting within
them. Individual people in a mob and individual people in a corporation
should be held morally responsible for any wrongdoing they commit,

according to the legal aggregate theory. But French feels that corporations and mobs have an important difference, which the LA theory fails to acknowledge. This difference is part of what makes corporations more orderly than mobs.

5.10   That important difference is that corporations, but not mobs, are guided by a corporate internal decision-making structure (CID). Employees in corporations use the CID to decide what to do when the actions must be carried out by many people. The CID is first of all an employment hierarchy: it explains which supervisors make the decisions for which groups of employees. It also explains the principles that the supervisors are to use in making their decisions. These principles define the corporation's "corporate identity," as discussed further below. Finally, the CID explains how to resolve disputes among people at the same level of the employment hierarchy.

5.11   In this sense, the CID allows people to coordinate with one another and regulate their actions in ways that are impossible for mobs. The CID also makes it the case that people are not totally responsible for their actions, in the way that the LA theory requires. In the Ford Pinto case, for example, the Pinto engineers decided to use the weaker gas tank in order to save weight and money, meeting the orders that their boss, Lee Iacocca, gave them: under 2,000 pounds and less than 2,000 dollars. Without that direction, the Pinto engineers might have preferred a different gas tank. But Iacocca just gave the direction: he did not actually select the tanks. Considering the corporation's CID structure in evaluating the employee's actions thus demonstrates that it is impossible to see the Pinto fiasco as being the product of any one person completely. Ford employees were acting together in such a way that it can make sense to hold the Ford Motor Company *itself* responsible for the Pinto fiasco.

5.12   There is still the problem, though, that a corporation is quite straightforwardly *not* a moral person in the way that Martin Luther King, Jr. and Aung San Suu Kyi are. Whereas King and Suu Kyi have bodies and minds, the corporation is an abstract construction that has no flesh. If it is a person, it can only be a *non-biological* person. To explain how responsibility is to be attributed to non-biological persons, French develops his *fiction* theory of corporate personhood. According to this view, persons are creations of the law itself. Because persons are created by the law, biology has no role in personhood. So, how exactly does the law create persons? The law creates persons by calling them so. There was a time when women, people of color, and poor white men were not considered "persons" in the United States. (This meant that their rights were not legally recognized.) In the same way that the law was changed to include all human beings as moral persons, French argues that corporations can also be included in the moral community.

French's view is called the fiction theory, in this sense, because it under- 5.13 stands personhood as itself being fictional: whatever we decide it is. People decide which entities should be considered persons in the same way that they decide to pretend that the fictional people that they read about in novels are real people, about whom they should care. If these fictional characters were seen as being only words on a page, they would be far less interesting. Their *fiction* is what gives them life. French is not saying that we have to pretend that corporations are people, while knowing in our hearts that this is not so. Rather, he thinks that personhood is essentially fictional. Any entity can be a person if we decide—for good reason—that the entity should be a person.

French still needs to explain, though, why it is a good idea to include 5.14 corporations in the moral community. Even if we accept that personhood is fictional, this does not mean that we are going to be willing to include just anyone in the moral community. The fiction theory suggests that a kitchen table could be considered a moral person, if only we decide that it should be. But that is preposterous: there is no good reason to include kitchen tables in the moral community. French thinks that there *are* good reasons to include corporations in the community, however. He explains these good reasons by defining several kinds of personhood and explaining why he believes that corporations meet the standards to be considered some kinds of persons, but not others. The kinds of personhood he discusses are legal personhood, moral personhood, and metaphysical personhood. He thinks that corporations are legal and moral persons but not metaphysical persons.

Let us understand what French means by each of these terms. First, legal 5.15 personhood. This is the sense of personhood that we discussed in the fiction theory: persons are whatever the law says they are. Legal persons are entities that are the subjects of legal rights and legal responsibilities. It is a fact about U.S. law that businesses are considered legal persons. They are legal persons in the sense that they can do legal things: they can obey the law, can break the law, can enter into contracts, can sue and be sued. Businesses become legal persons in the process of being "incorporated." But the mere fact that a business is a legal person does not mean that it is a member of the moral community.

A moral person is a member of the moral community. Moral persons are 5.16 defined, for French, as being accountable for their actions. This means that they can be blamed for their bad actions and praised for their good actions. Moral persons like you and me are praised and blamed for our actions because we freely decided to do them: no one forced us and we made up our own minds. That is to say, we are responsible for our actions because we are metaphysical persons. Metaphysical persons are defined, for French, as entities that are able to act freely. Are corporations able to act freely? This question seems difficult to answer. Think back to the Ford Pinto case. The engineers decided to install the weak gas tank—but this was not "their" decision in a very strong sense. They were acting under orders from their supervisor, Lee Iacocca. Iacocca did not "force" them to choose a particular tank because Iacocca did not have the engineering expertise to decide which tank was appropriate for the Pinto. But he strongly influenced the decision the engineers were able to make. So their actions as Ford employees do not seem "free" in the sense required for metaphysical personhood. In this sense, Ford is not a metaphysical person.

5.17   French, though, thinks that corporations like Ford are moral persons. So Ford is morally responsible for the damage caused by its faulty Pintos. But Ford did not "freely decide" to make the faulty Pintos. Therefore, French needs to provide a different explanation of corporations like Ford are morally responsible for actions that they do not freely undertake. And French does have an explanation ready. He thinks that entities can be considered morally responsible if they demonstrate what he calls *intentionality*. And French thinks that corporations do have intentionality.

5.18   So, why do corporations have intentionality? First, we need to define this term. Intentionality is a quality that people have when they form an *intention* to act. Think back to our discussion concerning Kantian ethics (Chapter 4). There, we considered a person's intention in acting to be a rule underlying that action. More generally, an intention is the thought that a person gives to an action, before the person carries out the action. It is a part of decision-making.

5.19   French thinks that corporations do form intentions as part of their decision-making. We can see their intentions by referring to the CID structure discussed above. How does the CID structure allow corporations to form decisions? As noted above, the CID establishes an employment hierarchy: who gives orders to whom. So, even if a corporate decision is made at a lower level, the CID explains who must ratify this decision in order for it to count as the corporation's own. The CID also establishes the corporation's *corporate policy*: its rules for making corporate decisions. Part of this corporate policy is the corporation's *corporate identity*, which offers general guidelines about what kind of decision-maker the corporation hopes to be.

In the same way that your personal identity guides you to form intentions 5.20
about which actions to take, the corporate identity guides the corporation's
intentions about what it will decide to do. Because the corporation thus
forms intentions, it is possible to hold it morally responsible for the actions
it undertakes.

Sidebar Exercise

Raise an objection to French's view of corporate personhood and offer
a response on French's behalf.

Sidebar Exercise

Apply French's view of corporate personhood to the Enron case. How
does French's view help to evaluate the case? What problems, if any,
does French's view encounter in evaluating the Enron case? Can you
think of any way of improving the view so as to gain more insight into
the case?

Businesses as Bureaucracies

In his ([1989] 2009) book, *Moral Mazes*, Robert Jackall raises an important 5.21
challenge to French's account of businesses' CID structures. Unlike Mill's
challenge to Bentham's view (described in Chapter 2), however, Jackall
does not directly criticize French's account. Rather, he offers an independent theory of corporate organization, which we can use to criticize French's
account. On French's view, the CID structure facilitates clear, *centralized*
decision-making: the kind of centralized decision-making in which individual human beings engage. (Individual human decision-making is centralized in the sense that there is only one person, with one brain,
"centering" the decision.) Jackall argues, though, that businesses are not
centrally organized at all. In fact, on his view, businesses are essentially
bureaucracies.

Jackall and French thus have a dispute about corporate personhood (or, 5.22
we can interpret them as having this disagreement, though they do not

actually engage with one another's views). Each one thinks that a business is a different kind of thing. For French, corporations are simple, centralized persons. Jackall holds—by contrast—that they are complicated, chaotic bureaucracies. And their bureaucratic natures challenge the extent to which businesses can be held responsible for anything.

5.23   To understand the dispute between French and Jackall, we need to understand why Jackall thinks that businesses are bureaucracies rather than centralized decision-makers. First, a definition of bureaucracies. Bureaucracies are the complicated systems that administer large organizations like corporations. The word is somewhat derisive, in that calling something a "bureaucracy" is typically a way of criticizing that thing. The term suggests that it is very hard to get things done, that the channels of communication are not clear, and that people often have to do things completely unrelated to accomplishing their goals in order to accomplish those goals. That is because bureaucracies generally require members to follow elaborate routines in order to accomplish even simple tasks.

5.24   According to Jackson, the routines that people must follow in bureaucracies largely involve currying favor. What French's approach neglects, that is, is that all of the people working at the corporation are still *people*, interested in achieving success and other goals. They do not give up their individuality just because they are working as part of a larger group. In fact, it is part of Jackall's argument that bureaucratic workers achieve success largely by pleasing and submitting to their supervisors. Taken all together, the individual self-interest and universal incentive to flatter—directed throughout the organization—make it impossible for the corporation to act in a centralized manner about anything.

5.25   Jackall argues that corporations should be considered bureaucracies because of their complicated organizational structures. These structures include:

- an administrative chain of command;
- standard work processes;
- regular schedules;
- uniform policies;
- central control.

Jackall's argument depends, in this sense, on the fact that corporations actually have the aspects of their organizations listed here. (In the same way, French's argument requires that corporations actually use CID structures to make their decisions.) But how do we, on the outside, know whether a particular business has such structures? We can start by re-examining the business ethics-controversies that we have looked at so far (Chapter 3) and using our knowledge of corporations.

First, an administrative chain of command. This means that businesses 5.26 have a hierarchy of power, such that people closer to the top of the hierarchy make decisions that people lower on the hierarchy must follow. Typically, the top of the hierarchy is the chief executive officer (CEO) followed by other C-suite executives (COO, CFO, and so on, as discussed in Chapter 2). Lower down on the hierarchy, we find various vice presidents, such as Lee Iacocca; still lower, we find the Pinto engineers at Ford, the brokers at Enron, store managers at Walmart, and so on. This is generally the way that corporations are structured. Moreover, French also thinks that corporations have an administrative hierarchy: so this is not a point of disagreement between the two views.

Next, standard work processes, regular schedules, and uniform policies. 5.27 These aspects of corporate organization mean that the corporation has a standard way of doing things, including a regular timetable by which it brings its products to market and policies that affect all workers in the same way. These descriptions of corporate organization do seem in line with the cases we have examined so far. We have not seen specific examples of standard work processes, regular schedules, and uniform policies as yet, so we should remain somewhat cautious here. But it makes sense that Ford engineers, Enron brokers, and Walmart employees all do their work following a standard process, along regular schedules, following uniform policies. Although French does not explicitly discuss standard work processes, this seems to be in keeping with his view, as well.

Finally, central control. This aspect of corporations seems to be more 5.28 questionable. What evidence do we see for central control in the Pinto case? We believe that engineers were influenced by Iacocca's belief that "safety doesn't sell" and his requirement that the car cost under $2,000, to choose a weak gas tank. We think that Ford's devotion to cost-benefit analysis was influenced by CEO Robert McNamara's background as an accountant. This standard for bureaucracies also seems vaguer than the first four. We will have to wait and see how important it is to Jackall's overall view.

For now, let us assume that Jackall has successfully established that 5.29 corporations are bureaucracies. The next step in his argument is to demonstrate how corporations' complicated organizational structures shape managers' moral outlooks. This includes: the CEO's influence, the reporting system, and what causes employees to succeed or fail.

5.30   Jackall writes that each company is a self-sufficient organization, like its own little country with the CEO at the top as the king or queen. Like a monarch, the CEO has a lot of power. The CEO's subordinates know this. They also know that the fastest way for them to gain power for themselves is by pleasing the CEO.

5.31   The desire to please the CEO takes several characteristic forms. The first is the *ritual deference* that employees extend to the boss. This means that employees defer to their supervisor almost as a matter of habit. The second is the effort to protect the CEO: to keep the boss from making mistakes and, especially, to keep any mistakes from being made public. Employees who are further down the administrative hierarchy extend the same kind of subordination to their immediate supervisors.

5.32   Another effect of the CEO's power is the so-called *reporting system*. All employees report to their manager and, ultimately, all managers report to the CEO. The CEO, in turn, provides goals to his or her subordinates. The details of the goals are never spelled out and it is up to the subordinate to figure out how to achieve the goals. Jackall calls the bureaucratic management style "management-by-objectives."

5.33   According to this style, details are delegated to subordinates while credit is kept for superiors. As an example, a boss might tell an employee to: "Build ten oil wells in the Gulf of Mexico. Call me when they are ready to pump." It is up to the employee to figure out how to achieve the boss's goal. Because they are unfamiliar with the details of how the goal is achieved, bosses expect triumphs with no tradeoffs. The employees are under intense pressure to make any problems go away: not only so they may transmit good news but also so they may protect their bosses. By pleasing their bosses, employees hope that they also will be rewarded.

5.34   What brings about success for executive managers, in this sense, is setting hard-to-reach goals and forcing their subordinates to reach them. What brings about success for employees, though, is simply pleasing their bosses. They are acculturated to put on an agreeable appearance and never complain. Ambitious employees hesitate to express moral qualms that could make their bosses worry. They simply strive to meet the boss's goals—especially as regards profit commitments—as fully as possible.

5.35   Jackall does not specifically argue that all of these bureaucratic shenanigans prevent the corporation from acting as a single person. By examining his ideas in the context of Peter French's view, though, we can see how the bureaucratic nature of corporations—if real—could prevent them from acting in a centralized manner.

Take French's requirement that the corporation demonstrate intention- 5.36 ality, for example. Jackall might not disagree that corporations have CID structures as part of their administrative hierarchy. But his analysis of the reasons why employees of a corporation are acting undermines the impor- tance of that hierarchy. According to Jackall's analysis, employees act so as to protect and please their supervisors—not so as to effect the decisions that have been handed down from above. Supervisors' instructions are intentions in only a very weak sense. They do not tell subordinates to do anything in particular but just to accomplish some goal. Thus, the actions that employees take are not the corporation's own. But the employees would not have taken the actions if not for the corporation. Under Jackall's view of corporate organization, it looks like it will be very difficult to hold anyone associated with the corporation responsible for anything: either the corporation itself or any corporate employee.

Sidebar Exercise

Consider one way in which the bureaucratic organization could have contributed to one of the business scandals we looked at in Chapter 3. Be specific in your analysis.

Sidebar Exercise

Raise an objection to Jackall's view of corporate organization. How could Jackall respond?

Businesses as Collective Persons

Peter French and Robert Jackall present starkly different views of corporate 5.37 organization, which lead to conflicting views of corporate responsibility. Whereas the corporation is morally responsible on French's view, it is not responsible when examined in light of Jackall's account. If French is correct, then we will be able to apply our ethical theories to corporate activities easily—as the corporation is just another moral person. If Jackall is correct, though, it could be more difficult to apply our ethical theories to corporate actions and hold the corporation morally responsible. So the dispute between them is an important one, for our purposes.

5.38   One way to resolve this dispute would be to show that Jackall's worries about corporate bureaucracy do not undermine our ability to hold corporations (or business people) morally responsible. Another way is to seek ethical theories that can hold corporate agents responsible—even if corporate agents are bureaucracies rather than moral persons. According to this argument, ethical theories that can only hold persons (individual agents) responsible would be less useful for business ethics students. Ethical theories that can hold bureaucracies (corporate agents) responsible, on the other hand, could be widely used in business ethics. In this section, we pursue the latter strategy, following an argument made by American business ethicist, Matthew Altman. (You might want to pursue the former strategy on your own, perhaps as a term paper.)

5.39   Let us begin by discussing Altman's criticisms of ethical theories that can evaluate only the actions of individual agents. Altman focuses on Kantian ethics, in particular. First, Altman argues that corporations are not morally responsible from a Kantian perspective. Corporations lack certain characteristics that moral persons require, for Kant. These characteristics include inclinations and rationality, as discussed further below. Second, he argues that Kant also struggles to attribute moral responsibility to the individual people who work in corporations. This is because of what he calls the *diffusion of responsibility* in corporations. The diffusion of responsibility in corporations means that responsibility is spread throughout the corporation in such a way that it is impossible to attach it to anyone in particular.

5.40   We examined the problem of the diffusion of responsibility (in the Pinto case) when discussing Jackall's view, above. It was Pinto engineers, not Lee Iacocca or Robert McNamara, who placed the weak gas tank in the Pinto's rear end. But the Pinto engineers were striving to fulfill a goal set for them by Iacocca. Although Iacocca did not tell them precisely how to meet that goal, the engineers would not have selected the weak gas tank if not for Iacocca's business model for the Pinto. Because Kantian ethics can only hold individual people morally responsible, then, Altman concludes that Kantian ethics will be unable to attribute moral responsibility in business ethics controversies. Business ethics students will have to use another ethical theory to do that.

In particular, business ethics students will have to use an ethical theory 5.41 that can attribute collective responsibility. Given the diffusion of responsibility in a bureaucracy, as discussed above, Altman feels that ethical theories must be able to attribute collective responsibility if they are to be useful in business ethics. Collective responsibility means that a *group* of people is responsible for a particular action—rather than individuals within that group. Moral theories can use collective responsibility to hold a group of people morally responsible for an action when it would have been impossible for any of them to have done that action on their own.

The Pinto case as discussed above seems to be a good example of collec- 5.42 tive responsibility. The Pinto engineers chose the defective tank. But they were fulfilling the directive of their boss, Lee Iacocca. Iacocca, though, did not tell them specifically to install a weak tank. He gave them a set of instructions that the engineers found impossible to follow in any other way.

This all sounds good so far. But why can't we use Kantian ethics to deliver 5.43 the analysis about Iacocca's and the engineers' wrongdoing? As noted above, Altman points out that, for Kantian ethics, moral agents must have inclinations and a capacity to reason. Inclinations are what you naturally feel like doing. Usually, this is not obeying the moral law. Rationality, or human intelligence, is what guides people to the moral law, for Kant. It is important to him that moral agents form maxims, test their maxims, and then hold themselves to the moral law. But businesses lack both inclinations and human rationality. They also lack collective intentions. In the Pinto case, for example, there is nothing that Iacocca, McNamara, and the Pinto engineers collectively intend to do. Rather, each have their own intentions: McNamara to run an automobile business like an accounting firm, Iacocca to keep the Pinto sticker price under $2,000, the engineers to please their supervisors. According to Altman's analysis, then, Kantian ethics have little to offer business decision-making.

A Kantian could object to this criticism by pointing out that corporations 5.44 *do* have collective intentions: as expressed in their corporate identities and corporate policies. This, in fact, was one of French's central claims in his argument that corporations are moral persons. Even if employees are self-centered and act to further their own interests, rather than to carry out their orders in an ethical and dutiful manner, this does not mean that they are not bound by the corporation's collective intentions. It could mean, rather, that they are acting unethically—in dereliction of their duty to fulfill the corporation's objectives.

5.45   Altman has a response to this objection. He argues that corporate policies can only *encourage* (or discourage) people to act in certain ways. The morality of a given action, though, is up to the people acting themselves. This is a central tenet of Kantian ethics, on his interpretation. People must overcome their inclinations and hold themselves to rational standards (as expressed by FUL and FH, which we discussed in Chapter 4). For example, some employees might wish to neglect their ethical responsibilities in order to please their supervisors and advance within the corporation. Using Kantian ethics, though, it is up to those employees to evaluate their possible actions and hold themselves to the moral law. The morality of what they decide to do, whatever it may be, cannot be determined by the corporation's policies.

5.46   Altman does not say which moral theory he thinks can account for collective intentions. But he does offer an alternative to French's and Jackall's theories of the metaphysics of business. French holds that the corporation is a moral person and that the corporation itself is morally responsible for any ethical wrongdoing in which it is involved. Jackall argues that the corporation is a bureaucracy. As such, we can infer that corporations cannot be morally responsible for any ethical wrongdoing in which they are involved. But individual people cannot be held responsible either, on his view. Altman offers an alternative to both of these positions. He does not say whether he thinks the corporation is a person, a bureaucracy, or something else. But he does say who is morally responsible: groups of people, acting collectively.

Sidebar Exercise

Altman focuses on Kantian ethics, only, as an ethical theory that is able to evaluate the actions of individual agents, only, and not the actions of corporate agents like Ford or Walmart. Consider the extent to which his criticisms of Kantian ethics apply to the other ethical theories we have studied, such as utilitarianism and virtue ethics. Should business ethics students use these theories to evaluate business actions? Or are they subject to the same criticisms as Kantian ethics?

Sidebar Exercise

Do you agree with Altman that Kantian ethics cannot account for collective actions? Raise an objection to Altman's view and consider his response.

Sidebar Exercise

Consider one way in which collective responsibility could help to make sense of the Enron, Walmart, or B.P. cases from Chapter 3. Be as specific as possible!

References and Further Reading

Altman, Matthew C. 2007. "The Decomposition of the Corporate Body: What Kant Cannot Contribute to Business Ethics." *Journal of Business Ethics*, 74(3): 253–266.

French, Peter A. 1979. "The Corporation as a Moral Person." *American Philosophical Quarterly*, 16(3): 207–215.

Jackall, Robert. [1989] 2009. *Moral Mazes: The World of Corporate Managers.* Oxford: Oxford University Press.

Totenberg, Nina. 2014. "When Did Companies Become People? Excavating the Legal Evolution." *NPR*, July 28. http://www.npr.org/2014/07/28/335288388/when-did-companies-become-people-excavating-the-legal-evolution

6

THEORIES OF POLITICAL ECONOMY

6.1 Now that our philosophical toolkit is full of powerful, ethical decision-making strategies (Chapter 4), and we have had an opportunity to consider some problems with those decision-making strategies (Chapters 4 and 5), we can add some fine-tuned tools. These new tools will help us to address the issues we considered concerning corporate personhood (Chapter 5) and to understand more deeply the background issues at play in our business ethics cases (Chapters 3 and 8–11). Including those background issues in our evaluations will allow us greater insight into the cases themselves. This insight, in turn, will help us to come up with solutions to ethical problems in business that are more likely to succeed.

6.2 As we progress in our business ethics studies, then, we will continue to use our ethical theories (Chapter 4) to evaluate case studies. We will supplement and challenge those decision-making strategies with our new conceptual tools concerning corporate personhood (Chapter 5). In this chapter, we add theories of political economy to our philosophical toolkit. The theories of political economy serve two purposes. First, they begin to address the issue of corporate bureaucracy that we examined in Chapter 5: by giving us ways to consider corporations as political and economic organizations rather than as individual people. Second, the theories of political economy offer perspectives for analyzing some of the dynamics at play in corporate activities, which ethical theories might neglect.

6.3 We begin, as always, by defining our terms. Theories of political economy are philosophical explanations for features of the economy. As will be discussed further, these philosophical explanations involve *justifying*

This is Business Ethics: An Introduction, First Edition. Tobey Scharding.
© 2018 John Wiley & Sons, Inc. Published 2018 by John Wiley & Sons, Inc.

aspects of the economy. Economies are (roughly) the social institutions and activities by which people buy and sell goods and services. Businesses are some of these social institutions and business activities are some of the activities involved in the economy. By understanding which aspects of the economy are justified and on what grounds, then, we can assess when business activities are justified—even if we cannot conceive of businesses as persons, as discussed in Chapter 5.

Economies have many aspects: private property, taxation, the printing of 6.4 currency, the establishing of a certain interest rate, the division of labor, and many others. In this chapter, we will be exploring competing justifications of: (1) private property; and (2) the division of labor. We focus on justifications of these aspects of the economy for two reasons. First, the justifications utilize a full range of perspectives on business activities: individual, society-wide, that of the most powerful, that of the least powerful. Second, the justifications were written by historically important theorists, are well argued, and have influenced many other theorists. The two discussions of private property provide the opportunity to reflect on whether ownership should be justified on an individual basis (the grounds by which an individual person comes to own something) or a society-wide basis (no property is justified unless we consider what everyone in society owns). The discussions of the division of labor, in turn, offer two different perspectives on what kinds of workplace conditions are justified: the view from the most powerful (in terms of overall productivity) and the view from the least powerful (individual employees as they perform their hard work).

Before getting into those specific topics, though, let us spend a bit of time 6.5 understanding what theories of political economy are. In introducing our ethical theories, we contrasted them with scientific theories. The same comparison is helpful in grasping what theories of political economy are. As is well known, scientific theories explain physical phenomena in cause-and-effect terms. One simple example is: when I drop an object, it falls to the ground. The explanation is that whenever X occurs (where X is defined as "a person drops an object"), Y results (where Y is defined as "the object falls to the ground). This explanation can be tested empirically. The tests either support or falsify the explanation. Over time, after many tests have been completed, scientists can have a very good idea if the explanation is true or not.

Theories of political economy, by contrast, explain features of the econ- 6.6 omy. They do not, however, explain why there *is* a particular economic feature, empirically speaking. Rather, theories of political economy attempt to *justify* the feature. Take the economic institution of taxation, for example.

An empirical theory might explain taxation as follows: when a government needs money, it taxes its citizens. This explanation is similar to the scientific observation offered above. Whenever X occurs (where X is defined as "a government needs money"), Y results (where Y is defined as "the government taxes its citizens"). This explanation, like the explanation from physics, above, can be tested empirically.

6.7   A theory of political economy would not explain when the government taxes its citizens but, rather, what *justifies* a government in taxing its citizens. So, a theory of political economy might claim that a society is justified in taxing its citizens in order to provide for the common defense or pay for the judiciary. Although many people might agree with this claim, it cannot be tested empirically in the same way as the empirical explanation. In this sense, theories of political economy resemble the ethical theories we examined in Chapter 4. Like those ethical theories, we do have grounds to accept or reject theories of political economy, even though they cannot be supported or falsified in an empirical sense. Instead, we have to decide if the theory of political economy agrees or disagrees with our intuitions about related matters. For example, if you and a group of friends wish to purchase something that you all need, like people in a society need a common defense or a judiciary, is it ethical for you to each pay for a portion of it? How you answer this question can help you to think about the right way to decide whether governments are justified in taxing their citizens, and for what purposes.

6.8   In this sense, theories of political economy seem quite philosophical. Why, then are they called theories of "political" economy instead of "philosophical" economy? This is a complicated question, and there might not be a single, really satisfying answer to it. But think about it this way. Theories of political economy usually try to justify some aspect of the economy in terms of the role it plays in the society's political structure. In the above discussion of taxation, for example, the theory explained that taxation is justified when the monies are needed to pay for the common defense and the judiciary. The common defense and the judiciary are political institutions. Theories of political economy generally do not give explanations that are purely philosophical in nature. What is a purely philosophical explanation? Philosophical explanations typically try to explain why something is justified in an absolute sense. In Chapter 4, for example, we saw that the formula of humanity claims that the right thing to do is to respect humanity as an end and never treat humanity as a mere means. This is always the right thing to do, no matter what the circumstances, for Kantian ethics. The justification of taxation, though, applies only to circumstances in which governments need money to pay for the common defense and judiciary. The government is not absolutely justified in taxing its citizens but just in those particular circumstances.

Okay, that is a lot to take in. And we have not even gotten to the theories 6.9 themselves yet. Hopefully the background information helps to explain why it is useful to study theories of political economy and to give you a better idea of the kinds of studies we will undertake in this chapter. We will begin by looking at two theories of the justification of private property: (1) the philosopher John Locke's strong defense of private property rights; and (2) the philosopher John Rawls's account of *distributive justice*. Distributive justice means that private property is only justified if it is distributed, or shared, across society in a certain way. Next, we will look at two theories of the justification of the division of labor: (1) Adam Smith's argument that the division of labor is justified because it increases overall prosperity; and (2) Karl Marx's argument that the division of labor is not justified because it alienates workers.

Private Property

Private property is an economic institution whereby people can gain *exclu-* 6.10 *sive control* over things like objects, places, and even ideas. Exclusive control means that no one but the owner can use these things without the owner's explicit permission. We are so used to the institution of private property that it is hard to imagine life without it. If we did not have private property, for example, it is possible to imagine that anyone could use your laptop whenever they pleased—it would not be yours exclusively, after all. That probably does not seem very convenient. The institution of private property also played a role in the cases we examined in Chapter 3. In the Pinto case, for example, the cars were sold to customers and became their private property. If customers did not gain exclusive control of the Pintos, though, Ford might have taken greater care with them. For example, if the cars were shared among customers, Ford engineers, Lee Iacocca, Robert McNamara, and other executives, executives might have decided to reinforce the rear axle, improve the bumper, support the tank, add a bladder, or surround the tank with a protective barrier, as discussed in Chapter 3.

Consider also the role of private property in the Walmart case. In that 6.11 case, we saw that Walmart had many low-skilled employees who felt that their employer did not treat them well. Despite being employed by a hugely profitable company, these employees were paid low wages. Some of them said that they had to choose between buying food and taking a sick child to the doctor: because they could only afford one or the other. These unfortunate situations, also, depend on the institution of private property. The aggrieved Walmart employees had very little private property in a society in which many people have a great deal more private property. This disparity can make life hard for those who have little private property. With a different conception of property, such as the one that John Rawls sets forth, these poor people might be able to own more property and have better lives. Let us now examine the theories of private property.

The justification of private property

6.12 As noted above, the institution of private property is so much a part of our daily lives that it is hard to imagine life without it. One of the reasons that private property plays such an important role in society is the foundational account offered by John Locke. Locke was an English philosopher who lived in the seventeenth century. He wrote a famous philosophy book called *Two Treatises of Government*. In this book, Locke explained why people are entitled—and even ethically required—to have exclusive control over certain physical objects as their private property. This is not to say that no one enjoyed "exclusive control" over objects, places, or ideas before John Locke wrote his book. Of course they did. The difference was that Locke gave an explanation of why people are justified in owning private property.

6.13 As a basis for this justification, Locke imagines a much earlier time in the history of the world, before human civilization really took off. This earlier time is called the *state of nature*. In the state of nature, there are no countries, cities, skyscrapers, or cars. People live solitary lives with only their family members and perhaps a few other acquaintances. They reside in caves or simple huts. Unlike the houses in which civilized people live—and know that they own—people in the state of nature do not feel that they are exclusively entitled to their caves and huts. Instead, everything is shared. Locke tries to imagine how people went from this way of living to their current societies, in which private property has so much importance.

6.14 His justification of private property is based on two claims, concerning: (1) humankind's original, common ownership of the world; and (2) people's original, exclusive ownership of their own bodies and minds. We will examine these claims in turn. Then, we discuss two philosophical skills that Locke uses in his work: raising objections and offering responses to those objections. Finally, we will consider some objections that other philosophers have raised against Locke's view—and see if we can respond to those objections on Locke's behalf.

First, Locke's claim about common world ownership. When Locke tries 6.15 to imagine what the world was like for people, before it was divided up into countries and cities, he imagines that there was no private property at all. Instead, he said that the world was owned by all people. Of this world, he wrote that "all the fruits it naturally produces, and beasts it feeds, belong to mankind in common." This means that the earth itself belonged to everybody; everything that the earth produces—fruits, nuts, deer, pigs—also belongs to everybody. In this sense, anyone can venture out to pick whatever fruits he or she wants and eat whatever animals he or she wants.

So, why does Locke think that the world originally belonged to people in 6.16 common? Locke was a devout Christian and on his interpretation of the Christian Scripture, God gave the world to people as their common property. The world is a gift from God to human beings. For Locke, this was a bountiful gift, but it came with strings attached. That is, God did not give the world to humankind so that they could do whatever they wanted with the world, including waste or squander it. No. God gave the world to human beings so that they can "make use of it to the best advantage of life and convenience." God wanted human beings to benefit from the world: to enjoy the good things in life and live comfortably.

Sidebar Exercise

Think of a reason why someone who is not Christian, or does not believe in God, might think the natural world belongs to all people in common. Do you personally agree with Locke's claim about original, common world ownership? Why or why not?

Worksheet Exercise

Explaining a philosophical claim

In looking at Locke's claims about common world ownership, we did some work together to figure out what he means by his claims. In explaining a claim, we began by quoting Locke's own writing. Then, we paraphrased the quotation using our own words. We sometimes gave examples to clarify Locke's meaning. He mentions that the "beasts" of the earth belong to everyone and we gave two examples of beasts that humans eat: deer (venison) and pigs (pork). Finally, we drew an inference from Locke's claims. An inference is when one of the philosopher's explicit statements implies that the philosopher believes something else as well. So, when Locke said that fruits and beasts belong to humankind in common, we inferred that people could pick whatever fruits they wanted, or hunt whatever animals, no matter where they were: close to their own home or far away.

Now, try to explain some other claims of Locke's related to the state of nature. Begin by paraphrasing the quotation using your own words. Then, give an example of the claim, or draw an inference from it, or both, to make it really clear what Locke means by his words.

> Men living according to reason, without a common superior on earth, to judge between them, is properly the state of nature.

> [C]hildren or servants could not cut the meat, which their father or master had provided for them in common, without assigning to every one his peculiar part.

> [N]o body has originally a private dominion, exclusive of the rest of mankind, in any of the[fruits and beasts], as they are thus in their natural state.

6.17   The fact that God wants human beings to benefit from the world means, for Locke, that there must be a way to divide up the common property among human beings. Remember those commonly owned fruits and beasts? Locke write that "there must of necessity be a means to appropriate them some way or other before they can be of any use at all beneficial to any man." Locke says that people must "appropriate" the fruits and beasts before they can benefit anyone. But he seems to be using this word in an unfamiliar manner. Indeed, the meaning that Locke uses was common in the seventeenth century and is less common now. By looking a little more closely, though, we can figure out what he means. Do you see any familiar word roots in "appropriate"? Perhaps some that are shared by the title of this section? By "appropriate," Locke means to "make property." Before human beings can benefit from fruits and beasts, they must figure out which fruits, and which beasts, belong to which people. They must make the natural world into private property.

Next, we explore Locke's claim concerning exclusive self-ownership. 6.18 The discussion of people's common ownership of the natural world shows that people must create private property, on Locke's view. It remains to be seen, though, exactly how people can remake the natural world into private property. Remember that on Locke's view the world isn't just unowned: it belongs to all people. So there has to be some justification for why a part of the world can stop being commonly owned and start belonging to only one person, as their exclusive property. Once an object, place, or idea is private property, no one else can use it—without the owner's explicit permission.

For Locke, the first step in dividing up the world is realizing that 6.19 not all of the world belongs to people in common. Each person already has exclusive property in one part of the natural world: in their own "person." (This is the word that Locke uses.) This means that each human being *owns* him- or herself. No one can take any action against them without their explicit permission. We call this state of owning oneself: *self-ownership*.

So, what does it mean to have *property* in your *person*? We do not usually 6.20 think of ourselves as property. We can *own* property, to be sure. But a person's relationship to him- or herself differs in an important way from his or her relationship to other kinds of property. That is, we can sell our property to someone else if we want to. We can even destroy our property if that is what we decide to do: it belongs to us alone, after all. But it doesn't seem ethical to do either of these things to ourselves.

How could Locke attempt to account for this problem? Well, one thing 6.21 that he might do is acknowledge that the way that we own ourselves *is* different from the way that we own other kinds of property. That is, he could say that our rights of self-ownership do not permit us to sell ourselves or destroy ourselves, even though the right of ownership does permit us to sell other property or destroy other property. Is this an arbitrary distinction or can Locke provide a good rationale for it? In Locke's opinion, he has a great rationale for the distinction between people's ownership of themselves and people's ownership of other kinds of property. He views human beings as kind of trustees over their persons, on behalf of God. God retains ultimate ownership over persons and we are not permitted to sell or destroy God's property.

Sidebar Exercise

Are you satisfied by Locke's response? Or would you criticize it further? What further criticisms could you raise against Locke's response?

6.22   Looking a little more deeply into Locke's view can help us to understand both (1) why Locke thinks that God owns us; and (2) how that rationale for ownership entitles human beings to gain private property in parts of the natural world. That is a little confusing. Let us begin with the second part first. Locke writes that human beings own themselves: each person owns his or her mind and his or her body as well. But self-ownership is not limited to ownership of one's arms and legs, one's ideas and decisions. On the basis of self-ownership, people also own everything that they can make with their arms, legs, ideas, and decisions. As Locke puts it: "Every man has a property in his own person; this nobody has any right to but himself. The labor of his body and the work of his hands we may say are properly his." People gain private property in the objects of the natural world that they labor on with their bodies and hands.

6.23   Consider an example. Remember, Locke is thinking about a world in which there is no private property in external objects and places yet. (People do, as noted above, already do have private property in their own persons.) One thing in this world might be a giant field in which an apple orchard is growing. The field and the apple orchard belong to no one in particular. One day, a man goes out into the field. He picks an armful of apples from a tree, laboring on that aspect of the natural world with his own mind (which decides to pick the apples) and his own arms (which remove the apples from the trees and carry them away). In virtue of this labor, Locke thinks that the man becomes the owner of the apples. Now, they do not belong to humankind in general but are the man's private property. So, he may do with the apples whatever he pleases. He may destroy them, say, by eating them. He may use them to make another product, such as an apple pie. He may trade them to someone else, gaining private property in something else that he wants. (At this time, there is no money, so the man is not yet able to gain cash, or earn a profit, on the apples.)

6.24   Now, think back to the first topic that we mentioned above: how looking more deeply into Locke's view can help us to understand why he thinks that God owns us. People gain private property in the parts of the natural world on which they labor. But God labored to create human beings themselves, on the Christian view. The fact that God created human beings is why God owns us, for Locke.

Sidebar Exercise

Can you think of any other objections to Locke's account of private property? Try to spell out the objections so that they are as powerful as possible. Then, consider Locke's response. Would he concede to your objection, as he conceded to the idea that self-ownership is different from other kinds of ownership? Or would he try to rebut your objection more directly? Imagine that you are having a conversation—like a friendly argument—with Locke about his view. See how many steps out you can take the argument.

Sidebar

In discussing Locke's claim that human beings own themselves, we raised an objection to that claim: people do not usually think of themselves as owning themselves. Raising an objection is one of the most important parts of philosophy. Because all philosophical views are controversial, considering objections to them helps us to improve the views, so that they become less controversial. As part of this improving process, we considered Locke's response to the objection. In his response, Locke did not deny the objection. In fact, he conceded it, admitting it was true. But then Locke tried to explain why the fact that people may not destroy themselves or sell themselves does not undermine his claim that people own themselves. Thus, in considering the objection and the response, we gained deeper insight into Locke's view.

Our next topic in Locke's philosophy of private property is the so-called 6.25 "Lockean proviso." There is another important difference between human ownership and divine ownership. God owns us outright because he created us. Our self-ownership is only as stewards for God. We gain private property in those aspects of the natural world on which we labor. But it turns out that our ownership of these natural products is not absolute either. (After all, God did create the natural world itself. So he retains an ownership interest in the world just like he retains an ownership interest in us.)

6.26   Locke thinks that there is a limit to people's abilities to gain private property in the natural world. That limit may be out of respect for God's ultimate creation of the natural world or it might be for some other reason. Locke himself does not say. What he does say is this: "Labor being the unquestionable property of the laborer, no man but he can have a right to what this is once joined to, at least where there is enough, and as good, left in common for others." This quotation is known as the *Lockean proviso*. There are a number of interesting things about this proviso. First, the name itself. "Proviso" is another one of those unfamiliar words. Remember, Locke was writing a long time ago! Different words were in common usage then. Note, though, that Locke does not explicitly use the term proviso in this quotation. One of Locke's commenters, who wrote about his view, came up with this term. Before you continue, look up this word so you are sure that you know what it means.

6.27   The second interesting thing about this quotation is the very strong defense that Locke gives in it of people's private property rights. He says that labor is the "unquestionable" property of the laborer. Think about the controversies we have been discussing in this book. Locke's point here is that it is *uncontroversial* that a person's labor belongs to him or her. Do you agree? Remember, we are not talking about whether any objects or places in the world can "unquestionably" belong to a person. Locke's claim about labor belonging to the laborer relates only to the actions that laborers can take— with their arms, legs, and minds—as they work on something.

6.28   Locke infers from the claim about labor belonging to the laborer in a very strong sense that no one can "have a right" to anything that the laborer "joins" his labor to. The laborer "joins" his labor to what he labors on in the sense discussed about in the apple orchard example. The apple picker labors on those apples, such that they apples are not the same as they were when they were just hanging on the tree. They now have labor attached to them. Thus, no one else has a right to them. Even someone who is really hungry does not have the right to take apples on which someone else has labored.

6.29   The third interesting thing in this quotation is, of course, the limit that Locke draws on private property rights. That's his *proviso*: people have strong private property rights in the state of nature, with the proviso, or condition, that they do not claim so much private property that others are unable to gain enough private property, and in as good a condition, as the person who has acquired the private property. So, according to Locke, people who are hungry cannot eat apples that someone else picked without the apple picker's permission. At the same time, though, the apple picker must leave enough apples on the trees for other people to collect. Moreover, they may not take all of the best apples and leave rotting apples, only, for other people. They must leave behind (some of) the best apples as well, so that other people have an opportunity to take them.

Sidebar Exercise

In this discussion of Locke's claims about property rights, we used an example to illustrate Locke's position. Our example to illustrate that claim was picking apples in an orchard that no one owns. In virtue of laboring on the apples, the apple picker gained private property rights in those apples: a right to exclusive control over the apples such that no one was entitled to take them without the apple owner's explicit permission. Using an example to illustrate a philosophical view is one of the most important philosophical skills. It really helps you to understand what philosophers mean by their claims. It also helps you, potentially, to start to figure out what might be problematic about some philosophical claims. Can you think of an example to illustrate the Lockean proviso? Write out your example. When you see the example of the Lockean proviso in action, do there seem to be any problems with how it would work?

The final aspect of Locke's justification of private property that we will 6.30 discuss is the objections he raises to his own view. We have already covered the topic of raising objections as an important philosophical skill. The fact that Locke raises objections to his own view is a good sign of what an important skill this is. Locke has set forth a provocative and tightly argued piece that people are entitled to own private property, even if the world and all of its resources originally belonged to everyone in common. In addition to setting forth an interesting philosophical view, Locke also demonstrates some key philosophical skills. Sidebar exercises throughout the chapter have explored these philosophical skills: explaining a philosophical claim, using concrete examples to illustrate and develop a philosophical claim, raising objections to a philosophical claim, offering responses to an objection. As we wrap up our chapter on Locke's defense of private property, let us take a close look at these last two philosophical skills. These are such an important part of philosophy that Locke himself raises objections against his own view and then tries to respond to the objections. That is, even though he believes that his own account is correct, he objects to it in order to try to improve the account. We will consider one objection that Locke raises to his account and Locke's response. Then, we will consider two objections raised by a more recent, twentieth-century philosopher who considers himself a "Lockean," or someone who has been deeply influenced by Locke and thinks his philosophical view is broadly correct.

6.31   The first objection, which Locke himself raises, is: "If gathering the acorns, or other fruits of the earth, etc., makes a right to them, then anyone may engross as much as he will." Paraphrasing the claim, this means that Locke is worried that his account of private property means that anyone can take as much private property from the natural world as they want to. All they need to do is gather up the parts of the world that they want to own, put a fence around the parts of the world that they want to earn, and so on.

Sidebar Exercise

Before looking at Locke's response, how would you respond to this objection on Locke's behalf? Does this raise a real worry about Locke's position? Or can Locke easily rebut the concern?

6.32   Locke rejects this way of understanding his account of property rights. As noted above, he thinks that there are limits to what property people are permitted to own. In particular, he thinks that people are only entitled to own property insofar as they can *enjoy* that property. He writes that "As much as anyone can make use of any advantage of life before it spoils, so much he may by his labor fix a property in; whatever is beyond this, is more than his share, and belongs to others." That means, for example, that people may only take possession of as many apples as they are able to eat before the apples spoil. Just as there are natural rights to property, Locke thinks that there are natural limits to the amount of property that people are entitled to own.

Sidebar Exercise

Are you satisfied by Locke's response to the objection? How might the objector counter-respond? Where does the conversation go next?

It is also helpful in understanding Locke's view to look at objections to   6.33
the view that other philosophers have raised. One philosopher who deeply admired and was strongly influenced by Locke was the twentieth-century American philosopher, Robert Nozick. Nozick's relationship with Locke resembled, in this sense, Mill's relationship with Bentham (except that Mill and Bentham lived much closer in time to one another). Nozick is Locke's philosophical frenemy. Nozick raised two interesting objections against Locke's view. We will set forth the objection and then it will be up to you to respond on Locke's behalf.

We looked at one way that Locke constrains his view of property rights.   6.34
Locke says that people may not own more property than they are able to use. For example, they may have property in only as many apples as they are about to eat. Nozick is also concerned that Locke does not specify enough limits to his account of property rights. Nozick objects that property rights in a knife allow the owner to do whatever he or she wants with the knife. But common-sense morality does not permit the owner of a knife to stab someone else in the chest with the knife. So, Nozick objects that Locke lacks an adequate account about what should constrain people's choices about their property.

Sidebar Exercise

How would Locke respond?

Nozick's second objection relates to Locke's account of how someone   6.35
comes to own some part of the natural world. As exemplified by the apple picker who became the owner of the apples that were picked, Locke says that mixing one's labor with something makes one the owner of it. Nozick objects, though, that if someone owns a bottle of juice and spills it into the ocean, the person loses the property in the juice rather than gaining ownership of the

ocean. (We will discuss this kind of example further in Chapter 7. It is a *counter-example* to the philosophical claim, which offers evidence that the claim is false.) This example suggests that mixing what a person owns with what the person does not own is a way of losing what the person owns rather than a way of gaining what the person does not (yet) own.

Sidebar Exercise

How would Locke respond?

Sidebar Exercise

How would you apply the Lockean proviso to the question of the "social responsibilities" of businesses? What are businesses' obligations to society, on Locke's view?

Distributive justice

6.36 In the previous section, we looked at a foundational defense of property rights written by John Locke. Toward the end of the section, we considered some ways in which Locke's defense of property rights appeared to be somewhat too strong. In this section, we consider another possible problem with Locke's defense of private property rights. That problem is potentially so serious that it we might want to start over with a completely new theory—in the same way that the serious problems with the dominant model (DM) inspired Freeman to cast aside that business decision-making strategy in favor of a new strategy, stakeholder theory (StakeT). If we are convinced about the problems in Locke's justification of property rights, we may wish to cast it aside in favor of John Rawls's account of how property should be distributed.

6.37   The name of this section is *distributive justice*. "Distributive" refers to the "distribution" of property in society, or an accounting of *who* is entitled to own *what*. It brings in the idea of the society as a whole in considering claims about private property. Whereas Locke considered private property rights from an individual perspective, distributive justice considers property rights across society. Thinking of all of society, who should be entitled to own what private property? The basic idea of distributive justice is that people do not gain private property rights as a result of their labor (as they do on Locke's account) but, rather, on the basis of everyone being entitled to property. So, the objection raised by concerns about distributive justice to Locke's view is: Locke's account of property rights is too individualistic. Under Locke's system, some people in society could wind up with not enough property.

The most famous theorist of distributive justice was another twentieth-century American philosopher, John Rawls. (As it so happened, Rawls was a colleague of Nozick's at the university, Harvard, where they both taught. Rawls and Nozick influenced each other but held quite different views of people's entitlements to private property. They were philosophical frenemies, too.) Unlike Locke, who thought that people could own property independently of society, Rawls thought that property rights only make sense once society has started. Because people own property only in society, society can have a say in how that property is distributed, or divided up. 6.38

Rawls's reasoning was as follows. According to Locke's view, people gain property in the state of nature, before civilization even gets started. But in the state of nature, there is no way to protect property rights. In civilization, for example, the police protect property rights. If someone steals your backpack, you can notify the police, who might be able to get it back for you. If someone steals your apples in the state of nature, though, you have no recourse. If you are big and strong, or smart and shrewd, you might be able to get the apples back: by intimidating or tricking the thief into giving them back to you. But if you are just an ordinary person, the thief is probably going to be able to get away with it. That means that by the time civilization gets started, and the police can start enforcing property rights, the share of property across society might already be very unequal. And there is nothing that anyone can do about this inequality under Locke's defense of property rights. Under Rawls's account, by contrast, the unequal distribution is *unfair*. To correct this unfairness, he claims that people's property rights begin in society, at the very same time that people are able to enforce their property rights. 6.39

So, once people are in society, how should society decide to distribute property rights? To answer this question, Rawls instructs us to look at the purposes of human society. He notes that human societies have two defining characteristics. First, societies are aimed at advancing their members' 6.40

interests. Second, societies are regulated by a conception of justice that everyone shares. A conception of justice is a set of principles for determining how society should work, including property rights. A just distribution of property rights in society, according to Rawls, should respect society's two purposes. The distribution should advance everyone's interests and should match a conception of justice that everyone shares.

6.41   How do we figure out what distribution of property will advance everyone's interests? And, how do we determine what conception of justice everyone shares? Like all things about society, Rawls thinks that the answers to these questions are up to the people in the society. They can decide whatever they want: and what they decide is the conception of justice that applies to them. We can contrast Rawls's view quite starkly, in this sense, with Locke's. Whereas Locke believed that human beings are bound by God's purposes for them, Rawls believes that people's purposes are up to themselves.

6.42   Rawls recommends a procedure that he thinks will do a good job in answering these questions. First, he thinks that the questions can be answered by *principles of justice*. Principles of justice are rules that the society invents to regulate how society will work. Rawls calls them principles "of justice" because they ensure that the society will be just, or fair. These principles determine a distribution of property that will further everyone's interests and express the society's shared conception of justice. The key thing is for the society to decide what, in particular, its principles of justice will be.

6.43   To decide what the principles of justice are, Rawls first notes that people must be able to agree on them. If we remember back to Chapter 3, in which the various ethical theories were defined, we can see that Rawls is using *contract theory* to ensure that his recommendations are ethical. In fact, Rawls was one of the philosophers who did the most to develop contract theory as an ethical theory.

6.44   As we know from living in society, though, it is rare that people agree on anything. It seems especially hard to achieve agreement over something as basic and important as principles of justice that regulate everything in society. But it is very important to Rawls that people agree on the principles of justice: their agreement is what guarantees that the principles of justice will be fair.

6.45   Thus, Rawls specifies a special decision-making procedure that people are to use to decide on the principles of justice. The principles are to be chosen in an *original position* behind a *veil of ignorance*. The original position is a kind of thought experiment. Have you ever imagined what it would be like to be someone else, like a famous person, and acted out a scene from this person's perspective? The original position requires you to undertake a similar kind of imaginative activity. Instead of acting out a scene from another person's perspective, though, people in the original person are supposed to imagine that they are at the very beginning of society, deciding how society is going to be organized. So they are at the original, or first, position in society. You can imagine that you are in such a position right now.

The original position has one very important characteristic. Everyone in the original position is behind the *veil of ignorance*, which makes them "ignorant" of anything about themselves in particular. So, behind the veil of ignorance we do not know whether we are rich or poor, male or female, black or white—or any other identifying characteristic. All that we know behind the veil of ignorance is that we are human beings, who are free and who are fundamentally equal to all other human beings. People behind the veil of ignorance know that they are free in the sense that they are able to make up their minds for themselves and decide for themselves what they are going to do. Thus, they are free in the sense of not being enslaved to anyone. They are equal in the sense of knowing that they have the same moral status as everyone else. They are nobody's slave and they are also nobody's master. 6.46

Because people choose the principles of justice based on their humanity (their freedom and equality), anyone who shares this basis (humanity) can agree to them. Thus, everyone can agree to the principles. For Rawls, this universal agreement means that the principles are fair. 6.47

Rawls thinks that people in the original position behind the veil of ignorance would choose *two* principles of justice, in particular. The first principle establishes people's political equality. The second principle establishes how property rights should be distributed across society. Another way of saying "how property rights should be distributed across society" is: which economic inequalities are just. So the first principle requires political equality and the second principle sets forth what kinds of economic inequalities are compatible with political equality. 6.48

The first principle says that each person has an equal right to the greatest liberty possible, limited only by the need to provide "a like liberty for all." This means that people are entitled to political rights like those in the U.S. Bill of Rights. As you know, these include: the right to free speech, the right to jury trials, and so on. People should have as many of those rights 6.49

as are compatible with everyone having the same rights, according to the first principle of justice. So, for example, no one could have a right to have a million dollars because it is not possible (in the current economy) for everyone to have a million dollars. Rawls does not say which rights, in particular, people would think that they were guaranteed in the original position: just that they would think that they are guaranteed as many rights as possible.

6.50   Second, Rawls thinks that people in the original position would decide that economic inequalities must meet the following standards: they benefit everyone and the jobs that produce the inequalities are open to all. Jobs "produce" inequalities in the sense that some jobs pay high salaries and others pay low salaries. The second part of this requirement, jobs being open to all, means that there would be no false limits on employment. For example, no one could be denied a job because of being a woman, being a member of a racial or ethnic minority, or having poor parents. People could only be denied jobs because they were not qualified for the job or because they were outcompeted for the job by someone who was better qualified. Rawls holds that people are entitled to *fair equality of opportunity*, which means that people who have the same level of natural talent, and are equally ambitious, should have an equal chance of securing desirable jobs (such as those that pay high salaries).

6.51   The first part of the second principle of justice, the idea that economic inequalities must benefit everyone, is a little more complicated. Rawls sometimes calls this idea the *difference* principle because it sets forth what economic differences, or inequalities, are permitted. To relate back to our investigation of justifications of private property, we can understand "permitted economic inequalities" as "permitted differences in ownership of private property." What does it mean to require that economic inequalities benefit everyone? It means that people can only become wealthy if their wealth-creating activities benefit poor people as well. No one can make themselves economically better off at someone else's expense. Everyone must benefit from economic activities.

6.52   Why does Rawls need to specify that poor people must benefit from the activities that allow some people to become rich? It might not seem obvious how people could become better off at someone else's expense. We usually think that people become wealthy as a result of their hard work and good ideas.

6.53   That kind of wealth creation, and property ownership, is still possible in Rawls's conception of society. But think back to the Walmart case that we covered in Chapter 3. In the Walmart case, the owners of the Walmart company became very rich partially as a result of paying their employees very low wages. That kind of discrepancy might not be possible under the difference principle. If the Waltons were using the difference principle to think about Walmart employees' wages, they would have to make sure that the Walmart employees were benefiting from Walmart's economic activities, along with the Waltons.

Sidebar Exercise

Do the wages that Walmart employees earn satisfy the difference principle? Why or why not? What would people in the original position think about the Waltons' activities? Remember that people in the original position would not know whether they were a Walton or a Walmart employee. What do you think that people in this position would decide about Walmart employees' wages and Walton family's profits?

The property rights available under Rawls's system of distributive justice, 6.54 then, seem like they would be more restricted than those under Locke's justification of private property. Whereas Locke thought that people were entitled to whatever they labor on in the state of nature, so long as they leave as much and as good for others, Rawls thinks that people are entitled to enrich themselves only if their self-enriching activities benefit everyone else, along with themselves.

Sidebar Exercise

Would Locke agree or disagree with Rawls's proposals? How do Rawls's ideas relate to the Lockean proviso? What objection might Locke raise against Rawls's ideas? How would Rawls respond? Imagine that the two philosophers are having a conversation—a friendly argument. They take each other's views seriously and try to explain how their view can accommodate the other person's concerns (or why the concerns are less important than what the view does do).

Sidebar Exercise

How would you apply the difference principle to the question of businesses' "social responsibilities"? What are businesses' obligations to society, on Rawls's view?

The Division of Labor

6.55   In this section, we will be investigating a second economic convention, the division of labor. The division of labor is the social convention such that individual people work in different jobs. Some of these jobs are more or less interesting. Some of these jobs have higher salaries and are more prestigious than others. We will look at two different accounts of the division of labor: one defense and one criticism. The defense comes from the eighteenth-century Scottish philosopher, Adam Smith. Smith supports the division of labor because he thinks that the division of labor increases productivity. The criticism comes from the nineteenth-century German philosopher, Karl Marx. Marx criticizes the division of labor because he thinks that the division of labor alienates workers. We will look at Smith's view first.

Smith's productivity-based defense of the division

6.56   Adam Smith is best known for being an important early theorist of capitalism. Capitalism is an economic system that developed as a response to the improvements in industrial efficiency brought about by the Industrial Revolution. It involves freely trading (buying and selling) private property in a marketplace. Smith was the first philosopher to describe capitalism systematically: explaining the nature, benefits, harms, and justification of capitalism as a theory. Capitalist economic processes were already occurring in society. Smith's theory of these processes served to persuade many people that they were justified. Others, though, were not convinced—as we will see in the next section.

6.57   One of the economic conventions that was present in Smith's society was the *division of labor*. The division of labor is a way that people can perform work together. Say you have five people making sandwiches. They can make sandwiches in two different ways. First, *undivided* labor. In this way of

making a sandwich, each person makes sandwiches independently: taking the bread out of the bag and separating it on the counter; spreading mustard on one slice and mayonnaise on the other; stacking lettuce, then tomato, then turkey, then cheese on the bottom slice; placing the second slice on top and cutting the sandwich diagonally; wrapping the sandwich in a piece of tissue paper. When labor is *divided*, by contrast, each worker performs only one of these functions. The sandwich travels along an assembly line with five stations. At each station, a worker performs one of the tasks listed above.

Smith claims that the division of labor "occasions, in every art, a propor- 6.58
tionate increase of the productive powers of labor." The increase in the quantity of work that the same number of people are capable of performing owes to three factors, according to Smith. First, by focusing on only on task in a system of divided labor, workers become better at performing that task. Second, workers save time that was lost in undivided workplaces, in which workers had to move from one kind of work to another. Third, divided workplaces are more productive because they inspire entrepreneurs to invent machines that can replace the single tasks that workers are performing.

Take the sandwich-making example discussed above. First, the worker 6.59
taking the bread out of the bag and placing it on the assembly line becomes better skilled at performing this task because it is the only thing that the worker is doing. The worker does not have to split his or her attention between a variety of different tasks but can focus on performing the one task well.

Second, the workers save time by not having to move around from sta- 6.60
tion to station. The worker who cuts the sandwich does not have to worry about going to the supply cabinet to get more tissues because the worker who wraps the sandwich in a piece of tissue handles that responsibility. Because the tissue responsibilities are all that worker does, he or she can plan ahead to minimize the time taken in restocking supplies.

Third, dividing labor makes it easy to use machines to further expedite 6.61
work. In the sandwich-making example, dividing the labor of the five workers allows them to use an assembly line, which increases their efficiency. Dividing the workers' labor also helps to isolate which aspects of the labor can be mechanized, further enhancing efficiency. In the sandwich-making example, placing the bread on the assembly line is probably the easiest to mechanize, as it involves the least human labor. Dividing the workers' labor, in this sense, helps to make clear how the work can be made even more efficient.

6.62   Smith argues that the division of labor is justified because it allows workers to be more efficient, producing more goods and more happiness. He appears to offer, in this sense, a *utilitarian* rationale for the division of labor. Smith claims that the consequence of the division of labor is the creation of universal wealth: "It is the great multiplication of the productions of the different arts, in consequence of the division of labor, which occasions, in a well-governed society, that universal opulence which extends itself to the lowest ranks of the people." Under the division of labor, all workers produce more products than they can use. This produces huge profits for the people who own the means of production. It produces wealth for the workers as well, as they have more than they need and can exchange their surplus for things that they merely want. Therefore, everyone in society becomes wealthier under the division of labor—not just business owners.

6.63   Smith thinks that additional ethical support for the division of labor can be found beyond utilitarianism, however. He thinks that there is a natural basis for the division of labor. Whereas other animals are independent upon maturity, Smith notes that human beings depend on one another even as adults.

Sidebar Exercise

Which ethical theory is most associated with the "natural basis" rationale that Smith offers to support the division of labor? Is this a convincing rationale? Is it more or less convincing than the utilitarian rationale? Say why you answer this question as you do.

6.64   As a third justification for the division of labor, Smith offers the idea that the division of labor benefits all of society. This is different from the utilitarian rationale offered above. In this justification, Smith is not primarily concerned with the division of labor insofar as it *maximizes* social wealth. Rather, he feels that the division of labor is good for society because it allows more work to be performed and creates incentives for people to perform more difficult work.

6.65   The *way* that the division of labor benefits society in this sense is, interestingly, through people's self-interest. Under the division of labor, Smith claims that every individual is always seeking the most lucrative employment for him- or herself. Workers search for better jobs because of self-interest: they

wish to have more income, which will allow them to buy more of the things they wish to own. By pursuing the highest-paying careers, though, workers naturally gravitate to the most difficult careers. The most difficult careers, Smith believes, have the greatest social benefits. Why does Smith think that the careers with the greatest social benefits will be the most well paid? He believed that those are the careers that society will most want to be performed and so, to encourage the best-qualified people to accept these positions, they will compensate the positions handsomely.

Sidebar Exercise

Are you convinced by Smith's claim that the best-compensated jobs are the most socially beneficial? Think of an example that supports this claim: a well-compensated job that is socially beneficial. Then, think of an example that challenges the claim: either a well-compensated job that is not socially beneficial OR a socially beneficial job that is not well compensated. Overall, say whether you agree or disagree with Smith's claim.

Sidebar Exercise

How would StakeT evaluate Smith's defense of the productivity of the division of labor?

Marx's alienation-based criticism of the division

Karl Marx is perhaps best known as the founder of communism. 6.66 Communism is an economic system defined in opposition to capitalism. Unlike capitalism, communism is based on the *public* ownership of important social resources. We will not be examining Marx's communist theories in this textbook, as they are not widely used in business. In addition to creating the economic philosophy of communism, however, Marx was also a great critic of capitalism: one of the sharpest and most intelligent critics that capitalism has ever had. It is those aspects of Marx's thought that we will be examining, as they are highly relevant to the study of business ethics.

6.67   Marx agrees with Smith that the division of labor increases productivity. But he thinks that the division of labor creates very serious harms that appear to outweigh its benefits. We should strive, in this sense, to find ways to replace the division of labor. Marx discusses both the *impoverishment* and the *alienation* of labor. First, the impoverishment of labor: this is the idea that the worker becomes poorer even as he or she is creating more wealth for society. It is a confusing idea, which seems paradoxical. As Smith noted, workers gain higher wages as a result of the division of labor than they would earn if they were working in undivided workplaces. But Marx asserts that these capitalist workers nonetheless become impoverished as a result of working in systems of divided labor.

6.68   This paradox can be explained by looking more closely at what Marx means by "impoverished." He does not mean "poor," in a financial sense. Let us examine three alternative senses, then, in which Marx holds that systems of divided labor impoverish workers. First, an impoverished *inner life*. Marx holds that the more the worker expends himself in work, "the poorer he becomes in his inner life, and the less he belongs to himself." Think back to the sandwich makers. Although they may become very good at slicing bread or arranging cheese while working in this capacity, slicing bread and arranging cheese are probably not the most interesting activities. But they are all the work activities that workers have under the division of labor. Thus their inner lives—their thoughts as they are working—are less vibrant and full than they would be if the workers were performing more engaging or challenging tasks.

6.69   Divided labor also impoverishes the worker by devaluing the worker. As noted above, the division of labor helps to isolate which work tasks can be mechanized. So by performing their work well, workers may make themselves obsolete. Being obsolete means: a machine can replace them. Finally, divided work impoverishes workers by making them overly focused on material goods. This criticism of the division of labor implicates low-skilled workers and higher-level workers as well. Because more material things become available to purchase under systems of divided labor, workers tend to focus more on these things than on the aspects of life that could be considered more important: relationships, nature, human development.

6.70   Next, the alienation of labor. In addition to impoverishing the worker, Marx argues that the division of labor alienates workers. There are five senses in which the worker becomes alienated, on Marx's analysis. First, workers become alienated in that the work is "external" to the worker. It is outside of the worker or alien to the worker's nature. What does Marx mean by the worker's "nature"? Here, Marx seems to be talking about the worker's human nature, or what human beings might have been like in the state of nature. Before the advent of civilization and the industrial revolution, people were concerned to perform activities to sustain their own existences and nurture their relationships. Working in an assembly line seems alien to these human concerns.

Second, work in a system of divided labor is alienating in the sense that   6.71
workers do not fulfill themselves in work. Rather, workers must put aside their essential needs and desires. We can see this again in the sandwich assembly line. Workers do not find this boring work fulfilling. It forces them to deny their needs for fulfilling work and their desires to do more interesting and fulfilling things.

Third, and relatedly, workers are alienated because they feel miserable   6.72
rather than well while working. Work does not help to develop their well-being or their human capacities. Fourth, the division of labor prevents workers from freely developing their mental and physical energies, as more healthful activities develop people's intellects and physiques. Rather, Marx claims that workers are physically exhausted and mentally debased. Because of this, finally, workers feel at home only in their free time. At work, workers feel homeless.

Sidebar Exercise

Are you convinced by Marx's claims about the impoverishment and alienation of labor? Think of an example that supports each claim. Then, think of an example that opposes each claim. How would Smith respond to his criticisms of the division of labor? Overall, who has the better argument: Smith or Marx? Why?

Sidebar Exercise

How would the DM evaluate Marx's criticisms of the alienating qualities of divided labor?

References and Further Reading

Barry, Christian. 2014. "Redistribution." In *Stanford Encyclopedia of Philosophy*. http://plato.stanford.edu/archives/spr2014/entries/redistribution/

D'Agostino, Fred, Gerald Gaus, and John Thrasher. 2017. "Contemporary Approaches to the Social Contract." In *Stanford Encyclopedia of Philosophy*. https://plato.stanford.edu/archives/sum2017/entries/contractarianism-contemporary/

Fleischacker, Samuel. 2013 "Adam Smith's Moral and Political Philosophy." In *Stanford Encyclopedia of Philosophy*. http://plato.stanford.edu/archives/spr2013/entries/smith-moral-political/

Lamont, Julian and Christi Favor. 2013. "Distributive Justice." In *Stanford Encyclopedia of Philosophy*. http://plato.stanford.edu/archives/spr2013/entries/justice-distributive/

Locke, John. 1763. "Two Treatises of Government." http://www.gutenberg.org/files/7370/7370-h/7370-h.htm

Marx, Karl, 1867, tr. Samuel Moore and Edward Aveling (ed.). Frederick Engels, 1887, Capital: A Critique of Political Economy, https://www.marxists.org/archive/marx/works/download/pdf/Capital-Volume-I.pdf

Murphy, Mark. 2011. "The Natural Law Tradition in Ethics." In *Stanford Encyclopedia of Philosophy*. https://plato.stanford.edu/archives/win2011/entries/natural-law-ethics/

Rawls, John. 2005. "A theory of justice." Cambridge, Mass: Belknap Press.

Smith, Adam. 1776. "An Inquiry into the Nature and Causes of the Wealth of Nations." http://www.econlib.org/library/Smith/smWN.html

Tuckness, Alex. 2012. "Locke's Political Philosophy." In *Stanford Encyclopedia of Philosophy*. http://plato.stanford.edu/archives/win2012/entries/locke-political/

Waldron, Jeremy. 2012. "Property and Ownership." In *Stanford Encyclopedia of Philosophy*. http://plato.stanford.edu/archives/spr2012/entries/property/

Wolff, Jonathan. 2011. "Karl Marx." *The Stanford Encyclopedia of Philosophy*. http://plato.stanford.edu/archives/sum2011/entries/marx/

Part III

CONTEMPORARY CASE STUDIES

Now that our business ethics "toolkit" is full of different strategies with which we can evaluate business ethics controversies, it is time to begin evaluating actual controversies. We will examine 20 ethical issues related to five aspects of business: employment (Chapter 7), advertising (Chapter 8), finance (Chapter 9), the environment (Chapter 10), and globalization (Chapter 11). Each chapter presents four case studies involving the applied issue upon which that chapter focuses. We will refer back to Parts I and II in order to develop our understanding of the cases, while also using the cases to enhance and refine our understanding of the theoretical issues addressed in the first two Parts of this book.

This is Business Ethics: An Introduction, First Edition. Tobey Scharding.
© 2018 John Wiley & Sons, Inc. Published 2018 by John Wiley & Sons, Inc.

Part III
CONTEMPORARY CASE STUDIES

7
BUSINESS ETHICS IN EMPLOYMENT

In our first applied topic, business ethics in employment, we discuss ethical 7.1
dilemmas that arise for employees and for the executives who manage
employees. The topics include: (1) employment at will, or the condition of
employment such that employees may be fired for any reason, good or bad
(except for reasons prohibited by law); (2) executive compensation, including questions about how much more than workers ethics permits executive
management to earn; (3) anti-discrimination; and (4) the work-life balance.

Employment at Will: The Bechtel Case

The Case

A longtime employee of the Bechtel Corporation was terminated
when his work unit was eliminated. He sued for (1) breach of an
implied contract to be terminated only for good cause; (2) breach of
an implied covenant of good faith and fair dealing; and (3) age discrimination. The court ruled that his employment contract was "at
will" and no "implied covenant" can decree otherwise.

The Ethical Questions

Is it ethical to terminate long-time employees without good cause?
What are the best arguments for and against?

This is Business Ethics: An Introduction, First Edition. Tobey Scharding.
© 2018 John Wiley & Sons, Inc. Published 2018 by John Wiley & Sons, Inc.

7.2 Many college students have part-time jobs. These jobs, along with the full-time jobs that they will work when they graduate from college, are generally governed by an *at will* condition of employment. This condition of employment means that the employer may terminate the employee whenever the employer wishes, or "wills" to. At-will employees are similarly free to quit their jobs whenever they wish. In this case study, we will try to achieve a fuller understanding of the ethical issues associated with this condition of employment. Our focus is an employee who was terminated in what the employee considered to be an unethical manner.

Bechtel's corporate identity

7.3 Our first case study concerns Bechtel Corporation. Bechtel is an engineering, construction, and project management company. It performs work for the federal government, primarily the Departments of Energy and Defense. This work focuses on infrastructure: airports, bridges, highways, ports, rail, sports venues, urban development, and more.

7.4 Bechtel, like other members of its industry, operates from project to project: bidding on new projects when they become available. Because of its dependence on competitive bidding, its workload varies.

Sidebar Exercise

Based on Peter A. French's account of the corporation as a moral person and Bechtel's corporate identity, what kind of policy do you think it should have vis-à-vis employment decisions?

Facts of the case

7.5 The Bechtel case involves the termination of a longtime Bechtel employee, John Guz. Guz was hired in 1971 as an administrative assistant at an initial salary of $750 per month. From 1986 until his termination in 1993, Guz was employed in Bechtel's management information work unit: the BNI Management Information Group (BNI-MI). Between 1986 and 1991,

BNI-MI's size shrank from thirteen to six persons. During this same time, its budget was reduced from $748,000 to $400,000.

Between 1986 and 1991, Guz received regular raises and promotions. His performance reviews were mostly favorable. Close to his termination, an evaluation in March 1992 criticized his computer illiteracy and noted that he should become "fully computer literate in order to improve his long-term job success." 7.6

In April 1992, BNI-MI was targeted to reduce staff to three people and budget to $365,000. In December 1992, BNI-MI was disbanded and Guz was informed that he was being laid off. The two youngest members of BNI-MI, one of whom had excellent computer skills, were transferred to the work unit that would assume BNI-MI's responsibilities. Guz did not apply and was not considered for any positions in the new work unit. He was officially terminated in June 1993. 7.7

In October 1994, Guz sued Bechtel for wrongful termination. He alleged breach of an implied employment contract, breach of the covenant of good faith and fair dealing, and age discrimination. 7.8

From June 1991, Bechtel had governed its employment termination policies with Personnel Policy 1101 (Policy 1101). Policy 1101 mandates that "Bechtel employees have no employment agreements guaranteeing continuous service and may resign at their option or be terminated at the option of Bechtel." 7.9

Policy 1101 specifies several different "Categories of Termination," including "Layoff" and "Unsatisfactory Performance." Employees could be terminated for unsatisfactory performance if they "fail to perform their jobs in a satisfactory manner...provided the employees have been advised of the specific shortcomings and given an opportunity to improve their performance." Employees could be laid off if Bechtel initiated "a reduction in workload, reorganizations, changes in job requirements, or other circumstances." In his court case, Guz testified that he understood that Policy 1101 applied to him. 7.10

Sidebar Exercise

How would Bentham's utilitarianism evaluate Bechtel's decision to terminate Guz?

Sidebar Exercise

How would virtue ethics evaluate Guz's decision to sue Bechtel?

What happened

7.11 The trial court granted *summary judgment*, which means that the judge rules that the case does not raise a question of law: the existing law already fully sets forth what is the right thing to do, legally speaking. The court reasoned that Guz was an at-will employee. Guz did not establish "that he was ever told at any time that he had permanent employment or that he would be retained as long as he was doing a good job." The court found that Guz was unable to rebut Bechtel's legitimate business reason for his termination.

7.12 Guz appealed and the appeals court reversed the lower court's summary judgment. The appeals court's reasoning was that Guz's longevity, promotions, raises, and favorable performance reviews, together with Bechtel's written progressive discipline policy and Bechtel officials' statements of company practices, raised a triable issue. Namely, Guz's employment record gave him an "implied-in-fact" contract to be dismissed for good cause, only. There was evidence that Bechtel breached this term by eliminating BNI-MI, on the false ground that workload was declining, as a pretext to weed out poor performers without applying the company's progressive discipline procedures.

7.13 The case then went to the Supreme Court of California. That court ruled that Guz's "implied covenant" cause of action could not limit the termination rights to which Bechtel and Guz had actually agreed. At-will termination was upheld.

Historical significance

7.14 The California Supreme Court's decision was a watershed moment for employment rights. For the quarter century preceding the decision, at-will employment had been attacked in courts across the country. Those cases used a traditional contract-law principle, the implied covenant of good faith and fair dealing, to limit employers' ability to discharge longtime employees. Under that theory, at-will employment gradually became just-cause employment, aided by nothing other than the passage of time. *Guz vs. Bechtel*, by contrast, upheld the legitimacy of the EAW doctrine.

Sidebar Exercise

How does EAW relate to property rights, such as those discussed by Locke and Rawls?

Ethical significance: conditions of employment

The court case upheld EAW legally. As discussed in Chapter 2, though, 7.15 what is legal is not always ethical (and vice versa). In this section, we begin by defining EAW more precisely. Then, we examine two popular views about the ethics of employment at will: one criticizing EAW on ethical grounds and the other defending the doctrine on ethical grounds. The first view was set forth by business ethics professors Patricia Werhane and Tara Radin; law professor Richard Epstein argued for the second. Both the critics and the defender claim three reasons supporting their position.

First, the definition. EAW is technically defined is as the condition of 7.16 employment such that employees may be terminated for *good* cause, for *bad* cause, or for *no* cause. The only reasons for which employees at will may not be terminated are several protected reasons, for which it is illegal (according to U.S. federal law) to terminate employees. These will be discussed below.

Before getting to the several exceptions to EAW, let us attempt to under- 7.17 stand what this condition of employment entails. What is a "good" cause to terminate someone? Generally speaking, failing to perform their job well, or engaging in illegal or unethical behavior while on the job, are good reasons to terminate an employee. Spending too much time surfing the web, stealing office supplies, or failing to meet certain performance standards are classic examples of "good" reasons for termination.

Bad reasons for termination, by contrast, do not relate to work perfor- 7.18 mance. A bad reason to terminate an employee might be that the employee supports a different football team from the manager or dresses in a way that the manager finds unfashionable. When Henry Ford II fired Lee Iacocca from the Ford Motor Company, for example, he is rumored to have said, "Why am I firing you? Because I just don't like you!" That would be a bad reason to fire someone. It is bad because it has nothing to do with the terminated employee's work performance.

Some of these "bad" reasons for termination might strike us as being 7.19 unethical. After all, in the cases discussed above, the employee really did nothing wrong. Termination is a serious event and it might seem unfair in these cases. This issue is controversial. We can examine it in greater detail in the case concerning the Bechtel company. For now, the important thing to understand is just that termination for bad cause is permitted under EAW. The only reasons that employees may not be terminated relate to certain federal laws. As discussed in Chapter 2, for example, Title VII of the Civil Rights Act of 1964 makes it illegal to terminate an employee based on the employee's race, ethnicity, religion, or national origin.

7.20　It is also permissible under EAW to terminate an employee for "no" reason. What does it mean to terminate an employee for no reason? The classic example of a no cause termination is a lay-off, in which employees are let go for reasons utterly unrelated to anything about them. A business might lay off employees because of a downturn in business or because it has decided to eliminate one of its business units, for example.

7.21　As noted above, employees at will are free to resign their employment when they wish to. Like the reasons for which employers may terminate employees under EAW, employees may quit for good, bad, or no reason.

7.22　To understand more completely the nature of EAW as a condition of employment, it is helpful to contrast EAW with other possible conditions of employment. The two most prominent possibilities are contractual employment and just-cause-termination employment. Some jobs, such as those held by professional athletes, are contractual in nature. When a job is contractual in nature, the employee must complete the full term of employment that the contract specifies: they are not free to quit whenever they wish to. Similarly, the employer is obliged to provide employment for the employee, under the conditions specified by the contract, for the full length of the term of employment specified by the contract.

7.23　Under just-cause-termination employment, an employee may only be terminated for "good" cause. This means that employers are permitted to terminate employees when they fail to perform their jobs well but they are not permitted to terminate employees for bad cause or no cause. Even if the employer discontinues the business unit in which an employee is employed, then, the business must find some other job for the employee under this kind of employment.

7.24　Next, the ethical evaluation. We begin with two critics of EAW, business ethicists Werhane and Radin. Werhane and Radin raise three important challenges to the ethics of EAW: *rights, fairness,* and *public policy*. According to the rights-based challenge, EAW interferes with certain *guaranteed political rights*. Whereas employers continue to enjoy these rights on the job, EAW prevents employees from exercising them. The rights include free speech, privacy, due process, democratic participation, and even property rights.

How does EAW limit free speech? Werhane and Radin are concerned 7.25 that employers, but not employees, can exercise free speech on the job. Consider the example of a bad reason for termination offered above: an employee who supports a different football team from the employee's supervisor. Whereas supervisors are able to declare support for whichever sports teams they choose, employees' speech is not free in the same way. They, but not supervisors, can be terminated for supporting the "wrong" team.

Sidebar Exercise

How could Werhane and Radin support their claim that EAW undermines employees' privacy rights on the job?

Next, *due process*. The U.S. Constitution guarantees people a due process in 7.26 a criminal context. The "due" process, or process that an accused person is owed, includes a trial decided by a jury of their peers. Werhane and Radin point out that when EAW is a condition of employment, there is no due process. Employees can be fired at any time and for any reason. They are not guaranteed that their employers will follow a set procedure to decide whether they should be terminated.

Sidebar Exercise

How could Werhane and Radin support their claim that EAW undermines employees' right to democratic participation on the job?

Finally, *property rights*. The U.S. Constitution protects property rights. 7.27 Werhane and Radin argue that people have property in their jobs. Why would they think that people have property in their jobs? Well, the jobs *belong* to the employees, in the sense that particular jobs are identified with the particular workers who perform the jobs' duties. Their jobs are *worth something* to the employees, in the sense that they provide the employees' livelihoods. If people have property rights in their jobs, then employers might be constitutionally prohibited from unlawfully seizing those jobs.

Sidebar Exercise

Can you think of any objections to the rights-based reasons for challenging EAW? How might Werhane and Radin respond?

7.28 Their second reason for challenging EAW concerns *fairness*. Werhane and Radin argue that EAW allows employers and employees to treat each other arbitrarily and unfairly. John Guz, for example, did not expect—or wish—to be terminated by Bechtel. He felt that the termination harmed him and was unfair.

Sidebar Exercise

Do you agree with this reason for challenging EAW? Was Guz correct that his termination was unfair? Can you think of an example, from real life or a movie, that supports Werhane and Radin's claim that EAW allows employers and employees to treat each other unethically?

7.29 Their third reason for challenging EAW is *public policy*-based. The authors point out that businesses' abilities to terminate their employees are already limited by federal law. We discussed some of these laws above. They include: Title VII of the Civil Rights Act of 1964, the Age Discrimination in Employment Act, the Pregnancy Discrimination Act, and the Americans with Disabilities Act. Wehane and Radin seek to use these laws as a springboard to establish other limitations on the reasons for which employers may terminate their employees.

7.30   Ultimately, Werhane and Radin argue that the at-will condition of employment is unethical. It should be replaced by a more ethical conditional of employment, in which employees could be terminated for just cause, or good reason, only.

7.31   Epstein, by contrast, argues that EAW is perfectly ethical. Like Werhane and Radin, he offers three reasons to support his position. One of these reasons is even the *same* as one that Werhane and Radin discuss. That is, Epstein thinks that EAW is *fair*. The other two reasons are EAW's *effects on utility* and EAW's *distributional consequences*.

Let us begin with Epstein's account of EAW's effects on *utility*. Epstein 7.32
observes that almost all jobs are at will; EAW is spread throughout the
world and is found in many different businesses and professions. He infers
that EAW must produce utility for both employers and employees. If it did
not, employers and employees would not enter this condition of employment so readily. Epstein observes that EAW also helps companies to survive economic uncertainty. When business is slow, companies can stay in
business by eliminating less profitable employment units, terminating all of
the at-will employees.

Further, EAW allows employers to monitor employee behavior, provid- 7.33
ing an incentive for employees to work hard and a disincentive for them to
steal from their employers. EAW also protects employees: if their supervisors are too demanding, employees at will are free to quit and find less
demanding work elsewhere. Epstein concludes that EAW benefits both
employers and employees. It also helps to enhance the overall efficiency of
the marketplace.

His second reason for supporting EAW is *fairness*. In examining this rea- 7.34
son to support EAW, we will have to be careful to understand how Epstein's
understanding of the concept of fairness differs from (or resembles)
Werhane's and Radin's understanding. Remember, Werhane and Radin
think that conditions of fairness challenge EAW but Epstein thinks that
fairness supports this condition of employment. Epstein argues that EAW is
fair because both parties—the employer and the employee—agree that this
is the condition that will govern their employment relation. Epstein considers this aspect of EAW (that both parties agree to it) to be very ethically
important. He writes that the freedom to make this agreement is as important as other freedoms: the freedom of speech, the freedom of religion. He
thinks that people should be able to make their own employment choices,
including choosing to be employed in an at-will capacity.

Sidebar Exercise

Werhane and Radin argue that EAW is unfair because it allows employees
and employers to treat each other unethically. Epstein says EAW is fair
because employees and employers agree that this is the condition that
will govern their employment relationship. With which definition do
you agree? How do the definitions differ from one another?

7.35 His final reason to support EAW is its distributional consequences. Epstein does not think that this reason is as important, or as strong, as the other two. It is not as important or as strong because he does not think that EAW will have very significant distributional consequences. Epstein takes a Rawlsian perspective on distributional consequences. He does not think that eliminating EAW would help to transfer wealth from the well-off to the disadvantaged. In fact, Epstein notes that employees share many of their employers' interests. If the company goes bankrupt due to being unable to adapt to changing market conditions, for example, the employees will be out of their jobs anyway.

Sidebar Exercise

Could feminist ethics provide support for either of these arguments about EAW? Which one and on what grounds?

Executive Compensation: The A.I.G. Case

The Case

After playing a major role in the 2008 financial crisis, the American International Group (A.I.G.) avoided bankruptcy only after receiving $170 billion in bailout money from the U.S. government. Almost immediately, it paid $165 million in bonuses to certain executives, many of whom were directly responsible for the crisis.

The Ethical Questions

Was it ethical to pay these bonuses? To how much compensation are executives entitled and for what reasons?

7.36 Some jobs pay more than others. The United States does not have a centralized governmental committee that decides the salaries for various jobs: so the reason that some jobs earn a lot, and other jobs earn only a little, can seem somewhat mysterious. In this case, we look at the high end of salaries, executives in multinational companies, and ask why they are paid so much. Along the way, we investigate many other questions about executive compensation.

A.I.G.'s corporate identity

The case concerns an American multinational insurance company, 7.37 American International Group (A.I.G.). A.I.G. earned huge profits on some of the financial derivatives associated with the housing boom of the early 2000s and the 2008 financial crisis. In particular, it sold a kind of insurance that was used to support the market in mortgage-backed securities (MBSs). That market will be discussed further below. In 2006, at the peak of the housing boom, A.I.G. earned $14 billion in profit on revenue of $113.4 billion. It had 106,000 employees, 69 million customers, and assets worth nearly $1 trillion.

Facts of the case

In the run-up to the 2008 financial crisis, A.I.G.'s financial products unit 7.38 sold hundreds of billions of dollars' worth of a financial product called "credit-default swaps" (CDSs). CDSs were used as a kind of insurance for MBSs. MBSs were one of the main financial products involved in the crisis.

An MBS is created from a group of residential mortgages: the loans on 7.39 the houses people own. The group of mortgages is "securitized," or made into a financial product that can be bought and sold. That financial product is called an MBS. Then, the bank sells the MBS to an investor. Instead of receiving the homeowner's mortgage payments (and interest) over time, the bank receives an up-front payment. The investor, in turn, receives the mortgage and interest payments over the term of the loan. How is insurance involved in this? The CDSs that A.I.G. was selling allowed investors to make bets about whether borrowers will default on their mortgages. An MBS investor can buy a CDS so that if the borrowers in the MBS default, the MBS investor receives a payment from A.I.G. In this sense, the CDS is like insurance against the possibility of the borrowers not making their scheduled payments.

Early in 2008, many borrowers stopped making payments on their 7.40 mortgages. (The reasons for this downturn will be further discussed in Chapter 9's Countrywide and Lehman Brothers cases.) Investors began demanding payments for their CDSs. Observing that the payments threatened A.I.G.'s financial integrity, a number of employees in A.I.G.'s financial products unit prepared to leave the company at this time. To encourage them to stay, A.I.G created a special bonus pool for that employment unit. The pool was worth $450 million. A.I.G. intended to make bonus payments in a series of installments. Four hundred employees were eligible to receive bonuses. The bonuses ranged in size from $1,000 to $6.5 million.

7.41   By the autumn of 2008, the MBS and CDS markets had completely unraveled, contributing to the 2008 financial crisis. We will examine this crisis in greater detail in the Lehman Brothers case. For now, we simply note that the markets *did* unravel. Many large financial institutions lost hundreds of billions of dollars in late 2008. In the aftermath of their catastrophic losses, a number of them received "bailouts," or cash loans, from the federal government. The bailouts were intended to allow the banks to avoid bankruptcy and survive the crisis.

7.42   A.I.G. received a larger bailout than any other financial institution. Its bailout was worth $170 billion. Many Americans considered this bailout outrageous: A.I.G. was widely regarded as having engaged in some of the most reckless investing practices of any firm prior to the crisis, which directly contributed to the crisis. At the time of its bailout in the fall of 2008, A.I.G. had paid part of the bonuses to the financial products unit. It paid $55 million more in December 2008. The ethical controversy arose in March 2009, when the Treasury Department questioned A.I.G.'s claim that it was required to pay about $165 million of additional bonuses.

7.43   At that time, Treasury Secretary Timothy Geithner demanded that A.I.G. renegotiate the bonuses. A.I.G. refused to renegotiate on the grounds that it was contractually obligated to pay the bonuses. Edward Liddy, who served as interim chairman after the government takeover, claimed that the bonuses were needed to keep the most capable executives from defecting to another firm.

Sidebar Exercise

In Chapter 4's section on Kantian ethics, we discussed some reasons why this ethical theory views renegotiating contracts as unethical. Why is renegotiating a signed contract unethical, for Kantians? Is it unethical for utilitarianism, virtue ethics, or the other ethical views we have examined?

Sidebar Exercise

To what extent does A.I.G. seem like a bureaucracy, in Robert Jackall's sense? Does A.I.G.'s bureaucratic nature (to the extent that you find A.I.G. to be a bureaucracy) challenge our ability to use Kantian ethics to evaluate its decision-making about bonuses? Why or why not?

What happened

After performing its own analysis, the Treasury Department concluded 7.44 that A.I.G. was legally obligated to honor the bonus contracts. A.I.G. reduced the bonuses for which it was not under contractual obligations. Liddy agreed to reduce by 30 percent A.I.G.'s bonuses for the next year, 2009. The top 25 highest-paid executives in the financial products division agreed to reduce their salaries to one dollar (per executive) for the rest of 2009.

Over time, A.I.G. repaid the cost of the bonuses to the government, 7.45 along with the other bailout monies it had received. In 2013, it announced that it had completely repaid the bailout monies, plus an additional $22.7 billion in fees associated with the bailout, to the U.S. government. It earned $9.1 billion in profit in 2013 and $7.5 billion in 2014.

Sidebar Exercise

How would virtue ethics evaluate A.I.G.'s decision to reduce the company's 2009 bonus contracts?

Historical significance

The 2008 financial crisis motivated a moral crisis about widening inequal- 7.46 ity in the United States and other countries. The gulf between wealthy people, middle-class people, and low-income people had increased from previous generations. Many people were concerned that these inequalities (1) would have bad social consequences and (2) were unfair. A debate about executive compensation began around this time, with many people arguing that executives were paid far too much in comparison with workers.

Ethical significance: executive compensation

7.47 In this section, we examine three views of the ethics of executive compensation. First, Moriarty argues that very high CEO salaries are not justified by three accounts of justice in wages. Second, Dillon defends high executive salaries against several concerns. Finally, Borsch and Khurana argue that high executive compensation creates perverse incentives. Let us examine these theories of ethical executive compensation in turn.

7.48 First, Moriarty notes that the 365 largest U.S. corporations paid their CEOs an average of $8 million in 2003. This was 301 times as much as factory workers earned. His thesis is that very high CEO salaries are not justified by three popular accounts of justice in wages: what he calls the *agreement* account, the *desert* account, and the *utility* account. The popular accounts' failure to justify the high salaries suggests that the salaries are, ultimately speaking, unjustified.

7.49 Under the agreement account, just wages emerge from *impartial* negotiations between *informed* parties. They must be impartial in the sense that the parties negotiating on behalf of the company represent the company's, rather than the potential CEO's, interests. All parties should be familiar with typical CEO pay and what justifies different levels of pay. According to Moriarty, this account of justice in executive compensation fails to justify high CEO salaries because (1) the negotiations for CEO salaries are not impartial and (2) negotiating parties are typically not well informed. They are not impartial because parties may be motivated by hidden agendas. For example, the parties representing the company may be friendly with the CEO or seek to curry favor with an incoming chief executive. They are not well informed because it is very difficult to know what CEOs' salaries should be, as discussed further below.

7.50 Under the desert account, workers deserve certain wages for performing certain kinds of work, such as difficult work, work that has a lot of responsibility, work that requires a lot of effort, or work that makes a large contribution to the firm. Moriarty argues that the desert account fails to justify large salaries for executives because it is implausible that executives have 301 times as much difficulty and responsibility, or that they make 301 times the effort and contributions, as compared to workers.

7.51 Under the utility account, wages are incentives for future work, rather than compensation for past work. This explanation of why CEOs are entitled to earn high salaries also seems implausible. Moriarty argues that CEOs would work just as hard if they were paid a lower wage.

Second, Dillon's main concern is to address whether company share- 7.52
holders should have a voice in determining CEOs' (and other employees')
pay. He considers reasons supporting shareholders having a role in determining the firm's salaries and reasons opposing this role. On the *pro* side,
Dillon notes that excessive bonuses and compensation in the run-up to the
2008 financial crisis appear to have encouraged reckless risk-taking. Giving
shareholders a say in executive compensation could allow them to exercise
needed restraint on the company's main decision-makers.

On the *con* side, Dillon worries that shareholder interference in firm pay 7.53
policies could make it more difficult for executive management to run the
company. Executives would constantly need to interrupt their decision-
making processes to seek shareholder approval. He feels that inviting shareholders to offer their opinions on compensation policies could also open
the door to involving them in innumerable company activities: employee
working conditions, the company's carbon footprint, where to establish a
new location. Such interference could drastically undermine the firm's
effectiveness. He concludes by noting that some companies pay CEOs tens
of millions of dollars. But the profits of those companies are in the billions
of dollars. In this sense, Dillon argues that CEOs' shares of profits are not
actually that high. High CEO salaries are justified, on Dillon's view.

Third, by contrast, Lorsch and Khurana argue that executives are paid 7.54
too much. Lorsch and Khurana believe that executives' excessive salaries
point to a deep, structural problem in business. To understand if executive
salaries are too high, they reflect on the purpose of this compensation. For
what does executive compensation provide an incentive? They further
question how this incentive relates to the purpose of business in American
society and whether that purpose is a good one.

Lorsch and Khurana argue that high executive salaries rely on two prob- 7.55
lematic assumptions. First, high executive salaries assume that executives
work most effectively when their monetary reward is tied to the results they
achieve. This assumption seems false because (1) executives often do not
control the results they are rewarded for achieving; and (2) these results are
brought about by groups of employees rather than by a single person.

The second problematic assumption is that an executive's compensation 7.56
should be measured against what other executives are earning. The problem with this assumption, according to Lorsch and Khurana, is that it tends
to drive up executive salaries: because no company wants to pay its CEO a
below-average salary. There is even a sense that merely raising the executive's salary can make the company appear more successful.

7.57   They conclude that the two assumptions make it difficult to address the problem of excessive CEO salaries. Businesses typically address ethical shortcomings by making the behaviors associated with the ethical problem difficult or legally risky to carry out. But when the unethical behavior occurs as a result of unexamined (and fallacious) assumptions, it is less clear how to proceed. They recommend that we rethink the "American business paradigm" so that executives will build companies that serve society.

Sidebar Exercise

Could natural law theory provide support for any of these arguments for limiting executive compensation? Which one and on what grounds?

Preventing Discrimination and Achieving Diversity: The Google Case

The Case

One of the biggest technology companies takes steps to improve its diversity: percentage women employees and percentage employees of color.

The Ethical Questions

What challenges do women and people of color face in the workplace? What steps *may* employers ethically take to improve the numbers of women and people of color that they employ? What steps *should* they take?

7.58   The Google case involves a problem of demographics: technology companies like Google tend to employ more men than women and more white people than people of color. For a variety of reasons, companies wish to have more diverse workforces. As a leader in its industry, Google hoped to recreate employment structures in a way that would lead to greater diversity in its staff and, by extension, the staffs of other technology companies—perhaps even in leadership positions throughout society. This case study examines the steps by which the company attempted to become more diverse.

Google's corporate identity

Google is an information technology company, headquartered in Mountain View, California. It is best known for its popular web search service. The company also offers email (Gmail), storage devices (Google Drive), an internet browser (Google Chrome), and a variety of application programming interfaces (APIs) including Google Maps, Google Translate, and Google Scholar. 7.59

In 2014, Google had more than 55,000 employees, in more than 70 offices, in more than 40 countries around the world. Its revenue that year was $55.5 billion. It earns most of its money through AdWords, an advertising service that broadcasts advertisements to users who search for keywords specified by the advertiser. These advertisements are marked as "sponsored content" in the user's search result so as to differentiate them from the sites generated using Google's search algorithm. 7.60

The company states its philosophy in a list of "ten things we know to be true" on the company website. The list includes: "Focus on the user and all else will follow," "You can make money without doing evil" and "Great just isn't good enough." 7.61

The company emphasizes its casual, collaborative atmosphere. In explaining the Google culture, the company website notes: 7.62

> It's really the people that make Google the kind of company it is. We hire people who are smart and determined, and we favor ability over experience. Although we share common goals and visions for the company, we hail from all walks of life and speak dozens of languages, reflecting the global audience that we serve.

Google offers an employment policy called "Innovation Time Off." This policy allows Google engineers to devote 20 percent of their work time to projects that personally interest them. Many of Google's most popular and profitable services were created by engineers during Innovation Time Off. Some of these services include: Gmail, Google News, and AdSense, an advertising program that allows website owners to embed Google advertisements on their websites, earning revenue when the ads are clicked.

7.63   In 2007, 2008, 2012, 2013, 2014, and 2015, *Fortune* magazine ranked Google the very best company to work for. The company ranked fourth in 2009, 2010 and 2011. Google is one of the only companies in the world that has the financial and human resources to undertake the innovative experiments in diversifying their workforce that they propose to carry out.

Facts of the case

7.64 It is well known that the technology industry is dominated by white men. In order to draw attention to this issue in May 2014, Google published demographic information about its employees: 70 percent were male, 3 percent were Latino, 2 percent were African-American.

7.65   Google's motivation for publishing the data was twofold. First, public discussion had increased the pressure on companies to prioritize increasing diversity. This discussion had been mediated, and amplified, by social media. Second, research had shown that diverse workforces achieve better results than non-diverse workforces. Especially in technology, many feared that a lack of diversity led to technological products being narrowly tailored to meet a limited range of interests, leaving many needs unaddressed.

7.66   Google's report motivated Facebook, Apple, Yahoo, and other technology companies to disclose demographic information about their employees. These companies' employment data revealed similar underrepresentation of women and people of color.

7.67   Google responded to its own publication of demographic data by creating a version of its Innovation Time Off called "Diversity Core." This program aims to increase diversity among Google employees and serve as a model for other technology companies. Employees who participate in the program use 20 percent of their work time to develop programs designed to hire and retain more women and people of color. Some of these programs include: increasing recruitment efforts at colleges that have large numbers of students of color, working with the computer science departments of colleges that are popular with minorities to ensure that they are well prepared for a career in the technology industry, and offering internships to students.

7.68   Five hundred employees in 53 offices have participated in Diversity Core. They are interested in understanding why women and people of color are underrepresented in technology and in changing the culture so as better to include women and people of color. Allowing employees to devote part of their work time to increasing diversity "institutionalizes" these efforts, according to one employee. Once diversification is institutionalized, it prevents employees having to devote extra energy to these efforts, in addition to everything else they have to do.

As a separate initiative, Google is also investigating the role of uncon- 7.69 scious bias in (1) limiting opportunities for female and minority employees; and (2) creating a hostile work environment for them. The company posted four steps to reduce unconscious bias on its website:

1. Gather facts. It's hard to know you're improving if you're not measuring. We collect data on things like gender representation in our doodles and at our conferences.
2. Create a structure for making decisions. Define clear criteria to evaluate the merits of each option, and use them consistently. Using the same standards to evaluate all options can reduce bias. This is why we use structured interviews in hiring, applying the same selection and evaluation methods for all.
3. Be mindful of subtle cues. Who's included and who's excluded? In 2013, Googlers pointed out that of the dozens of conference rooms named after famous scientists, only a few were female. Was this our vision for the future? No. So we changed Ferdinand von Zeppelin to Florence Nightingale—along with many others—to create more balanced representation. Small changes can have big effects.
4. Foster awareness. Hold yourself and your colleagues accountable. We're encouraging Googlers to call out bias. For example, we share a "bias busting checklist" at performance reviews.

Sidebar Exercise

How would Kantian ethics evaluate Google's decision to implement Diversity Core? Raise an objection to this evaluation from Matthew Altman's perspective and consider how a Kantian would respond.

What happened

In June 2015, Google published updated information about its employees. 7.70 Google separates its demographic information by technical employees, non-technical employees, and employees in leadership roles. The publication revealed that, overall, 70 percent of all employees were men (unchanged from the previous year); 60 percent were white; 31 percent were Asian. Latinos comprised 3 percent of employees and African-Americans comprised 2 percent.

7.71   In technical roles, women rose from 17 percent to 18 percent. The percentages of African-American and Latino technical employees were unchanged at 1 percent and 2 percent, respectively. Among non-technical employees, the percentage of African-Americans increased from 3 percent to 4 percent. The percentage of women decreased from 48 percent to 47 percent. The percentage of Latino employees, 4 percent, did not change from the previous year. In leadership, the percentage of female employees rose from 21 percent to 22 percent. African-American and Latino percentages, though, did not increase.

7.72   Regarding the largely unchanged numbers, a Google executive noted the size of the company and that making substantial change takes time. Google has a "deep commitment and the sustained commitment" to increase diversity "over the long run." Google pledged to spend $150 million in 2015 on its diversity initiatives, including searching more widely for qualified female and minority job candidates and changing the social perception that the people who work in technology should be white and Asian men.

Sidebar Exercise

How would Mill's utilitarianism evaluate Google's commitment to diversity over the long run? Do you agree with this evaluation? On what grounds?

Sidebar Exercise

Can natural law theory provide support for Google's commitment to diversity over the long run?

7.73   As noted above in the A.I.G. case study, people became increasingly concerned about inequality in the early twenty-first century. Concern was directed at both economic inequalities, as discussed above with respect to that case, and inequalities between men and women, on the one hand, and white people and people of color, on the other. Google's efforts to highlight and mitigate these differences was an early step in what might become a much broader social movement.

Ethical significance: unconscious bias

One of the things that is most ethically interesting about this case is Google's 7.74 attempts to reduce unconscious bias among its employees. In this section, we explore some ethical issues associated with unconscious bias, including: (1) the ethical importance of recognizing unconscious bias; (2) the ethical importance of attempting to reduce the effects of unconscious biases; and (3) the ethical importance for each person to free themselves of unconscious bias, so their actions reflect their "true character." We discuss each of these issues in turn.

First, the importance of awareness of unconscious bias. Thinking of 7.75 ourselves as being ethically responsible for our unconscious biases might seem strange. After all, people usually think that they are only responsible for what they are aware of.

It is possible though, that people *ought* to be aware of their implicit 7.76 biases, even if they are not already aware. Some philosophers argue that people should take stock of their *likely* biases and try to interfere with those biases. We tend to hold people of earlier generations less responsible for their unethical biases because of their overall social conditions. For example, George Washington was a slaveholder but many people still think that he was a great man. No one, though, would think that someone who owns slaves today could be a great person—no matter what else he or she did.

In this spirit, these philosophers advise that people are responsible for 7.77 thinking about their current societies and the way in which unconscious biases might harm certain groups of people, such as by discouraging them from joining a technology company or by making it more difficult for them to do so.

Sidebar Exercise

Do you agree that people should try to be aware of their unconscious biases? Why or why not? Are you aware of any biases that influence the way that you treat other people or what you expect from them?

Sidebar Exercise

How would virtue ethics evaluate unconscious bias? Does the *phronimos* show unconscious bias?

7.78   Second, an argument for the ethical importance of controlling the effect of one's unconscious biases. Even if one is aware of one's biases, it might seem difficult to control the effects of these biases. Some behaviors associated with unconscious bias seem to unfold outside of the person's control. For example, one common unconscious bias involves automatically crossing the street when a person sees members of different races approaching.

7.79   Some philosophers argue that people should try to program themselves (like they program a computer) to act in a way that they find ethically acceptable. When people become aware that they have engaged in automatic, discriminatory behavior, they should reflect on this behavior and on what they intend to do differently the next time a similar situation arises.

7.80   In the same way that we hold people responsible for things that they do not directly control, such as being able to speak a foreign language, they can be held responsible for controlling the effects of their unconscious biases. Just as learning a language takes indirect control over time, people can learn to avoid acting in discriminatory ways.

7.81   Third and finally, is the ethical importance that one's actions reflect one's true character. This topic builds on the idea that what people *do* reflects who they *are* and that it is important for people to ensure that they are good people acting from good characters.

7.82   One question that immediately arises is whether it is possible that some of the things that people do *fail* to reflect who they truly are. Many philosophers believe that the answer to this question is "yes": sometimes our actions do not reflect our characters. People commonly act without reflection, for example, and simply do things without having thought deeply about them. This is generally not considered to be an ethically acceptable way of conducting one's life, however. We may excuse ourselves for occasionally acting without thought—but only if we generally try to ensure that our actions do reflect our characters.

7.83   Philosophers sometimes say that people are responsible for the actions that could be modified by their rational judgments. So, think back to Kantian ethics. Any action that you can formulate in a maxim, you can be responsible for. In this sense, using ethical theories to think about what is the right thing to do in light of the fact that unconscious biases sometimes manipulate us into doing what we do not truly want to do, can help us to live up to our conception of the person we most want to be.

Sidebar Exercise

Use FUL to investigate the unconscious bias of automatically crossing the street when someone of a different race approaches. What is the maxim of this action? Can it be universalized? Why or why not?

Sidebar Exercise

Are a person's unconscious biases something that he or she owns according to Locke's account of self-ownership? Why or why not?

Work-Life Balance: The Amazon Case

The Case

A company relies on a demanding, cutthroat culture that leaves little time for employees to pursue any interests outside of work.

The Ethical Questions

From an ethical perspective, how much may companies demand of their employees? How much should workers be willing to give?

Work is part of life. Almost everyone works for their living and many people   7.84
are deeply committed to their work. These hard workers are passionate about contributing to their business's success. But isn't there more to life than work? In recent years, many people have become interested in finding the right *work-life balance*. They want to ensure that they have enough time to spend with their families during the week: both enjoying the people they love and fulfilling responsibilities to care for dependents. They also want to

set aside time to pursue personal interests. Although work is a very important part of who a person is, the recent upswing in interest in work-life balance highlights that work is not all we are.

Amazon's corporate identity

7.85 To explore this topic, we examine Amazon's very demanding workplace. Amazon is an American multinational online retail corporation that sells merchandise from its website and ships it to customers around the world. Its corporate headquarters are in Seattle, Washington.

7.86   Amazon was founded in 1994, during the internet boom. It is one of the companies that most helped to popularize online shopping. Amazon became the biggest retailer by market value in the United States in 2015, surpassing Walmart. At that time, its market valuation was $250 billion. At that time, its CEO, Jeff Bezos, was the fifth-wealthiest person in the world, according to *Forbes* magazine.

Facts of the case

7.87 A 2015 investigation by the *New York Times* described Amazon's cutthroat workplace culture. One aspect of this culture is that workers are constantly *on call*: expected to respond to texts and emails. They must attend to business on holidays, on vacation, and late at night.

7.88   Amazon is at the cutting edge of the "always on call" workplace. This goes beyond workers' responsibilities to respond to texts and emails. Even when not actively responding to customers' and supervisors' requests, employees are being monitored. The company uses data to measure worker performance at all times. It also encourages employees to keep an eye on one another and report what they see. Amazon's "Anytime Feedback Tool" allows employees to praise or criticize their colleagues, secretly, to their colleagues' supervisors.

7.89   A second aspect of Amazon's culture, as described in the *New York Times* article, is that workers are expected to be very critical, rather than encouraging, of other workers' ideas. The company values criticism because it wants to assure that it has the very best product possible. It believes that flaws creep into products that are not relentlessly reviewed. The constant scrutiny and harsh appraisals are hard on employees, however. Employees can often be seen crying in public spaces.

Third, Amazon uses *rank and yank* to cull its less productive employees. 7.90
We examined this employment condition in the Enron case (Chapter 3).
Employees are periodically ranked according to productivity; the least
productive employees are terminated. Other large employers—such as
Microsoft, General Electric, and Accenture Consulting—had stopped using
this ranking system around 2015. Perhaps it seemed pointless to these companies to terminate well-performing employees simply because they are not
the *top*-performing employees.

Finally, workers who experienced medical and personal emergencies 7.91
were pressured to accept less prestigious positions or leave Amazon. An
employee was expected to go on a business trip the day after surgery for
miscarrying twins, for example. Another received a poor performance
review after having been treated for cancer. Supervisors discourage parent-
hood because it interferes with the long hours that employees are expected
to work. These policies put the company in stark relief from other large
companies. Google and Facebook, for example, offer employment perks
designed to make working there more fun. Companies like Netflix have
begun offering up to a year of paid parental leave.

Sidebar Exercise

How would ethics of care evaluate Amazon's employment policies?

Sidebar Exercise

How would contract theory evaluate Amazon's employment policies?

What happened

Two months after the *New York Times* piece was published, Jay Carney, 7.92
Senior Vice President for Global Affairs at Amazon, published a rebuttal of
the article on the website, medium.com. Carney denied that the piece represented Amazon work culture accurately. The *Times* responded on the same
website, defending its article. As of early 2016, the controversy is ongoing.

Historical significance

7.93 As noted above, Amazon's demanding workplace culture is at the cutting edge of using data to monitor employees' behavior and performance. The policies continue those found in other demanding workplaces, such as Enron's rank and yank policy. They are consistent with the heightened competition, shorter employment tenure, and heightened productivity found in a large number of contemporary workplaces. Many twenty-first-century workers have found that they must work longer hours in order to afford the things they want to buy. At the same time, though, Amazon's culture is at odds with the friendly, casual workplaces of other internet-based companies, such as Google and Facebook.

Ethical significance: work-life balance

7.94 The differences in these workplaces are part of a contemporary, society-wide discussion about work-life balance. In this section, we survey two views of this balance. First, Weinstein, argues that it is unethical to work too much. He argues that "Just as managing your career well means allocating your time wisely among the different projects and people you oversee, managing your life wisely means giving due time not just to work but to family, friends, community, self, and spirit." In this sense, people who work too hard are showing too little regard for their family and personal lives. Overlooking those aspects of life is an ethical lapse, for Weinstein.

Sidebar Exercise

Which ethical theories (if any) could support Weinstein's view? Which (if any) could oppose it? With which position do you agree? Why? Does it matter if employees are working hard to afford the necessities of life (food, shelter, clothing) or if they are working hard to afford luxuries? What if they just like working hard?

7.95 Second, Scitovsky, an economist, argues that the workweek should be shortened. Companies can hire unemployed people to do the work that their regular employees now cannot perform. He believes that shortening the workweek would have important benefits for families and for society.

Sidebar Exercise

How might shortening the workweek benefit society? Can you think of any possible problems with Scitovsky's plan? How would he attempt to respond to your worries?

References and Further Reading

Alba, Davey. 2015. "Meet the Exec Pushing Google to Fix its Dismal Diversity." *Wired* (June 3). https://www.wired.com/2015/06/google-diversity-nancy-lee/

Andrews, Edmund L. and Peter Baker. 2009. "A.I.G. Planning Huge Bonuses After $170 Billion Bailout." *The New York Times* (March 15). http://www.nytimes.com/2009/03/15/business/15AIG.html?_r=0&pagewanted=print

Baer, Drake. 2014. "Here's What Google Teaches Employees in its Course on Unconscious Bias." *Business Insider* (Sept. 26). http://www.businessinsider.com/google-course-on-unconscious-bias-2014-9

Brownstein, Michael. 2015. "Implicit Bias." In *Stanford Encyclopedia of Philosophy*. https://plato.stanford.edu/entries/implicit-bias/

David, Javier E. 2013. "AIG Makes Final Repayment to Government for Bailout." *CNBC.com* (Mar. 1), pp. 1–2.

Dillon, Karen. 2009. "The Coming Battle Over Executive Pay." *Harvard Business Review* (Sept.). https://hbr.org/2009/09/the-coming-battle-over-executive-pay

Epstein Richard A. 1984. "In Defense of the Contract at Will." *University of Chicago Law Review* 51(947). http://chicagounbound.uchicago.edu/cgi/viewcontent.cgi?article=2290&context=journal_articles

Guynn, Jessica. 2015a. "Google's 'Bias-Busting' Workshops Target Hidden Prejudices." *USA Today* (May 12). http://www.usatoday.com/story/tech/2015/05/12/google-unconscious-bias-diversity/27055485/

Guynn, Jessica. 2015b. "Google Gives Employees 20% Time to Work on Diversity." *USA Today* (May 14). http://www.usatoday.com/story/tech/2015/05/13/google-twenty-percent-time-diversity/27208475/

Guynn, Jessica. 2015c. "Google's Nearly Static Diversity Numbers Point to Long Road Ahead." *USA Today* (June 1). http://www.usatoday.com/story/tech/2015/06/01/google-diversity-workforce-numbers/28308271/

Harkinson, Josh. 2015. "Google's New Diversity Stats Are Only Slightly Less Embarrassing than They Were Last Year." *Mother Jones* (June 2). https://www.motherjones.com/politics/2015/06/google-diversity-statistics-barely-impoved/

Kantor, Jodi and David Streitfeld. 2015. "Inside Amazon: Wrestling Big Ideas in a Bruising Workplace." *The New York Times* (Aug. 15). https://www.nytimes.com/2015/08/16/technology/inside-amazon-wrestling-big-ideas-in-a-bruising-workplace.html

Lorsch, Jay and Rakesh Khurana. 2010. "The Pay Problem: Time for a New Paradigm for Executive Compensation." *Harvard Magazine* (May–June).

Moriarty, Jeffrey. 2005. "Do CEOs Get Paid Too Much?" *Business Ethics Quarterly*, 15(2): 257–281.

Schulman, Miriam. 2000. "Long Hours Put the Squeeze on Workers and Their Families." *Markkula Center for Applied Ethics of Santa Clara University*. http://www.scu.edu/ethics/publications/iie/v8n1/timetogohome.html

Starr, Michael and Jordan Lippner. 2000. "Implied Covenants." *The National Law Journal* (Dec.).

Weinstein, Bruce. 2009. "The Ethics of Work-Life Balance." *Bloomberg Businessweek* (March 27). https://www.bloomberg.com/news/articles/2009-03-27/the-ethics-of-work-life-balance

Werhane, Patricia H. and Tara J. Radin. 2003. "Employment-at-Will, Employee Rights, and Future Directions for Employment." *Business Ethics Quarterly*, 13(2): 113–130.

Case Cited

Guz v. Bechtel National, Inc., 8 P.3d 1089, 100 Cal. Rptr. 2d 352, 24 Cal. 4th 317 (2000).

8
BUSINESS ETHICS IN ADVERTISING

Numerous business ethics issues arise about advertising, including: (1) manip- 8.1 ulative advertising, or the idea that it is unethical for businesses to try to trick consumers into purchasing their products, rather than appealing to their intellects; (2) the new practice of targeting advertising directly to particular consumers, which raises questions about who owns the information that social media users post online and to what purposes such information may ethically be put, (3) the dependence effect, or the idea that consumers only desire products that advertising causes them to desire; and (4) discriminatory advertising, or advertising that harms historically oppressed social groups.

Manipulative Advertising: The Four Loko Case

The Case

A malt beverage that mixes caffeine with alcohol is accused of marketing to minors.

The Ethical Questions

What role does consumer safety play in profit-seeking activity? To what extent may businesses attempt to manipulate their customers via advertising? May businesses encourage (potential) customers to act illegally?

This is Business Ethics: An Introduction, First Edition. Tobey Scharding.
© 2018 John Wiley & Sons, Inc. Published 2018 by John Wiley & Sons, Inc.

8.2 As business ethics students, we are learning how to make arguments so as to persuade others of our ideas (and even to find out if the intuitions that we find within ourselves are correct, upon inspection). A great example of argumentative or persuasive speech is advertisements. Is that a surprising thing to say? Think about it. We all know that when we see advertisements on the internet or in the media, they are designed by a business to try to convince us to purchase their products. Most people don't spend much time thinking about *how* advertisements (try to) convince us to buy certain products, though. The point of this case study is to examine several ways in which advertisements might try to influence our consumer activities: by persuading us, by manipulating us, or by coercing us. In particular, we will be asking when, if ever, it is ethically acceptable for an advertisement to influence our buying preferences by manipulating us.

Phusion Projects' corporate identity

8.3 The case focuses on advertisements for a particular product, the fruit-flavored malt liquor beverage, Four Loko. Four Loko is manufactured by Phusion Projects. Based in Chicago, Phusion Projects is an alcoholic beverage producer with approximately 80 employees as of 2015.

Facts of the case

8.4 Until 2011, Four Loko contained caffeine in addition to alcohol. (The "Four" in its name refers to its original four ingredients: alcohol, caffeine, taurine, and guarana.) A 24-ounce can of the pre-2011 beverage had as much alcohol as four beers and as much caffeine as a strong cup of coffee. That's enough alcohol to intoxicate a consumer. Because of the caffeine, though, that drunk consumer would also be *alert*—and thus able to drink more.

8.5 The combination of alcohol and caffeine thus made Four Loko a potentially dangerous drink. People could continue to drink well past the point of intoxication. They could potentially consume fatal amounts of alcohol. In non-caffeinated alcoholic beverages, by contrast, consumers often lose consciousness as they become extremely drunk. This (obviously) prevents them from drinking further. Four Loko lacked that safeguard.

8.6 Legal drinkers (over the age of 21) are typically able to navigate this situation. Because they have experience with alcohol, they know not to consume too much: even if they still feel alert. But Four Loko was popular with a younger, less knowledgeable crowd. And the company was accused of directing its marketing specifically to this population, comprised of people who were least able to drink responsibly.

Critics raised the following issues with Four Loko's advertising. Senator 8.7 Chuck Schumer (D-NY) criticized the product's misspelled names, its neon-colored cans and jagged fonts, and its low price: 2 dollars per can. Models in the advertisements appeared very young: possibly younger than the legal drinking age. Others noted that the beverage failed to notify consumers about the special dangers associated with alcoholic beverages that contain caffeine.

Others defended Four Loko. They argued that banning Four Loko might 8.8 prevent some college students from harming themselves. But the ban would not itself improve their judgment: they would be just as likely to consume unsafely some other substance. Four Loko's defenders noted that Four Loko's dangers were straightforward. No ban was necessary to protect informed consumers. The problem was with some young consumers' judgments in (1) drinking underage and (2) drinking excessively.

Sidebar Exercise

How would FH evaluate Four Loko's advertising policies? Raise an objection to this evaluation and respond to the evaluation from the perspective of a Kantian ethicist.

What happened

In response to the controversy, Phusion Projects, agreed to the following: 8.9

- To remove caffeine from Four Loko.
- Not to promote mixing Four Loko with caffeinated products.
- Not to hire models or actors for its advertisements who are younger than 25 or who look younger than 21.
- Not to market on college property.
- Not to use the identifying characteristics (like name or mascot) of any school, college, university, student organization, sorority, or fraternity in its advertisements.

Historical significance

8.10 The controversy about Four Loko arose in the wake of other protests about the advertising of products judged to be dangerous. In the 1970s, 1980s, and 1990s, protesters successfully limited advertisements for cigarettes. Cigarette companies were legally banned from advertising on television in the 1970s, from advertising on billboards in the 1990s, and from advertising in magazines in the 2000s. The controversy about Four Loko is one of various efforts to regulate advertisements for potentially dangerous products. These products include other forms of alcohol and other forms of sugary sodas.

Ethical significance: manipulative advertising

8.11 Four Loko decided to change its marketing approach. That doesn't mean that its advertisements were unethical. The company decided that it did not want to use the controversial strategy anymore: perhaps because it agreed with critics that the advertisements were ethically questionable or perhaps because it decided that a less controversial strategy would help them to sell more malt liquor beverages. In this section, we investigate the controversy using new concepts related to the ethics of advertising: persuasion, manipulation, and coercion. The aim of this investigation is to understand more thoroughly (1) what about the controversial advertisements is ethically significant; and (2) if the controversial advertisements are unethical.

8.12   We will be using concepts provided by the business ethicist, Tom Beauchamp, in his analysis of advertising ethics. Beauchamp focuses on the different ways that advertisements convince consumers to purchase the advertised product. He claims that there is a continuum of influences on free choice: from coercion, in which the advertisement completely controls the consumer, so there is no free choice, to persuasion, in which the advertisement offers the consumer reasons. When an advertisement persuades them to purchase a product, consumers make up their minds for themselves.

8.13   In between coercion and persuasion is the difficult concept of manipulation. Manipulation is sometimes deceptive and sometimes not deceptive. Beauchamp criticizes deceptive manipulation as unethical. He seems to consider non-deceptive manipulation to be ethically acceptable. Persuasion, though, remains the ethical ideal for advertisements. Beauchamp's thesis is that persuasive advertisements are ethical and manipulative advertisements are unethical, especially when the manipulation is deceptive. In order to understand his argument more deeply—and decide whether we agree with it—let us examine the concepts of coercion, manipulation, and persuasion in greater detail.

To understand the concepts, we must first investigate the idea of a free 8.14 choice. Beauchamp seems to consider this idea very important, from an ethical perspective. Free choice is a special capacity that human beings have. It is a cognitive ability, which people use when they choose between different consumer products and decide to purchase the ones that best serve their distinctive aims in life. It is one of the most important parts of people's *humanity*, in the sense of Kant's Formula of Humanity, discussed above.

When someone is coerced, it prevents them from making a choice freely. 8.15 Someone who is mugged at gunpoint, for example, is coerced into handing over his wallet. He only hands over the wallet because the robber has a gun. It is not a free choice to give the robber the wallet.

How could an advertisement coerce you into doing something? If the 8.16 advertised product did not reveal that you had to buy another product in order to use the advertised product, for example, the advertisement would coerce you into buying the second product.

Persuasion, by contrast, explains the reasons that support making a par- 8.17 ticular choice. It leaves the choice itself, though, up to the consumer. If your parents want to persuade you to major in philosophy, for example, they will list all of the good reasons to major in philosophy—learning critical thinking skills, being well prepared for employment in a variety of contexts— while leaving the ultimate choice up to you. If they want to coerce you, by contrast, they might refuse to pay your college tuition unless you major in philosophy.

In an advertising context, think of an advertisement that straightfor- 8.18 wardly presents the product and explains the reasons that support purchasing the product. A persuasive argument may even disclose some of the weaknesses of the product, so that consumers can make truly informed decisions. It would not attempt to distract the consumer in any way, such as by using neon colors, jagged fonts, or celebrity endorsements.

It is probably fairly difficult to think of products that use a truly persuasive 8.19 advertising strategy. Most advertisements are somewhat manipulative. From Beauchamp's perspective, only those manipulative advertisements that use deception are truly unethical (though persuasive advertising is still his ethical model). Let us examine his reasoning about manipulation more closely, considering some examples of manipulative advertisements. In each case, it will be hard to determine whether the manipulation is deceptive or non-deceptive. But remember that, for Beauchamp, making this distinction is very important to determining whether an advertisement is ethically acceptable.

8.20   The first kind of example is an advertisement for a cell phone service that requires the cell phone user to agree to a term of service, such as two years. The advertisement emphasizes that the fee for the first month of service is very low, while failing to say (or writing only in very small letters) what the price will be for the rest of the term of the service.

8.21   This kind of advertisement is manipulative because it tries to distract consumers with the low cost of the service for the first month, so that they will not think through the true costs of the cell phone service, to decide if it is really a good purchase for them. A persuasive advertisement would say what are the good and bad aspects of the service, while allowing consumers to make up their minds for themselves. The manipulation could be considered deceptive because the advertisement misleads consumers about the true cost of the product. On the other hand, the information is there for consumers to read, if they just squint a little. In this sense, the advertisement might be considered non-deceptive. It depends on how small the font is and how hard it is for the consumers to find the information they need to make a free choice.

8.22   Beauchamp's second example of manipulative marketing are advertisements for unhealthy foods that mislead consumers about the products. For example, the food might be processed, high in fat and cholesterol, but advertised as being "low carb."

Sidebar Exercise

Think of a particular example of a food advertisement that is manipulative in this sense. Is the particular advertisement you selected deceptive or non-deceptive? Explain your reasoning for considering the advertisement deceptive or non-deceptive.

Sidebar Exercise

Which ethical theories can provide support for Beauchamp's criticisms of manipulative advertising? On what grounds? Are there any ethical theories that would support manipulative advertising? On what grounds?

The third kind of manipulative advertisement that Beauchamp discusses is 8.23 a "lifestyle" advertisement that does not discuss the features of a product but associates it with a desirable lifestyle. For example, the advertisement might show attractive people using the product in an affluent setting or might associate the product with a celebrity spokesperson.

Sidebar Exercise

Think of a particular example of an advertisement that is manipulative in this sense. Is the particular advertisement you selected deceptive or non-deceptive? Explain your reasoning for considering the advertisement deceptive or non-deceptive.

Sidebar Exercise

How would the DM evaluate manipulative advertising? Raise an objection to this evaluation from the perspective of one of the ethical theories (your choice which ethical theory). Do you agree with the objection or the original evaluation? Defend your preference.

Targeted Advertising: The Facebook Case

The Case

A website allows users to post private information and share it with a social network. The social network uses that private information and social network to target advertising to the users.

The Ethical Questions

Who owns the content that users post on social media? Is it permissible for social media websites to use that information for marketing purposes?

8.24 Companies transmit advertisements to potential consumers in the hope that those potential consumers will become actual consumers. They broadcast the advertisements wherever interested consumers are most likely to be found. Emerging internet technology allows companies to display their advertisements to certain potential consumers only: based on those potential consumers' internet browsing history and other personal information. In this case study, we examine ethical issues associated with these "targeted ads." Some of the ethical issues refer back to the theories of private property that we investigated in Chapter 5. Others will be introduced in this section.

Facebook's corporate identity

8.25 Facebook, the American multinational social media technology company, was one of the earliest users of targeted advertising. Facebook was created in 2004 in a college dorm room as an online version of the college "facebook," a directory of students at the college that included a photograph and contact information for each student.

8.26 Facebook subsequently expanded to include all college students. Eventually, it permitted anyone over the age of 13 to join the site. Through Facebook's website, users can communicate with other users designated as "friends." Until 2007, Facebook conducted little commerce through its social media services.

8.27 Facebook's principles state that users should: (1) control their personal information; and (2) have access to the information others want to share. These principles inform: what information Facebook collects; why Facebook collects it; who has access to it; and how users can get rid of information.

Facts of the case

8.28 As Facebook's number of users grew, two features of the information it collected from its users drew the interest of advertisers: (1) personal information about individual users; and (2) information about the connections between friends.

8.29 In November 2007, Facebook began offering a free tool, Beacon, to *partners* (or advertising clients) Blockbuster, *The New York Times*, and overstock.com. Once Beacon was embedded in a partner's website, it recorded users' activities and broadcast them to the user's Facebook friends. Beacon was praised as a way to target potential customers based on their social network and through friends' implied recommendations.

This form of advertising is known as *targeted* or *behavioral* advertising. 8.30 Behavioral advertising involves the tracking of a potential consumer's online activities—including web searches conducted, web pages visited, and content viewed—in order to deliver advertising targeted to the individual consumer's interests. These ads blur the boundary between content and paid advertising.

The activism website, MoveOn.org, created a Facebook group called 8.31 "Petition: Facebook, stop invading my privacy." The petition read: "Sites like Facebook must respect my privacy. They should not tell my friends what I buy on other sites—or let companies use my name to endorse their products—without my explicit permission." The Facebook group had 2,000 members within the first 24 hours. The petition eventually grew to over 80,000 names.

What happened

Facebook user Sean Lane, a California resident, filed a lawsuit against 8.32 Facebook in 2008. Facebook had posted Lane's purchase on overstock.com: an engagement ring for his then girlfriend. Lane filed a class action lawsuit on behalf of other Facebook users whose privacy had been violated by Beacon. The lawsuit alleged that Facebook's use of Beacon violated numerous laws, including the Video Privacy Protection Act, the Electronic Communication Privacy Act, and the Computer Fraud and Abuse Act.

Facebook settled the case for $9.5 million in 2009. Aa part of the settle- 8.33 ment, Facebook agreed to stop using the Beacon program. As of 2015, Facebook continues to use other forms of targeted advertising on its website.

Historical significance

Advertising changed and adapted to each new form of media as it became 8.34 available: newspapers, radio, television, cable television, and now the internet. Internet-based targeted advertising is an emerging form of marketing, which may come to define advertising in the twenty-first century.

Ethical significance: targeted advertising

8.35 The use of personal information in targeted advertising raises ethical concerns about manipulation, such as those discussed in the Four Loko case. It also raises questions about who owns personal data and to what use personal data may be put.

Sidebar Exercise

Use Locke's account of private property to analyze who owns the information that Facebook users post online. On the basis of your analysis, is it ethical for Facebook to use this personal information for advertising purposes? Why or why not?

The Dependence Effect: The Lipitor Case

The Case

A cholesterol-lowering drug, Lipitor, uses extensive advertising to convince customers to purchase it rather than similar generics that cost much less.

The Ethical Questions

To what extent may advertisers attempt to create desires in consumers? To what extent should consumers decide what to purchase based on advertisements?

8.36 Some advertisements are extremely effective. The make a product seem so enticing—so absolutely necessary—that they create a longing for the product in potential consumers. Even if people who view the advertisement did not know that the product existed before seeing the advertisement, they are filled with a sense that they must have that product. In this case study, we examine the ethics of this phenomenon. It was named the *dependence effect* by Canadian-American economist John Kenneth Galbraith. We do so by examining a 2010 advertising campaign for a cholesterol-reducing drug, Lipitor.

Pfizer's corporate identity

In 2010, Lipitor was the most successful drug manufactured by the phar- 8.37
maceutical company, Pfizer. Pfizer is an American multinational pharmaceutical company. Its corporate headquarters are in New York City and its
research headquarters are in Groton, Connecticut. It is one of the world's
largest pharmaceutical companies. Pfizer's 2010 revenue was $67.8 billion.
It employed 113,800 people that year.

In its Code of Conduct, Pfizer notes that integrity is its core value. 8.38
It guides employee conduct with the acronym O.W.N.I.T.:

- *Own* your part of the business by taking risks and accepting
  responsibility.
- *Win* by producing long-term strategies that further the company's
  mission.
- *No jerks* by challenging colleagues' egotistical and obnoxious behavior.
- *Impact* by following through on one's plans.
- *Trust* by telling other employees the truth, in a constructive spirit, about
  their ideas.

Facts of the case

In 2010, there were many other cholesterol-lowing drugs on the market, 8.39
including generic drugs that cost much less than Lipitor. To compete with
generics, Pfizer used an advertising campaign featuring the inventor of the
artificial heart, Robert Jarvik. In a context in which he appears to have just
completed an athletic activity, Jarvik explains the virtues of Lipitor over generics. The advertisements featuring Jarvik became closely associated with his
claim that "I take Lipitor instead of a generic." They warned patients against
pharmacists or physicians who might recommend a generic over Lipitor.

In the advertisements, Jarvik appeared to be a practicing physician 8.40
accepting funds to advocate for a particular pharmaceutical product, which
would have been a conflict of interest. The truth, though, was that Jarvik
was not a practicing physician. The athletic aspects of the advertisement
were performed by a body double, not Jarvik himself. The advertisements
did not include explicit falsehoods but encouraged potential customers to
form an incorrect impression of Jarvik's recommendation.

Generic versions of brand-name pharmaceuticals are significantly less 8.41
expensive than the brand-name originals. For most consumers, brand-name

pharmaceuticals are prohibitively expensive. The successful advertising campaigns of Lipitor and other drugs persuaded consumers to make choices that were not in the best interest of their personal bottom line. To the extent that medical expenses are shared across society, the advertisements encouraged consumers to make choices that were not in society's best interest (at least financially).

Sidebar Exercise

How would feminist ethics evaluate Lipitor's advertisement?

Sidebar Exercise

How would Bentham's utilitarianism evaluate Lipitor's advertisement?

What happened

8.42 Congressman John Dingell's (D-MI) Committee on Energy and Commerce used the advertisement as an example of deception in pharmaceutical marketing. A Pfizer executive testified that each statement included in the advertisements was defensible. Ultimately, no fines or penalties were levied and the regulation of pharmaceutical marketing was unchanged. Pfizer began using advertisements featuring ordinary people rather than experts.

8.43 Lipitor's patent expired in 2011. At that time, the company lowered its price to compete with generics.

Historical significance

8.44 Pharmaceutical companies create large profits by persuading potential consumers to purchase expensive, name-brand drugs rather than less expensive, generic versions of those drugs. The generic versions are chemically identical to the name-brand pharmaceuticals. In the 2000s, the high cost of prescription drugs began to concern more and more people. Their concern was heightened by pharmaceutical companies' aggressive marketing techniques for these drugs. One major concern is that this marketing manipulates patients, manipulates physicians, interferes with the physician-patient relationship, and prevents patients from receiving the best treatment for (and advice about) their medical conditions. The Lipitor case was the first widely publicized case of a physician publicly advocating for a pharmaceutical product.

Ethical significance: the dependence effect

Galbraith (1952) criticizes the "dependence effect," or the idea that people's 8.45 desires to own things for which they have seen advertisements depend on the advertisements themselves: the desires are created by the ads. For Galbraith, this means that advertising-created desires are less important than natural desires. It matters less that people are able to fill them. (So Galbraith might argue that people should just take the generic version of Lipitor.)

Hayek criticizes Galbraith's argument by pointing out that few natural 8.46 needs are truly original to the human being in the sense of not being influenced by what other people in the person's social group are doing and buying. (So Hayek (1961) might argue that it is fine for Pfizer to advertise Lipitor aggressively. People should do as they choose.)

Sidebar Exercise

Use natural law theory to evaluate the Lipitor case. Was Pfizer's advertising campaign ethical, according to this ethical theory? Why or why not? Then, raise an objection to your natural law theory evaluation from the standpoint of a different ethical theory. Which ethical theory's concern is more important? Why?

Discriminatory Advertising: The Abercrombie & Fitch Case

The Case

A clothing retailer that markets a trendy, "All-American" style is accused of featuring predominantly white models in its advertisements, to the discriminatory exclusion of models of color.

The Ethical Question

Must advertisements feature diverse models?

8.47 In the United States today, many people believe that it is a matter of deep ethical importance that institutions are *inclusive*, welcoming people from many different racial and ethnic backgrounds. Institutions include first and foremost the various divisions of the government itself: the Department of Labor, the Department of Justice, and so on. In the Google case, we saw that institutions can also include businesses, especially large and powerful businesses like Google and other technology companies. In the Google case, we examined a company's efforts to make its workforce more diverse. In this case, we ask a question about a company's customers. As a matter of ethics, must businesses seek out diverse customers for their products? How far should businesses strive to be inclusive in their marketing, from an ethical point of view?

Abercrombie & Fitch's corporate identity

8.48 The case focuses on the American multinational company, Abercrombie & Fitch, in the early 2000s. The company itself has a long history. It was founded in the late 1800s as a sporting goods retailer. Early customers included Theodore Roosevelt, Ernest Hemingway, and Charles Lindbergh. After a period of decline in the twentieth century, it was brought back to life when Mike Jeffries took over as CEO in 1992.

8.49   Jeffries' vision for Abercrombie is central to our case study. He wished to sell quintessentially American clothes—according to a very specific, 1950s-era concept of what "All-American" looks like. Men's and women's clothes were starkly designed according to traditional notions of masculinity and femininity: bulging biceps and tiny waists. Jeffries describes the Abercrombie & Fitch style as "cool," "beautiful," "funny," "masculine," "optimistic," and never "cynical" or "moody." He has called his brand the "essence of privilege and casual luxury."

8.50   In a controversial 2006 interview, featured on Salon.com, Jeffries discussed his preference that Abercrombie & Fitch sales associates be very attractive. He noted that "Good-looking people attract other good-looking people, and we want to market to cool, good-looking people. We don't market to anyone other than that." Jeffries added, "We go after the cool kids. We go after the attractive all-American kid with a great attitude and a lot of friends. A lot of people don't belong, and they can't belong. Are we exclusionary? Absolutely."

Jeffries explained the company's "exclusionary" marketing as follows. 8.51
Retailers who market to all demographics ("young, old, fat, skinny") are
"totally vanilla." He criticized that approach because "You don't alienate
anybody, but you don't excite anybody, either."

Facts of the case

In 2003, several Hispanic, African-American, and Asian-American employees 8.52
sued Abercrombie & Fitch for discrimination in hiring and promotions. They
alleged that the company failed to hire them in the front-of-the-store sales
positions for which they applied. Instead, they were hired for back-of-the-
store custodial positions. Though this case focused on discrimination in
employment (rather than marketing), it reflected the broader concern that the
company's image was focused on white people to the neglect of people of color.

In 2005, customers protested that the companies tee-shirts were offensive. 8.53
The tee-shirts to which they objected included ones that read: "Who Needs
a Brain When You Have These?"; "Gentlemen Prefer Tig Ol' Bitties"; and
"Wong Brothers Laundry Service—Two Wongs Can Make It White." This
protest demonstrated some consumers' concern that the company's marketing was disrespectful to women and people of color and exclusionary.

Sidebar Exercise

How would FH evaluate Abercrombie & Fitch's tee-shirts?

Sidebar Exercise

How would feminist ethics evaluate Abercrombie & Fitch's tee-shirts?
Do you agree with this evaluation? Why or why not?

What happened

In the settlement of the legal case, Abercrombie & Fitch agreed to pay $40 8.54
million to the plaintiffs of color to settle their claims of discrimination in
hiring and promotions. The company also agreed to take measures so that

its hiring and promotion of employees of color would reflect the diversity of its applicant pool. It discontinued the controversial tee-shirts. The company did not admit guilt in the settlement.

8.55   Abercrombie & Fitch also agreed to include more models of color in its advertisements and catalogs, which had previously featured predominantly white models. Plaintiffs demanded that the company add models of color to its marketing materials so as not to create the impression that people of color were not welcome at the company. Regarding the settlement, CEO Jeffries noted:

> I don't think we were in any sense guilty of racism, but I think we just didn't work hard enough as a company to create more balance and diversity. And we have, and I think that's made us a better company. We have minority recruiters. And if you go into our stores you see great-looking kids of all races.

By 2013, Abercrombie's sales had dropped 10 percent and its stock value had fallen 18 percent. Analysts attributed part of the reason for the fall to competition from less expensive retailers like Forever 21 and H&M. Part of the reason, though, seemed to be backlash for the ethical controversies. Jeffries resigned at the end of 2014. At that time, acting CEO Arthur Martinez commented: "The world moved on, and the company has to move on."

Historical significance

8.56 The Abercrombie & Fitch controversy was one of the first times that a company's choice of models for its advertisements was used to support claims of racial discrimination against a company. The case highlights changing norms about inclusion in the United States: inclusion has become one of the biggest ethical topics of the early twenty-first century. The controversy also reflects the changing definition of "All-American" from 1950s to 2000s to reflect the diverse population of the United States.

Ethical significance: discriminatory advertising

8.57 The case raises questions about whether it is ethically acceptable (1) to limit a company's freedom of expression in order to (2) force conformity to the new set of values. About the tee-shirt controversy, CEO Jeffries commented:

> Listen, do we go too far sometimes? Absolutely. But we push the envelope, and we try to be funny, and we try to stay authentic and relevant to our target customer. I really don't care what anyone other than our target customer thinks.

Other companies market to particular groups of people, such as specialty stores that feature cuisine or clothing associated with particular cultures. In this sense, it might seem ethically acceptable for Abercrombie & Fitch to focus on a narrow slice of the population and market aggressively to that slice. This marketing strategy would be part of the company's freedom of expression: to choose to whom it markets its clothes.

References and Further Reading

Beauchamp, Tom L. 1984. "Manipulative Advertising." *Business and Professional Ethics Journal*, 3(3–4): 1–22.

Berfield, Susan and Lindsey Rupp. 2015. "The Aging of Abercrombie & Fitch: Behind the Decline of Abercrombie & Fitch and the Fall of its Mastermind, Michael Jeffries." *Bloomberg Businessweek* (Jan. 22). http://www.bloomberg.com/news/features/2015-01-22/the-aging-of-abercrombie-fitch-i58ltcqx

CBS News. 2015. "San Francisco Sued Over Soda Warnings, Advertising Ban." (Jul. 27). http://www.cbsnews.com/news/san-francisco-soda-warnings-advertising-ban-lawsuit/

Chapman, Simon. 1996. "The Ethics of Tobacco Advertising and Advertising Bans." *British Medical Bulletin*, 32(1): 121–131.

Denizet-Lewis, Benoit. 2006. "The Man Behind Abercrombie & Fitch." *Salon* (Jan. 24). http://media.salon.com/2006/01/the_man_behind_abercrombie_fitch.jpg

Donohue, Julie M., et al. 2007. "A Decade of Direct-to-Consumer Advertising of Prescription Drugs." *The New England Journal of Medicine*, 357: 673–681.

Duke, Alan. 2010. "'Blackout in a Can' Blamed for Student Party Illnesses." *CNN* (Oct. 26). http://www.cnn.com/2010/US/10/25/washington.students.overdose/

Feldman, Brian. 2014. "R.I.P. Four Loko, 2005–2014." *The Atlantic* (Mar. 26). http://www.theatlantic.com/national/archive/2014/03/rip-four-loko/359602/

Field, Abigail. 2010. "The Case Against Banning Four Loko." *Daily Finance* (Nov. 15). http://www.dailyfinance.com/2010/11/15/the-case-against-banning-four-loko/

Galbraith, John Kenneth. 1952. "The Dependence Effect." In *The Affluent Society*. Boston: Houghton Mifflin. http://sites.middlebury.edu/econ0450f10/files/2010/08/galbraith.pdf

Godoy, Maria. 2013. "Four Loko Cans Will Now Make Clear They're Loaded with Alcohol." *NPR* (Feb. 13). http://www.npr.org/sections/thesalt/2013/02/13/171890650/four-loko-cans-will-now-make-clear-theyre-loaded-with-alcohol

Greene, Jeremy A. 2010. "'For Me There Is No Substitute'— Authenticity, Uniqueness, and the Lessons of Lipitor." *AMA Journal of Ethics*, 12(10): 818–823. http://journalofethics.ama-assn.org/2010/10/msoc2-1010.html

Greenhouse, Stephen. 2004. "Abercrombie & Fitch Bias Case Is Settled." *The New York Times* (Nov. 17). http://www.nytimes.com/2004/11/17/us/abercrombie-fitch-bias-case-is-settled.html

Hayek, F. A. 1961. "The Non Sequitur of the 'Dependence Effect.'" *Southern Economic Journal*, 27(4): 346–348.

Layton, Lyndsey.2010. "New FDA Rules Will Greatly Restrict Tobacco Advertising and Sales." *The Washington Post* (Mar. 20). http://www.washingtonpost.com/wp-dyn/content/article/2010/03/18/AR2010031803004.html

Lutz, Ashley. 2013. "13 Reasons Why People Hate Abercrombie & Fitch." *Business Insider* (Aug. 22). http://www.businessinsider.com/abercrombie-and-fitch-worst-controversies-2013-8?op=1

Martin, Kirsten E. 2010. "Facebook: Beacon and Privacy." *Business Roundtable Institute for Corporate Ethics.* http://www.corporate-ethics.org/pdf/Facebook%20_A_business_ethics_case_bri-1006a.pdf

Marwick, Alice E. 2014. "How Your Data Are Being Deeply Mined." *The New York Review of Books* (Jan. 9). http://www.nybooks.com/articles/archives/2014/jan/09/how-your-data-are-being-deeply-mined/

Parker, R. Stephen and Charles E. Pettijohn. 2003. "Ethical Considerations in the Use of Direct-to-Consumer Advertising and Pharmaceutical Promotions: The Impact on Pharmaceutical Sales and Physicians." *Journal of Business Ethics*, 48(3): 279–290.

Sauer, Abe. 2010. "Four Loko Declines to Own Its Marketing Strategy." *Brandchannel* (Oct. 28). http://brandchannel.com/2010/10/28/four-loko-declines-to-own-its-marketing-strategy/

Selinger, Evan and Shaun Foster. 2012. "How'd My Avatar Get into That Sneaker Ad? The Ethical Questions Surrounding Building Consumers into Commercial Advertising." *Slate* (Jan. 4). http://www.slate.com/articles/technology/future_tense/2012/01/behaviorally_targeted_ads_and_the_ethical_dilemmas_behind_building_consumers_into_ads_.html

Temin, Davia. 2013. "How a CEO Can Wreck a Brand in One Interview: Lessons from Abercrombie & Fitch vs. Dove." *Forbes* (May 13). https://www.forbes.com/sites/daviatemin/2013/05/13/abercrombie-and-fitch-v-dove-or-how-a-ceo-can-wreck-a-brand-in-1-interview-7-years-ago/#1d9e02ce73a0

Worland, Justin. 2015. "Here's What Alcohol Advertising Does to Kids." *Time* (Jan. 19). http://time.com/3672188/alcohol-advertising-kids/

9

BUSINESS ETHICS IN THE FINANCIAL SECTOR

This section of case studies relates to the emerging field of financial ethics. 9.1
Many of these cases involve the lead-up to the 2008 financial crisis, including
ethical criticism of (1) "predatory" behavior in finance; (2) excessive investment
risk; (3) the practice of short selling; and (4) the activity of insider trading.

Predatory Lending: The Countrywide Financial Case

The Case

A mortgage-lending business targets low-income borrowers for high-
priced loans.

The Ethical Questions

How much more may banks ethically charge people with bad credit
than people with good credit for home mortgages as a matter of ethics? Must businesses always inform people of the best deals to which
they are entitled?

Purchasing a first home can be overwhelming. Choosing a suitable home, 9.2
negotiating with the current owners—and we haven't even begun addressing the financial aspects. As we will explore in this section, finance can be a

This is Business Ethics: An Introduction, First Edition. Tobey Scharding.
© 2018 John Wiley & Sons, Inc. Published 2018 by John Wiley & Sons, Inc.

tricky business. Generally, speaking, *finance* refers to strategies for managing a business's (or a person's) monetary resources over time. Because the strategies are implemented over many years, and unexpected events can change the future in unforeseeable ways, finance involves a lot of uncertainty and risk. This is what makes it so difficult. We never know what will happen and there are many approaches to managing uncertainty and risk. So finance is very complicated. In the Countrywide Financial case, one of the questions we will be examining is: how much help must a mortgage-lender provide its customers in navigating the difficult world of finance?

Countrywide Financial's corporate identity

9.3   Countrywide Financial was an American mortgage-lending business. Founded in 1968, Countrywide gave loans to people for their home mortgages until 2008, when it was purchased by Bank of America. Countrywide *securitized* most of the loans it made. As discussed in the A.I.G. case, securitizing a loan means that the mortgage-lending business legally transforms its mortgage into financial instruments, or *securities*, that can be bought and sold. Once the mortgages were securitized, Countrywide sold these *mortgage-backed securities* (MBS) to investors.

9.4   Countrywide loaned money to both *prime* and *subprime* borrowers. Prime borrowers have good credit and pay low interest rates. Subprime borrowers have bad credit and pay higher interest rates. It also did business in *loan servicing*, handling the process through which borrowers made interest and principal payments to repay their loans.

9.5   The company was co-founded by Angelo Mozilo, who was the firm's CEO at the time of the ethical controversy that this case study examines, between 2006 and 2007. During this time, Countrywide financed almost $500 billion in home mortgages: $41 billion, or 177,000–240,000 loans, every month. It had 62,000 employees, 900 offices, and assets of $200 billion. In 2006, Countrywide's revenue was $11.4 billion, $2.06 billion of which was generated by mortgage banking.

Facts of the case

9.6   The ethical controversy in this case concerns Countrywide's subprime mortgage business. Three claims of unethical activities will be examined. First, Countrywide gave higher-interest subprime loans to customers who qualified for prime (less expensive) loans. Second, Countrywide made loans to subprime customers who were very likely to default on their loans. Third, Countrywide's incentive structure encouraged the first two unethical practices.

First, the claim about targeting some prime customers to subprime 9.7 loans. This claim involves the computer system in Countrywide's subprime unit. The system was programmed not to include borrowers' *cash reserves* (or savings) when determining their loan eligibility. For some low-income borrowers, their cash reserves would have allowed them to qualify for prime loans. Without the cash reserves, though, these low-income borrowers did not qualify for prime loans.

In this sense, Countrywide directed low-income borrowers to high-cost 9.8 subprime loans even when the borrowers' credit scores qualified them for prime loans. The more expensive loans produced higher profits for Countrywide because they were subject to a higher interest rate and charged higher fees. Countrywide also avoided offering low-income borrowers Federal Housing Administration (FHA) loans, which are well suited to low-income borrowers but do not generate high fees.

Sidebar Exercise

Consider the following example of two ways to structure a fixed-rate, $275,000 loan with a 30-year term and a 10 percent down-payment for a borrower with fully documented income and a credit score of 620.

An FHA loan has a 7 percent interest rate and a monthly payment of $1,829. Countrywide's subprime loan has an interest rate of 9.875 percent and a monthly payment of $2,387. That amounts to a difference of $558 a month, or $6,696 a year—a big difference to a low-income borrower.

Use rule utilitarianism to evaluate whether it is ethical for Countrywide to lead the low-income borrower to take out a subprime loan rather than an FHA loan.

Second, the firm is accused of signing off on loans that borrowers were 9.9 unlikely to be able to repay. For example, the firm offered *piggyback* loans such that borrowers could buy a house without putting down any of their own money. Although it might seem appealing to buy a house with no down-payment, this kind of mortgage is very precarious. Because the borrower has so little equity in the house, it is easier to lose the home if the borrower encounters any difficulty making loan payments.

9.10   Other unlikely-to-be-repaid loans are the following. The firm made loans that were worth more than 95 percent of a home's appraised value and required no documentation of a borrower's income. That means that a borrower could, in theory, lie about their income—and get away with it. Countrywide made loans to borrowers with bad credit grades. A borrower's credit grade rates how likely they are to repay their loans. Countrywide made a huge loan ($500,000) to a borrower rated C-minus, the second-riskiest grade. Finally, it made loans that left little income for borrowers' food, clothing and other living expenses. After paying their mortgage, a family of four might have only $1,000 in disposable income. A single person might have only $550 left over.

9.11   Third, Countrywide's incentive structure encouraged brokers to make controversial loans like those described above. Brokers received higher commissions for subprime loans: 0.50 percent of the loan's value for subprime loans, versus 0.20 percent on higher-quality "Alternate-A" (Alt-A) loans, which were just below prime loans. That means that they would earn a $500 commission for making a $100,000 loan subprime—but only $200 for making the same loan as Alt-A.

9.12   As a result of loans such as those described above, Countrywide earned huge profits. Penalty fees generated $212 million in 2005 and $268 million in 2006. Late charges generated $285 million in 2006. It earned additional revenue from closing fees associated with the loans: flood and tax certifications, appraisals, charges to email or FedEx paperwork. In 2006–2007, Countrywide completed 3.5 million flood certifications, and 1.3 million appraisals. Its loan closing services subsidiary, LandSafe Inc., charged $60 for tax service fees and $26 for flood certifications, for which other companies typically charge $12–14.

What happened

9.13   Countrywide challenged the charge that its computer system was unethical. First, the firm pointed out that it was only conforming to the industry norm for mortgage-lending services: other mortgage-lending businesses also used aggressive sales techniques. Second, it argued that it was ethical to steer some low-income borrowers into subprime loans, rather than less expensive FHA mortgages, because FHA mortgages have a maximum loan amount. Thus, they are difficult to use in markets with high real estate costs—where many of the low-income borrowers wanted to live.

Despite these arguments, the company eliminated its subprime com- 9.14
puter program in September 2006. As a result of losses associated with the
risky loans it had made, the company nearly went bankrupt in 2008. It was
rescued from bankruptcy only by being sold to Bank of America at a greatly
reduced valuation.

Sidebar Exercise

Are you convinced by Countrywide's response? Say why or why not.
Can any ethical theories be used to support the company's response?
How might you further object to Countrywide's response?

Sidebar Exercise

How would feminist ethics evaluate Countrywide's response? Are you
convinced by this evaluation? Why or why not?

Historical significance

The Countrywide case study involved state-of-the-art tools of financial 9.15
investment, including MBS and subprime lending. (These new tools, introduced in the A.I.G. case, will be further explored in the Lehman Brothers
case.) The tools make finance much more powerful. They extend financial
opportunities to low-income people in a way that presents great opportunities. The new opportunities also have serious risks, though, such as those
discussed in this case. The housing boom that underwrote the Countrywide
case is now over but the mortgage derivatives and subprime lending are
here to stay—so it is more important than ever to think about the ethical
issues that they involve.

Ethical significance: predatory lending

On the one hand, the creation and widespread granting of subprime mort- 9.16
gages represented a great extension of financial opportunity to low-income
borrowers. For the first time, people with bad credit were able to take out a
loan. In fact, as discussed above, Countrywide Financial actively sought
out low-income borrowers to take out loans. On the other, though, these

activities greatly harmed many low-income people. Many of them obtained loans that were more expensive than those for which they qualified. Others took out loans that were simply too risky. When the housing boom ended and housing prices began to decline, these low-income borrowers lost their homes, as well as any equity that they had invested in their homes.

9.17   In this sense, we have a conundrum. Financial innovation allows businesses to extend opportunities to low-income people. But the same financial innovation creates temptations for businesses to exploit low-income people for their own profit-seeking activities. What is the right way to deal with this conundrum? Is there any way to capture the redistributive possibilities of financial innovation without incurring the temptations to exploit low-income people?

Sidebar Exercise

How could a bureaucratic management style contribute to the problem discussed in the Countrywide case?

Investment Risk: The Lehman Brothers Case

The Case

Lehman Brothers, an investment bank, made a series of risky real estate investments during a housing boom and continued its risky investments when the boom ended. While investment banks that had made less risky investments were able to survive the economic slowdown, Lehman went bankrupt. Due to the interconnectedness of the financial system, Lehman's bankruptcy worsened a global financial catastrophe.

The Ethical Question

Is it ethically wrong to bear too much risk?

9.18 The Lehman Brothers case also concerns problems with mortgage-backed securities (MBS). In this case, we are not concerned with too much risk taking on the *borrowing* side of MBS (as we were in the Countrywide case).

The Lehman case examines a company that took on too much risk on the *investment* side.

How can a firm take on too much risk when investing in MBS? Remember 9.19 that Countrywide was not a traditional bank. It could not depend on customers' deposits to provide the cash for its mortgage-lending services the way traditional banks could. Thus, Countrywide depended on investment banks to purchase its securitized mortgages. That was the only way that it could get more cash to make more mortgages. One of the investment banks buying MBSs (though not necessarily from Countrywide) was Lehman Brothers. In the same way that the loans that borrowers took out were ethically questionable, Lehman's investment practices were ethically questionable. It bought too many MBSs that were too risky, in an ethical sense. Or, at least, this is the claim that we will investigate.

Lehman Brothers' corporate identity

Lehman Brothers was an American multinational investment bank (IB). It 9.20 was founded in the nineteenth century by the Lehman family and did business until 2008, when it went bankrupt. In 2008, it was one of the largest American IBs, fourth to Goldman Sachs, Morgan Stanley, and Merrill Lynch.

An IB is a kind of financial institution, different from the commercial 9.21 banks where ordinary people have savings accounts. IBs primarily serve businesses. One main function of IBs is raising capital to support business entrepreneurship. *Capital* is a technical term for money used for investing purposes. IBs raise capital by buying and selling financial instruments like mortgage-backed securities (MBS). IBs are financial middlemen between creditors and debtors. Creditors provide capital by buying the financial instruments. Debtors borrow this capital from IBs in order to develop existing businesses or create new businesses.

IBs thrive on risk. A basic principle of investment banking is: to gain 9.22 return requires taking risk and to gain greater return requires taking greater risk. *Return* is the profits IBs earn on their investments. *Leverage* is the main tool by which IBs seek return for risk. Leverage is defined as the ratio of debt to equity. *Equity* is another technical term for money, which highlights the business's ownership of the money. In the Countrywide case, for example, we spoke of borrowers' equity in the houses on which they were paying their mortgage. That equity was the part of the mortgage that the borrowers had already paid back.

The debt involved in leverage is a special kind of debt. It is debt bor- 9.23 rowed to pursue greater returns than those possible using only the bank's capital. Investing with borrowed money is risky because the firm has to repay its debt regardless of how well its investments do. Even if it loses all of its money, it still owes repayment—in the same way that people have to repay their mortgages and other debt even if they lose their jobs. That's pretty risky!

9.24   The board and senior management decides how much leverage a bank takes. Their decision defines the bank's *risk tolerance*. Historically, the industry ratio was under 20 to 1. Prior to the 2008 financial collapse, it was more than 30 to 1. Even 20 to 1 is a lot of debt, though. It's not exactly the same as the debt that an individual person takes on. To get a ballpark comparison, though, try thinking about it that way. Being levered 20 times is like purchasing a home with only 5 percent down: you put down $5,000 on a house worth $100,000 and are responsible for repaying the rest. Being levered 30 times is like buying a $100,000 home with a down-payment of only $3,333.

9.25   A few times before the 2008 financial crisis, banks whose leverage ratio was very high had encountered difficulty in paying back their loans when too many of their risky investments failed to pan out. This happened to the hedge fund Long Term Capital Management (LTCM) in 1998. At that time, the U.S. government engineered a bailout of the hedge fund. A bailout means that the fund was loaned money so that it could meet its repayment obligations. The fund paid that money back to its creditors later.

9.26   The government engineered the bailout because it decided that LTCM was of *systemic* importance to the U.S. economy. That means that the fund was so bound up in the U.S. economy that its failure would bring about many other failures as well. It would cause more failures because of leverage. LTCM owed money to other banks. If it failed, it would not make those payments. But then those other banks would fail. When they failed, they would miss payments to the financial institutions to which they owed money. And so on. There could be so many failures that the whole U.S. economy would fail. So, the U.S. government had a practice that certain firms would be bailed out if they were "too big to fail" (TBTF).

9.27   This all seems reasonable. The problem, though, is that the possibility of being bailed out if investments go bad leads to a special kind of ethical problem. That problem is called *moral hazard*. Moral hazard refers to a situation in which a business (or other actor) takes risks that it would not otherwise take because it believes that it has a benefactor that will rescue it if it gets into trouble. In the case of TBTF, that "benefactor" is the U.S.

government. So, an explicit policy of TBTF could lead big firms to take risks that they would not take if they believed that they were solely responsible for their own survival. This could lead to an economic situation that was worse for everyone. That's why the U.S. government never had an explicit policy of TBTF. Despite the absence of an explicit policy, though, some firms might have thought that they actually were TBTF. As noted above, Lehman was a big bank; it might have thought this, too (though we don't know for sure).

Facts of the case

In the early 2000s, Lehman increased its leverage ratio in order to compete 9.28 with larger rivals. A large percentage of its investments were in real estate, to capture profits associated with the MBS and subprime markets. Due to its high (30-to-1) leverage ratio, Lehman required its real estate holdings to perform favorably in order to remain profitable. That means that the value of the investments needed to do more than retain their value. The investments actually had to increase in value just for Lehman to continue to meet its repayment obligations.

At the same time, though, there were signs that the real estate market 9.29 was in trouble. As discussed in the Countrywide case, standards were being lowered for subprime mortgages. More loans were being given to people with bad credit and more loans were being given to people who were unlikely to be able to repay their loans. By the end of 2006, loan delinquencies and defaults were escalating. Many subprime lenders began to go out of business.

On March 4, 2007, HSBC, the European bank, reported an $11 billion 9.30 write-off to cover mounting losses from bad subprime loans. HSBC was Europe's largest bank and a top subprime lender in the United States. The bank's difficulties were a strong warning that the business had gone bad. But Lehman continued to expand its real estate activities.

Sidebar Exercise

How would virtue ethics evaluate Lehman's decision to expand its real estate activities?

What happened

9.31 Lehman's stock fell throughout 2008. In September, it was clear that the bank would fail without federal intervention. The U.S. government declined to apply its TBTF doctrine to Lehman, releasing systemic risk. In the ensuing global financial panic, trillions of dollars were lost.

Historical significance

9.32 Lehman's bankruptcy filing was the largest bankruptcy in U.S. history. It precipitated the most significant economic downturn in the United States since the Great Depression. Its effects were felt around the world. Moreover, acquiring certain parts of the defunct Lehman may have contributed to the ethical controversy that occurred in the Nomura case, discussed below. Other downstream effects might also occur.

Ethical significance: investment risk

9.33 The focus of this case is risk-taking. How can we know how much risk is too much, from an ethical perspective? Business ethicist Scharding poses two ethical questions about financial risk:

- May investment firms risk money in abstruse financial instruments that are highly complicated and interconnected in intricate ways?
- May investment firms rely on being bailed out, or rescued by an outside agency, when they put money at risk?

She argues that these investment practices are unethical in a Kantian sense when they risk the integrity of the financial system upon which the firm depends. She defends this thesis through two examples.

9.34   First, an example concerning abstruse investments. In 2004, the U.S. bank, Goldman Sachs, created a synthetic collateralized debt obligation (synthetic CDO), Abacus 2004-1. Synthetic CDOs are similar to MBSs in that they are derived from other financial instruments. But while MBSs are based on home mortgages (and the collateral that supports them), synthetic CDOs are based on *other* financial instruments. So they are much more complicated. Abacus was based on residential MBSs, existing CDOs, and commercial MBSs. The financial engineering behind this investment—including the combination of different kinds of MBSs and the investment's independence from cash assets—made it hard to understand and price.

Banks make different kinds of investments in synthetic CDOs. In 9.35
Abacus, investors could choose funded long, unfunded long, and unfunded
short positions. *Long* investments earn return when the underlying financial instruments—MBSs, other CDOs—perform well. *Short* investments
earn return when the underlying financial instruments perform poorly.
Funded means that the investor has its own money on the line, for example,
because the investor owns the MBSs and existing CDOs. *Unfunded* investments are bets about how the financial instruments will perform. With
respect to Abacus, the German bank, IKB, the asset management firm,
TCW Group, and the U.S. bank, Wachovia, invested $195 million in a
funded long position. Goldman itself was the largest funded long investor,
holding $1.8 billion in that position. These investors stood to make millions
if the loans were repaid.

TCW and GSC Partners, another asset management firm, became 9.36
unfunded long investors. These unfunded long investors did not pay initial
investments but would owe short investors if the borrowers defaulted. As
such, they could potentially gain, or lose, millions. The short investor was
also Goldman Sachs. Goldman bet $2 billion that the borrowers referenced
by Abacus would default.

Scharding analyzes GSC's decision to take an unfunded long position 9.37
from a Kantian perspective. If all firms take abstruse risks, some investments (and some firms) will fail, while others will succeed. Because the
investments are interconnected, even firms that win their abstruse-invest-
ment bets will lose money when all firms make abstruse investments.

Winning firms have counted on losing firms for loan repayments. 9.38
Because losing firms are now bankrupt, though, they will not honor their
obligations. Thus, firms that have money will be unwilling to loan, as those
who need money are the same as those who have just failed to meet repayment obligations.

Trust would evaporate. No one would be able to borrow money and the 9.39
financial system, which depends on a ready supply of cash to pursue investment opportunities, will be at a standstill. Investment activities would cease.
Thus, abstruse investing becomes self-defeating when universalized.

Next, an example of a bailed-out investment. This example relates to the 9.40
Federal National Mortgage Association's ("Fannie Mae's") decision to take
on additional loans in August 2007. The U.S. government created Fannie
Mae to encourage home ownership by establishing a "secondary market"
for mortgages, so commercial banks could sell their existing mortgages,
receiving funds with which to make more mortgages.

9.41   Fannie Mae is a publicly traded corporation but maintains close ties with the U.S. Treasury as a "government-sponsored enterprise" (GSE). Because of these close ties, many investors feel that the government "implicitly" guarantees the GSE. An implicit guarantee means that the government would be highly likely to bail out the GSE if trouble arose.

9.42   In the summer of 2007, commercial banks became less willing to make new mortgages. Because fewer investors wished to purchase MBSs in the weakening housing market, the available MBSs would cost the GSEs less than they would in a booming market.

9.43   At this time, Fannie Mae were already exposed to significant risk: it was responsible for $5.3 trillion in mortgages, close to its legal limit. (Yes, that is trillion, with a *t-r*. Fannie Mae was responsible for a lot of mortgages.)

9.44   On August 1, 2007, Fannie Mae CEO Daniel Mudd requested that the U.S. government lift its limits and allow Fannie to buy $150 billion of additional loans. Scharding analyzes this decision from a Kantian perspective.

9.45   If universalized, the U.S. government would bail out firms whenever their failure threatened the U.S. economy as a whole. Widespread bailouts would, however, change the nature of the economy. The government would own key economic players and the economy would be centralized, not market-based. As people in centralized economies lack private property to invest, making investments (that riskily rely on rescuers, or otherwise) in the context of such economies is impossible. Thus, she argues that bailed-out investing cannot be universalized.

Short Selling: The Herbalife Case

The Case

An investor, Bill Ackman, believed that a company, Herbalife, was overvalued. In 2013, Ackman decided to *short sell* the company's stock, which means that he will make a profit if the value of the stock goes down. Ackman then campaigned against Herbalife for being a *pyramid scheme*.

The Ethical Questions

Is it ethical to short sell, or bet against, stocks? To what extent may short sellers publicly criticize the companies in order to make their stocks go down?

In the Countrywide and the Lehman Brothers cases, we examined firms 9.46
that were behaving unethically and ended up losing a lot of money. Our
point in looking at those cases was to reflect on the ethical issues that they
involve. There is another point of interest in cases like that, though: badly
acting firms that are likely to fail can be a source of revenue for alert investors. How is that possible? The investing strategy of *short selling* allows
investors to make a bet that the price of the company's stock will decrease.
We briefly discussed short selling with respect to the Abacus synthetic
CDO in the Lehman case. In this case study, we examine the ethics of short
selling. Is this an effective way to call out businesses that are acting unethically? Or is short selling itself unethical?

Herbalife's corporate identity

The case study focuses on two firms: the short selling investment firm and 9.47
the business against which the firm made its investment bet. We will start
with business that was *shorted*. That was the American multinational
nutrition company, Herbalife. Founded in 1980 and based in Los Angeles,
Herbalife sells weight-loss products and nutritional supplements. It is a
multi-level marketer (MLM). MLM is a kind of business organization. It
means that Herbalife has no retail stores. It produces nutritional products
but does not sell them directly to the public. Instead, independent salespeople purchase the products from the company and sell them to clients
for a profit.

Herbalife's revenue was $5 billion in 2014; in 2013, it had more than 9.48
three million independent salespeople around the world. This revenue
does not derive from the products that the independent distributors sell.
Remember, because Herbalife is an MLM, its revenue comes from the
products that the independent distributors purchase from Herbalife.

Pershing Square Capital Management's corporate identity

The firm that shorted Herbalife was an American hedge fund, Pershing 9.49
Square Capital Management (PSCM). A hedge fund is a kind of investment firm. Hedge funds pool investors' money for the purpose of making
larger investments than the independent investors could make on their
own. Hedge funds tend to make riskier investments than other kinds of
investment pools, like mutual funds. Fort this reason, hedge fund investors
must be high net worth: so they can afford the kind of risky bets that hedge
funds undertake.

9.50   Bill Ackman founded PSCM in 2004 in New York City. In 2014, it had
assets of $12 billion. Its history is characterized by huge, high-risk bets.
Many, but far from all, of these bets have paid off handsomely. Major suc-
cesses included an investment in Canadian Pacific Rail, which generated
$1.4 billion. Shorting MBIA, the bond insurer, earned a $1.1 billion return.
Significant mistakes included an investment in J.C. Penney, which lost
more than $450 million. A failed investment in Target Corporation cost
$1.5 billion.

Facts of the case

9.51   So, why did PSCM short Herbalife? The main reason, of course, is that
Ackman thought that the value of the company's stock was likely to go
down. (Another way of saying this is that the stock was *overvalued*.)
Ackman thought that the company was overvalued for two reasons. One
reason relates to the company's business model and the other relates to
ethics. First, Ackman considers Herbalife to be a *pyramid scheme* or a
Ponzi scheme, as defined below, which are illegal forms of business organization. Second, Ackman believed that Herbalife preys on low-income
people.

9.52   The two reasons are related as follows. Most of Herbalife's independent
salespeople lose money, according to PSCM's analysis. PSCM determined
that Herbalife salespeople, most of whom are unemployed and sell Herbalife
products as a last-ditch effort to earn an income, have less than 1 percent
probability of earning $95,000 per year from their sales. That is an extremely
low likelihood of earning a decent living. But salespeople continue to purchase more products, while recruiting additional salespeople, to whose
sales they theoretically become entitled to a share under Herbalife's MLM
structure.

9.53   Allowing salespeople to earn a percentage of the sales earned by salespeople they have recruited is not inherently illegal (or unethical). This is a
classic strategy of recruiting new salespeople for MLM businesses. If the
company increases its profits *only* by convincing more people to become
salespeople, though, it could be considered an illegal pyramid or Ponzi
scheme. In that case, the company is sustained not because consumers find
its products useful. A pyramid scheme survives only by manipulating people to purchase its products. Herbalife salespeople, for example, continue to
purchase Herbalife products because they hope to sell them. A Ponzi

scheme is similar to a pyramid scheme except that Ponzi schemes focus on investing, only. Pyramid schemes can structure different kinds of businesses, not just investing.

Pyramid and Ponzi schemes are illegal under U.S. law. So, if Herbalife is 9.54 organized in this way, the government would force it out of business. If that happened, the company's stock would be worthless. Anyone who shorted Herbalife, though, would gain a huge profit.

When Ackman shorted Herbalife, its stock was worth about $40 per 9.55 share. Ackman put more than a billion dollars on the line in the short. Part of the money belonged to investors in Pershing Square Capital; part was Ackman's own money.

After shorting the stock, Ackman began a public campaign against 9.56 Herbalife. This campaign included denouncing the company publicly, accusing it of preying on poor people and people of color, organizing protests, and petitioning the Fair Trade Commission to close the company for violating its anti-pyramid-scheme laws. Ackman has solicited civil rights organizations to help him locate people of color who believed that the company targeted them, paying the organizations at least $130,000 for their efforts. In a CNBC interview in January 2015, Ackman said that his Herbalife investment was "the most philanthropic investment I have ever made."

Sidebar Exercise

How would virtue ethics evaluate Ackman's investment?

Sidebar Exercise

How would FH evaluate Ackman's investment?

What happened

Ackman admits that he thought other hedge funds might bet against him— 9.57 and, thus, that Herbalife's stock would go up. Indeed, other investors did take this *long* bet. A long bet, as discussed in the Lehman Brothers case, is the opposite of a short bet in the sense that the long investor wagers that the value of the stock will increase. Many of them seemed to do it for personal reasons: simply for the satisfaction of defeating Ackman. (Ackman sometimes seems arrogant in a way that annoys his peers.) This strategy is known as a *short squeeze*. In a short squeeze, a group of investors attempt to bid up a stock that has a bet against it so that the short seller will lose big.

9.58   One long investor felt that Herbalife was currently undervalued. This investor also reasoned that if the company tried to defend itself against the short by buying some of its own stock, driving up the price, Herbalife's value could increase even more.

9.59   As noted above, Ackman thought that the Federal Trade Commission (FTC) would close Herbalife for violating pyramid-scheme laws. The FTC has not, though shut down other MLMs, like Avon or Tupperware. To date, the FTC has not found that Herbalife is an illegal pyramid scheme. Ackman also believed that distributors would quit selling the products once they realized they were being deceived. So far, though, they have not done this.

9.60   As of August 2015, Ackman had lost at least $300 million on his investment. As of early 2016, Ackman is currently losing money on the short. He still maintains, though, that Herbalife's stock will eventually go to zero.

Historical significance

9.61 Short selling and high-risk bets are important parts of contemporary investing and contemporary business. The Herbalife short is one of the only shorts, though, in which the short seller has campaigned so aggressively against the company being shorted. As such, it brings into focus some ethically significant features of short selling. We examine those features in the next section.

Ethical significance: short selling

9.62 The highlighted ethical issue in the Herbalife case is short selling. Now that we have covered the case, let us examine this phenomenon in greater detail. First, a more technical definition than the one employed above. To short sell a stock, an investor borrows (for a fee) someone else's stock. The borrowed stock is then sold. Profits from the sale go to the investor. If the price of the stock goes down, the investor purchases the stock at the lower price and returns it to the original owner, earning a profit. If the stock's price increases, though, the investor must buy back the stock at the higher price, losing money. Because there is (in theory) no limit to how high the price can go, short selling is very risky.

According to business ethicists, Angel and McCabe, short selling could 9.63 be considered unethical because it involves profiting from other's bad fortune. Angel and McCabe argue that short selling is ethically acceptable, despite this problem, because of its social value: short selling improves the extent to which stock prices correctly express the value of a company, protecting investors from losing money on overvalued stocks. Short selling comprises about a quarter of the trading volume in the U.S. equity market, so it is a very significant business.

In the Herbalife case, the short seller went somewhat further than 9.64 merely betting against the company, though. He actively campaigned against the company. The short itself can serve to inform the market that a stock might be overvalued. And of course it is ethically acceptable to inform authorities that a company is violating the law. The Herbalife case, though, raises the question of whether it is ethically acceptable to draw law enforcement's attention to an ethical problem in a company's business practices *in order to* lower the value of the company's stock—thus apparently coopting the public function of the justice system for the sake of earning a private profit.

Sidebar Exercise

Use each of our ethical theories to evaluate this problem. Which (if any) ethical theories say that it is ethical to profit from a company's unethical conduct? Which (if any) ethical theories say that it is *unethical* to profit from a company's unethical conduct? Which do you agree with? Why?

Sidebar Exercise

Is PSCM a moral person in Peter French's sense? Why or why not? Discuss one way in which PSCM meets the standard for moral personhood and one way in which it fails to meet that standard.

Insider Trading: The Nomura Case

The Case

In 2010, people noticed suspicious trading in deals that the Japanese investment bank, Nomura Securities Company, was underwriting. Companies affected included Inpex, the oil and gas producer, Tokyo Electric Power, and Nippon Sheet Glass. The Japan Securities and Exchange Surveillance Commission (SESC) investigated and determined that Nomura employees had engaged in insider trading. Because Japanese law punished insider trading less harshly than other countries, the SESC was faced with a question about what to do.

The Ethical Questions

What is ethically problematic about insider trading? Should Japan punish insider trading more harshly? Should the United States, and other countries, punish insider trading less harshly?

9.65 In the Nomura case, we examine ethical issues about another way of making investments: insider trading. Insider trading occurs when an investor relies on non-public information in deciding to buy or sell a stock. This is an especially interesting topic for ethical analysis as it is subject to different regulation in different advanced economies. In the United States, for example, insider trading is illegal and punishments are stiff. In Japan, by contrast, insider trading is only frowned upon. Punishments are much more lenient. Thus, the Nomura case, in which a Japanese firm is accused of engaging in insider trading, is the perfect opportunity to examine the ethics, as opposed to the mere legality, of insider trading in greater depth.

Nomura's corporate identity

9.66 The Nomura Group is a Japanese multinational financial conglomerate. Nomura provides varied financial services to domestic and international businesses, including underwriting initial public offerings (IPOs), asset management, and capital investment. The company was established in 1925. By 2010, it was Japan's largest and most influential securities company.

In the aftermath of the 2008 financial crisis, it acquired Lehman Brothers India, a large portion of Lehman Brothers Asia, and a portion of Lehman's business in Europe and the Middle East.

Facts of the case

In 2010, Nomura was underwriting public offerings for three companies: 9.67
Tokyo Electric Power, Inpex Corporation, and Nippon Sheet Glass. Public offerings involve releasing new shares to the public. Releasing these new shares generally causes the value of existing shares to decline—as there are now more shares available. Immediately before new shares were issued, observers noticed suspicious trading activities. Chuo Mitsui Asset Trust, a hedge fund, had shorted Inpex. First New York Securities, another hedge fund, had shorted Tokyo Electric. These hedge funds thus profited when the stock prices of Inpex and Tokyo Electric declined upon the issuance of new shares.

Even if they provided information about the public offerings, Nomura 9.68
employees would not have profited directly from the shorts. It would have been likely, though, that the Chuo Mitsui and First New York fund managers would have promised to provide the Nomura employees with additional business. So, the information-giving Nomura employees could profit *indirectly* from providing the information. Nomura employees were under pressure from top executives to increase sales so that Nomura could be competitive on the world stage. There was all the more pressure to engage in insider trading due to the lenient nature of Japanese law, which punishes insider trading only if the person who provided the insider information profits from the resulting trade.

Sidebar Exercise

How would virtue ethics evaluate insider trading?

Sidebar Exercise

How would ethics of care evaluate insider trading?

Sidebar Exercise

How could a bureaucratic management style, in Robert Jackall's sense, contribute to the problems regarding insider trading that Nomura experienced?

What happened

9.69   The Japan Securities and Exchange Surveillance Commission (SESC) investigated and found that Nomura brokers had provided information about the public offerings to fund managers at Chuo Mitsui Asset Trust and First New York Securities.

9.70   CEO Kenichi Watanabe, who was responsible for the Lehman acquisitions, and other executives resigned in early 2012. In November 2012, the Tokyo Stock Exchange (TSE) fined Nomura 200 million yen. It was the largest fine the TSE had ever imposed but only 0.2 percent of Nomura's Fiscal Year 2011–2012 profits (85 billion yen).

9.71   As a result of the scandal, Nomura was excluded from lucrative underwriting opportunities for Japan Tobacco, Japan Housing Finance Agency, Resona Holdings, and Japan Airlines, reducing their opportunity for profits.

Historical significance

9.72   Following the Nomura insider trading scandal, there were widespread calls for Japan to strengthen its law against insider trading.

Ethical significance: insider trading

9.73   Now that we have covered the details of the case, we can examine the investment practice of insider trading in greater depth. This term refers to buying or selling the stock of a publicly held corporation based on information that is not public. Insider trading can be carried out by employees who gain access to private information or by non-employees with whom they share the information. In the United States, insider trading is subject to criminal prosecution. It is typically penalized by fines and/or by imprisonment. In Japan, insider trading is regulated. Punishments, when given, tend to be lighter than those in Western countries.

Business ethicists Werhane and Barnes criticize insider trading. Werhane 9.74
argues that insider trading undermines the free market. It allows different parties to operate under different rules, which is unfair. Ma and Sun defend insider trading against Werhane's argument. They counter that all players continue to operate under the same rules when insider trading occurs. According to their analysis, some players are simply *more informed* than other players.

Barnes argues that insider trading can be considered unethical both 9.75
because it violates the corporation's property rights and because it is unfair to other market participants. It violates property rights to the extent that the corporation owns information about itself and has a right to control that information. It is unfair to other market participants because other investors do not have access to the information that underlies the insider traders' strategies. If carried out on a large scale, insider trading could lead market participants to distrust the stock market and stop trading stocks, undermining the rightful functioning of the financial markets.

Business ethicists Ma and Sun defend insider trading, albeit in a quali- 9.76
fied way. They argue that insider trading could serve overall social interests by allowing corporations to maximize profits. If insider trading limits shareholder profits, then it should be considered unethical. Until business ethicists have empirically demonstrated such limitations, however, they should neither regard insider trading as necessarily unethical nor seek to regulate it overmuch.

Sidebar Exercise

Use each of our ethical theories to evaluate this problem. Which (if any) ethical theories say that it is ethical to use insider trading? Which (if any) ethical theories say that it is *unethical* to use insider trading? Which do you agree with? Why?

References and Further Reading

Angel, James J. and Douglas M. McCabe. 2009. "The Business Ethics of Short Selling and Naked Short Selling." *Journal of Business Ethics*, 85(Suppl.1): 239–249.

Barnes, David. 2012. "Insider Trading in Japan: The Nomura Case." *Seven Pillars Institute*. http://sevenpillarsinstitute.org/case-studies/insider-trading-in-japan-the-nomura-case

Boyle, Catherine. 2015. "Bill Ackman: Herbalife Short Is 'Philanthropic.'" *CNBC* (Jan. 14). http://www.cnbc.com/2015/01/14/bill-ackman-herbalife-short-is-philanthropic.html

Cohen, William D. 2015. "Bill Ackman, Dan Loeb, Carl Icahn, and Herbalife: The Big Short War." *Vanity Fair* (April). http://www.vanityfair.com/news/2013/04/bill-ackman-dan-loeb-herbalife

Hudson, Michael. 2011. "Countrywide Protected Fraudsters by Silencing Whistleblowers, Say Former Employees." *Center for Public Integrity* (Sept. 22). http://www.publicintegrity.org/2011/09/22/6687/countrywide-protected-fraudsters-silencing-whistleblowers-say-former-employees

Hyuga, Takahiko and Russell Ward. 2012. "Japan's Insider-Trading Carousel." *Bloomberg Businessweek* (Aug. 9). http://www.bloomberg.com/bw/articles/2012-08-09/japans-insider-trading-carousel

La Roche, Julia. 2015a. "Herbalife Shares Are Up 43% This Month, and Bill Ackman Is Getting Stomped." *Business Insider* (Mar. 23). http://www.businessinsider.com/ackman-losing-money-on-herbalife-short-2015-3

La Roche, Julia. 2015b. "Bill Ackman: Now Is a Better Time Than Ever to Short Herbalife's Stock." *Business Insider* (Apr. 13). http://www.businessinsider.com/bill-ackman-on-herbalife-short-2015-4

Ma, Yulong and Huey-Lian Sun. 1998. "Where Should the Line Be Drawn on Insider Trading Ethics?" *Journal of Business Ethics*, 17(1): 67–75.

McLannahan, Ben. 2012. "Nomura Hit by Another Insider Trading Case." *Financial Times* (Nov. 2). http://www.ft.com/intl/cms/s/0/41547818-24d1-11e2-8924-00144feabdc0.html#axzz3pvDsKVny

Morgenson, Gretchen. 2007. "Inside the Countrywide Lending Spree." *The New York Times* (Aug. 26). http://www.nytimes.com/2007/08/26/business/yourmoney/26country.html?_r=0&pagewanted=print

Olster, Scott. 2010. "How the Roof Fell in on Countrywide" *Fortune* (Dec. 23). http://fortune.com/2010/12/23/how-the-roof-fell-in-on-countrywide/

Scharding, Tobey K. 2015. "Imprudence and Immorality: A Kantian Approach to the Ethics of Financial Risk." *Business Ethics Quarterly*, 25(02): 243–265.

Schmidt, Michael S., et al. 2014. "After Big Bet, Hedge Fund Pulls the Levers of Power: Staking $1 Billion that Herbalife Will Fail, Then Lobbying to Bring It Down." *The New York Times* (Mar. 9). http://www.nytimes.com/2014/03/10/business/staking-1-billion-that-herbalife-will-fail-then-ackman-lobbying-to-bring-it-down.html?_r=0

Sorkin, Andrew Ross. 2008. "Lehman Files for Bankruptcy; Merrill Is Sold." (Sept. 15). http://www.nytimes.com/2008/09/15/business/15lehman.html?_r=0&pagewanted=print

Sterngold, James. 2010. "How Much Did Lehman CEO Dick Fuld Really Make?" *Bloomberg Businessweek* (Apr. 29). http://www.bloomberg.com/bw/magazine/content/10_19/b4177056214833.htm

Stewart, James B. and Peter Eavis. 2014. "Revisiting the Lehman Brothers Bailout That Never Was." *The New York Times* (Sept. 29). http://www.nytimes.com/2014/09/30/business/revisiting-the-lehman-brothers-bailout-that-never-was.html

Tabuchi, Hiroko. 2012. "Nomura Chief Resigns Over Insider Trading Scandal." *The New York Times* (July 26). http://dealbook.nytimes.com/2012/07/26/nomura-chief-resigns-amid-insider-trading-scandal/

Taylor, John. B. 2009. "How Government Created the Financial Crisis." *The Wall Street Journal* (Feb. 9). http://online.wsj.com/articles/SB123414310280561945#printMode

Vardi, Nathan. 2013. "Bill Ackman's Herbalife Nightmare Gets 100 Percent Worse." *Forbes* (Jul. 30). http://www.forbes.com/sites/nathanvardi/2013/07/30/bill-ackmans-herbalife-nightmare-gets-100-percent-worse/print/

Weissman, Jordan. 2011. "Countrywide's Racist Lending Practices Were Fueled by Greed." *The Atlantic* (Dec. 23). http://www.theatlantic.com/business/archive/2011/12/countrywides-racist-lending-practices-were-fueled-by-greed/250424/

Werhane, Patricia H. 1989. "The Ethics of Insider Trading." *Journal of Business Ethics*, 8(11): 841–845.

Wiggins, Rosalind Z., Thomas Piontek, and Andrew Metrick. 2014. "The Lehman Brothers Bankruptcy A: Overview." Yale Program on Financial Stability Case Study 2014-3A-V1, October. New Haven, CT: Yale University.

10

BUSINESS ETHICS IN THE ENVIRONMENT

10.1 As the twenty-first century progresses, concerns about the environment have loomed large in public thought. They have begun to play a larger role in business as well. Our cases in this chapter address businesses' ethical responsibilities as regards: (1) the water supply; (2) respect for indigenous populations; (3) the food supply; and (4) emissions.

Water Supply: The Coca-Cola India Case

The Case

Coca-Cola's operations in Rajasthan, India, bring it into conflict with the local population over the use of groundwater in this arid region.

The Ethical Questions

How much of a common resource like water may companies use? May the company itself decide or must it rely on a regulatory body to decide how much is the company's fair share?

10.2 In this case study, we examine a very famous concept from environmental ethics: the tragedy of the commons. The tragedy of the commons explains the difficulties that self-interested individuals (like businesses) encounter when using a limited resource that is shared among many parties.

This is Business Ethics: An Introduction, First Edition. Tobey Scharding.
© 2018 John Wiley & Sons, Inc. Published 2018 by John Wiley & Sons, Inc.

Coca-Cola India's corporate identity

The company encountering the problem of the tragedy of the commons is 10.3
Coca-Cola India, a subsidiary of the Coca-Cola Company. The Coca-Cola
Company is an American multinational beverage manufacturer based in
Atlanta, Georgia. It is the world's leading nonalcoholic beverage producer,
generating more than $1 billion in annual revenue.

Coca-Cola India was created in 1992 to serve consumers in India. It 10.4
maintains 56 bottling plants and employs more than 25,000 people directly,
as well as 150,000 people indirectly. It invested $2 billion in the country
between 1992 and 2011 and will invest another $5 billion between 2012
and 2020.

On its website, Coca-Cola India lists its mission as threefold: "To refresh 10.5
the world," "To inspire moments of optimism and happiness," and "To create
value and make a difference."

Sidebar Exercise

Is Coca-Cola India's corporate identity adequate to establish it as a
moral person, in Peter French's sense? Why or why not?

Facts of the case

The case concerns Coca-Cola India's operations in Rajasthan, a large state 10.6
in northwest India. In Rajasthan, the groundwater is a common resource:
anyone is allowed to use as much as they want. Water supply throughout
India, though, is scarce. India's 1.2 billion people are projected to exhaust
their freshwater supply by 2050.

In arid Rajasthan, the water shortage is especially acute. There is little 10.7
surface water and droughts are frequent. The state depends on subterranean
groundwater as its primary water source. Indian law does not restrict how
much or for what purpose people pump groundwater. Local farmers, businesses, and ordinary citizens all draw on the same groundwater. The law
does not give any of them greater rights to the groundwater than the others.

Coca-Cola India's Rajasthan plant is located in the village of Kaladera. 10.8
The Central Ground Water Board, which manages water supply in India, is
worried that Kaladera's watershed is vulnerable to exhaustion. As early as

1998, local people's water withdrawal rate surpassed the watershed's natural ability to replenish itself.

10.9 Coca-Cola India began producing beverages in Rajasthan in 1999. In its early years of operation, Coca-Cola India drew 200,000 cubic meters of groundwater per year, about 0.4 percent of total groundwater extraction in the area. By 2011, it had reduced water usage to 100,000 cubic meters annually, or about 0.2 percent of total water extraction. The main cause of the reduction was switching from glass to plastic bottling. Plastic bottles do not need to be washed before filling, saving water. Coca-Cola India remains one of the largest single users of water in Rajasthan.

10.10 Many activists, both Indians and foreigners, have objected to Coca-Cola India's water use in Rajasthan. They claim that Coca-Cola pumps excessive groundwater, depleting it, while farmers' and ordinary people's pumps go dry. Student protestors at the University of Michigan successfully petitioned the university to end its relationship with Coca-Cola. (After a brief hiatus in 2006, the University subsequently resumed doing business with Coca-Cola.)

What happened

10.11 Coca-Cola India faced a variety of possible actions. The company could:

- Reduce groundwater use further (to .1 percent or less).
- Increase rainwater harvesting to replenish the groundwater.
- Move operations from Rajasthan to a region with more available groundwater.
- Do nothing.

As of early 2016, what Coca-Cola India will do to address the problem in Rajasthan remains an open question.

Sidebar Exercise

Use each of our ethical theories to evaluate this problem. Do any of our ethical theories support any of the possible actions, listed above? (You might want to do additional research about the options the company faces.) Explain why or why not. Are there any other actions that Coca-Cola India could take? How would ethical theories evaluate those other possible actions?

Historical significance

Scientists have identified water shortage as the most worrisome current 10.12
environmental problem, next to global warming. India's water crisis is among
the most pressing. According to the United Nations' Food and Agriculture
Organization, India's citizens have 1,614 cubic meters of water available per
year, compared with 2,117 cubic meters per year for each Chinese citizen
and 9,943 cubic meters of water available per year for each U.S. citizen.

Ethical significance: tragedy of the commons

Karnani has argued that Coca-Cola India faces a *tragedy of the commons*. 10.13
The tragedy of the commons is an ethical problem about resource management. It was famously discussed by Garrett Hardin. We can think of it as a
kind of *thought experiment*.

Sidebar Exercise

What are some of the other thought experiments we have covered in
this book? Are thought experiments an effective way to think about
philosophical problems? Why or why not?

In considering the tragedy of the commons, we are to Imagine a pasture 10.14
that is open to all local shepherds: no one owns the pasture. Each shepherd
grazes as many animals as possible in the pasture because the expected benefits of grazing more animals (for the shepherd) are greater than expected
costs of doing so (for the shepherd). Each shepherd selfishly ignores the
costs imposed on the others. As the shepherds graze more and more sheep
in the pasture, it gradually becomes depleted. Thus, individual decisions
cumulate to tragic overuse. The commons is destroyed.

Sidebar Exercise

In what sense do Coca-Cola India and Rajasthan face a tragedy of
the commons? Analyze the problem in detail, supplementing with
original research about water use in Rajasthan. How can Coca-Cola

India and Rajasthan avoid a tragic outcome? List three different ways that they could avoid a tragic outcome. Then, explain why one strategy for avoiding a tragic outcome is preferable to the others.

Indigenous Populations: The TransCanada Case

The Case

TransCanada, a Canadian multinational oil company, plans to build a pipeline through part of Oklahoma to transport oil from Alberta to refineries in the Gulf of Mexico. Although the pipeline proceeds through privately-owned, not tribal, lands, local Native Americans claim that it may disrupt sacred burial grounds. They demand that TransCanada follow their directions in constructing the pipeline or abandon the project.

The Ethical Questions

What ethical obligations do businesses have to indigenous peoples with respect to natural resources and the environmental degradation of tribal lands? To what extent should indigenous peoples be included in business decision-making about natural resources and environmental degradation of tribal lands?

10.15 A company envisions building a pipeline to transport oil from oil fields to where oil is needed. The pipeline has many benefits. Transporting oil via pipeline is less risky than transporting it via railway. The oil fields will allow the country to become less dependent for its oil supply on the politically unstable countries upon which it currently depends for oil. It will be a great source of revenue for the company. But there is a serious ethical issue associated with the pipeline: it is virtually impossible to guarantee that the pipeline will not pass through the sacred burial grounds of indigenous peoples.

TransCanada's corporate identity

10.16 The company at issue is TransCanada, a Canadian multinational energy company. Based in Calgary, Alberta, TransCanada offers a range of services related to energy production and distribution, including electricity, natural gas, and crude oil. The company owns and operates more than 50,000 kilometers of pipelines that store and move natural gas. It provides 20 percent of North America's natural gas. Its net profit in 2014 was 1.7 billion CAD.

TransCanada is actively developing its oil distribution capacities. It 10.17 already owns an oil pipeline that moves oil from the tar-sands basin of Alberta, Canada, to Steel City, Nebraska. From Steel City, two pipelines transport the crude oil to refineries in Illinois or for distribution in Cushing, Oklahoma. TransCanada now seeks to build a new pipeline, Keystone XL, to connect Cushing to the Gulf of Mexico.

Facts of the case

The proposed Keystone XL extension could move 830,000 barrels of oil per 10.18 day, including oil from North Dakota's Bakken shale site. North Dakota currently transports its oil to the Eastern United States and Canada via rail. Rail travel is risky, however. Derailments have occurred, spilling oil in residential areas. Moving oil by pipeline would reduce the risk of residential spills.

Building the pipeline has another benefit. It would increase North 10.19 American energy independence from its largest suppliers. Gaining greater energy independence could be considered a worthwhile goal in itself, as it would give North America more control over its energy supply. Moreover, many of the countries that currently supply North America with oil are politically unstable. North America's main suppliers now are Venezuela, Saudi Arabia, and Nigeria. Their political instability makes them unreliable providers of vital energy resources.

The proposed pipeline also has significant downsides, though. First, it 10.20 would lead to the further (1) exploitation of oil; and (2) release of carbon dioxide emissions into the atmosphere, contributing to climate change. Second, 38 Native American tribes maintain sovereign land in Oklahoma. Cushing itself sits in the Sac and Fox Nation. Members of the these tribes believe that the pipeline could disrupt sacred burial grounds throughout the region.

The basis for this belief is as follows. The Sac and Fox tribe lived in the 10.21 Great Lakes region of North America prior to the European conquest. After a series of battles with U.S. troops in the nineteenth century, the tribe signed treaties with the federal government to resettle in Oklahoma around 1870. Many tribal members perished, from smallpox and other ailments, on the road to their reassigned sovereign land. Unmarked graves and other important sites occupy the land through which the pipeline would progress.

10.22   TransCanada attorneys believe that they are not legally required to obtain the tribe's consent before building the pipeline. They seek to cooperate with the Sac and Fox nation "because it's a good, neighborly thing to do." Native American attorneys, though, believe that nineteenth-century treaties oblige the company to respect the tribe's wishes. It is a disputed issue.

Sidebar Exercise

How would feminist ethics evaluate TransCanada's decision to build the pipeline? Are you convinced by this evaluation? Why or why not?

Sidebar Exercise

How would contract ethics evaluate TransCanada's decision to build the pipeline? Are you convinced by this evaluation? Why or why not?

What happened

10.23   As a compromise, TransCanada has hired groups of Native Americans to observe the pipeline's construction and serve as lookouts for burial and other remains. Tribal leaders have visited TransCanada's headquarters at TransCanada's expense. The company has also charted the pipeline's path to avoid around Indian lands, even though it would disturb the environment least by creating a straight route.

10.24   As of early 2016, the U.S. government had refused to grant permission for TransCanada to begin digging the pipeline. Because the pipeline crosses the U.S.-Canada border, the president's authorization is required by law. Thus, the fate of the Keystone XL pipeline remained undetermined at that time.

Historical significance

10.25 Native Americans have drawn parallels between the construction of Keystone XL and the Ponca Tribe's *Trail of Tears* (which is different from the better-known Cherokee Trail of Tears). The Ponca's Trail of Tears is the route that this Native American tribe followed on their forced relocation from their ancestral home in Nebraska to Oklahoma. First, the pipeline would cut through the lands that the tribe traversed during their journey. Second, the pipeline represents a further instance of the Canadian and U.S. governments disrupting the native populations of North America, and damaging their distinctive way of life, in order to exploit the continent's natural resources.

Ethical significance: indigenous populations

This case focuses on the control of natural resources. It inquires to what   10.26
extent indigenous peoples maintain authority over natural resources and to what extent businesses, who wish to exploit those natural resources, should consult with indigenous peoples. Indigenous peoples are the currently living descendants of the autonomous societies (sometimes known as *First Nations*) that occupied various lands prior to conquest by European powers. They retain certain legal rights against the government, preserved in treaties. Some people believe that they also possess moral authority with respect to natural resources. As the first (or at least prior) inhabitants of resource-rich lands, indigenous peoples appear to possess (quasi-) property rights with respect to those lands.

Sidebar Exercise

Would John Locke's view of private property support the claim that indigenous peoples have property rights (or something like them) with respect to the lands, and natural resources found in those lands, they inhabited prior to the European conquest? Why or why not? How would you criticize Locke's view in this respect?

Lertzman and Vredenburg (2005) argue that companies may not threaten   10.27
indigenous cultures so as to extract resources. Companies must respect indigenous people's wishes and needs when they interact. They base their argument in the Kantian idea that people should be respected as ends in themselves and not used as mere means, extending this idea to indigenous cultures. They also use utilitarianism in their analysis. They note that indigenous people are more knowledgeable about the ecosystems involved in

industrial development. Indigenous people should, therefore, be consulted so as to ensure that the ecosystems are developed in an environmentally sustainable way.

Food Supply: The FieldScripts Case

The Case

FieldScripts uses sophisticated data about soil, climate, and weather conditions to tell farmers which seeds to plant, where to plant them, and how to cultivate them. This data greatly increases crop yield but brings farmers into conflict with the data company.

The Ethical Questions

Who owns information about soil, climate, and weather conditions? May FieldScripts use the data provided by farmers to improve the performance of *rival* farms? Who is entitled the profits from the increased yields, as a matter of ethics?

10.28 In the Coca-Cola India case, we looked at a problem about water shortage. Concerns about the availability of clean water are becoming increasingly urgent in the contemporary world. This case examines a related issue: food supply. The population is always increasing but the world has a finite amount of natural resources such as arable land. Changing weather patterns due to global warming make the problem even more pressing. How will we assure that the world's 7.3 billion people can be fed?

10.29 An agricultural technology company, Monsanto, has come up with an ingenious answer to this problem. Monsanto claims that farmers can use data about the soil, the local climate, and even likely future weather conditions to produce more food from the same amount of natural resources. Monsanto's business is to sell farmers that data. In this case study, we examine questions about the relationship between property and data about that property. (Some of this builds on our work in the Facebook case.) Does the person who owns the property also have, as a matter of ethics, property rights in data about the property? Is the company obligated to protect the property owner's privacy regarding data about their property? And, finally, should farmers trust Monsanto to preserve their privacy?

Monsanto's corporate identity

The Monsanto Company is an American multinational agricultural tech-   10.30
nology firm based in St. Louis, Missouri. Monsanto is well known as a producer of genetically modified seed products. It is a Fortune 500 company,
which employs more than 21,000 people in 66 countries.

Monsanto sees its business as "empowering" farmers to gain greater crop   10.31
yields even as they farm more efficiently, using fewer natural resources. The
Monsanto pledge includes foundational commitments to "integrity," understood as encompassing honesty, decency, consistency, and courage, and
"dialogue"—respectfully discussing controversial topics with those who
disagree in an effort to broaden understanding.

Facts of the case

FieldScripts is a relatively new product of Monsanto's. Released in Spring   10.32
2014, FieldScripts tailors seeds and fertilizer to the soil conditions where
the crops will grow, specific to a 10 ft sq plot of land. The service uses satel-
lite imagery, soil samples, and information about the plots' yield over the
past two years. It recommends the Monsanto seeds that are most likely to
produce the highest yields for those soil and climate conditions. The prescription is transferred to the farmers' iPad, where it can direct the farmer's
planting activities.

Three ethical challenges have arisen concerning the product. First,   10.33
services like FieldScripts threaten the traditional practice of farming.
FieldScripts replaces farmers' intuition about planting with scientific information geared to optimal planting. Although there is a sense in which people must accept changing times and practices, farming maintains a crucial
role in human culture. It speaks to the important relationship between
human beings and the earth and, in particular, the dependence of the former on the latter. While FieldScripts' promises of greater productivity can
be liberating, they are also terrifying.

Second, the service is much better suited to big farms than to small farms.   10.34
Take an example from corn production. Farmers can currently sell corn for
about $4 per bushel. If FieldScripts can boost yields by 5–10 bushels per acre,
farm profits will increase by $20–40 per acre. The service currently costs
$10 per acre. A large farm of 5,000 acres will increase its revenue by
$100,000–200,000, for which it will pay $50,000. This profit margin will
allow it to comfortably update its planting equipment, or buy new tractors,
to insure compatibility with the FieldScripts application. A small farm of

500 acres, on the other hand, would earn $10,000–20,000 additional revenue, for which it would pay $5,000. This small profit margin would probably not cover the farm's costs of updating its equipment.

10.35   The situation is even more problematic for small farmers than this example reveals. The increased yields facilitated by FieldScripts are most dramatic when overall yield is low. In good years, FieldScripts will not contribute much to yields that are already substantial. In this sense, small farmers are taking on great additional risk by purchasing the FieldScripts seeds. This risk might not be worth it for small farms.

Sidebar Exercise

In the Lehman Brothers case, we used FUL to evaluate ethical issues associated with financial risk. The FieldScripts case presents farmers with another kind of business risk. Use FUL to evaluate this risk. Is it good business for small farmers to purchase FieldScripts seeds? Is it ethical? How could FieldScripts help farmers to mitigate this risk?

10.36   Third, the service threatens farmers' autonomy and even, perhaps, their livelihoods. As noted in the first problem, above, FieldScripts replaces farmers' intuitions as the standard for agricultural decision-making. In addition to subverting the natural relationship between human beings and the earth, mentioned above, farmers are reluctant to give up using their intuition as their guide. The reason for this is that farmers do not trust Monsanto.

10.37   Farmers worry about relying too heavily on data because it makes their farming vulnerable to "hostile takeovers" by rival farmers. The journal, *Modern Farmer*, offers an example:

> Farmer Jones gets his hands on Farmer Smith's yield data and finds out how much he's producing. Then Farmer Jones calls up Farmer Smith's landlord and promises bigger profits if he kicks Farmer Smith off that land and gives it to Farmer Jones.

There is reason for this worry, both because of the way that data has been used in other industries and because of the interest that investment firms take in agricultural data. Regarding the first reason, Sarathy and Robertson discuss pharmaceutical firms that have obtained information about the people who use their rivals' drugs. (They obtained this information from the pharmacies to which the firms sold their products.) The firms have used the information to create individually-targeted ads to market their own products to those pharmaceutical consumers.

Regarding the second reason, Monsanto might sell their farmers' data to 10.38 commodities traders, who could use information about the farm's yields for their own profits, potentially at the expense of the farmer's. Farmers also worry that the service could prescribe which seeds, sprays, and equipment they purchase: reducing farmers' control over their farms and potentially reducing their profits as well. In either case, farm profits are directed into someone else's hands, not the farmer's.

What happened

According to the *Wall Street Journal*, some farmers contemplate collecting 10.39 their own data, to allow them greater control over who can buy the data and to ensure that they will receive the revenue from the data sale.

In response, Monsanto has claimed that the aggregate information is 10.40 only available to Monsanto employees, not to rival farmers. They maintain that data privacy is one of their primary concerns.

Monsanto relies on the improvements the service can yield: both to pro- 10.41 ductivity and to sustainability. As one farmer notes:

> There's farmers out there that don't keep track of how much bushels are get-
> ting off each field, what spots are good. The people that keep score are the
> ones that are gonna be the ones farming 20 years from now.

Data-based planting prescriptions could increase world-wide revenue from crop production by $20 billion per year.

Sidebar Exercise

How would Mill's utilitarianism evaluate a farmer's decision to use FieldScripts? Are you convinced by this evaluation? Why or why not?

Sidebar Exercise

How would virtue ethics evaluate a farmer's decision to use FieldScripts? Are you convinced by this evaluation? Why or why not?

Historical significance

10.42 Food shortages and environmental degradation are two of the most pressing issues of the twenty-first century. FieldScripts offers a way to address both issues. One of the consequences of widespread use of the service, though, will be making human beings more dependent on technology and less in touch with the natural world.

Ethical significance: data privacy and trust in business

10.43 One ethical issue raised by the FieldScripts case relates to data privacy. Data privacy is the idea that sensitive information about a person or business should not be widely or publicly available. One way of assuring that sensitive data remains private is establishing that a person or business has private property rights in any information that is about them.

Sidebar Exercise

How could you use John Locke's theory of private property to support assigning property rights in personal information? Raise an objection to this account. How might Locke respond to the objection?

10.44 As discussed by legal scholar Litman (2000), conceiving of sensitive data as private property would give people more control over data that implicates them. On a Lockean picture, property ownership is pre-political. That means that people can own things, including personal data, independently of the government. People who dislike government regulation might resist permitting the government to make laws about acceptable uses about personal data. If people just own this information, independently of the government, then even anti-regulatory people could endorse limiting commerce in it.

There are some problems with considering personal information to be   10.45
private property. Litman, for example, worries that conceiving of sensitive
data as private property seems more likely to increase the market for sensitive data than to protect the privacy of this data. If personal information is
property, then people can sell it. Allowing people to sell their individual
data would obviously not reduce commerce in personal information. It
would, however, ensure that profits on the information go to the person
whose information it is.

A second ethical issue related to the FieldScripts case concerns trust in   10.46
business. Trust in business is not a thing or kind of knowledge. Rather,
according to business ethicist George Brenkert, trust in business is an attitude toward those with whom one interacts, "which consists of the willing-
ness to place oneself in situations in which one is vulnerable and in which
there is risk." Brenkert notes that philosophers, from the ancient Greeks
through the twentieth century, did not write much about trust. Contemporary
business ethicists take a greater interest in trust due to their focus on the
relationships between people and the background to those relationships.

One risk of cultivating greater trust in business, according to Brenkert   10.47
(1998), is that close and trusting relationships may facilitate nepotism,
favoritism, and cronyism. Benefits include that trust can reduce transaction
costs, facilitate information sharing and collaboration, and "provide a basis
for expanded moral relations in business."

Sidebar Exercise

Should there be more trust in business? Use an ethical theory to
support cultivating more trust in business. Then, raise an objection to
the ethical theory's evaluation.

Emissions: The VW Case

The Case

Volkswagen (VW) attempted to market its diesel-engined vehicles,
popular in Europe, to American consumers. Diesel engines create
fewer carbon dioxide (CO_2) emissions than gasoline-burning engines

but more nitrogen oxides (NOx). NOx emissions are associated with smog and other problems. The United States has more demanding standards for NOx emissions than Europe. In September 2015, it was revealed that VW met these demanding standards only by tricking the Environmental Protection Agency's (EPA) tests for diesel-engined cars. The software in several diesel-engined VWs was engineered to use NOx-controlling technology only when the software detected the predictable conditions associated with EPA tests. In normal driving conditions, the software switched off the NOx-controlling technology. When the technology was off, NOx emissions exceeded the legal limit by 40 times.

The Ethical Questions

What standards should govern software engineers? What kinds of corporate culture lead to such clear ethical violations? What can concerned people in society do to prevent such ethical lapses?

10.48   The 2015 revelations that Volkswagen had engineered its cars to trick environmental tests shocked people around the world. Many aspects of the case were surprising. First, Volkswagen had *deliberately* engineered the cars to deceive: a clear case of unethical behavior. There was nothing ambiguous or questionable about its wrongdoing. Second, Volkswagen had a reputation as a relatively environmentally friendly business. It was the last car maker that people expected to become embroiled in an ethical scandal. Finally, car emissions are among the most pressing environmental issues in the twenty-first-century era of climate change. It seemed outrageous that a reputable business would allow damaging emissions in order to achieve its goal of becoming the biggest automobile company in the world.

VW's corporate identity

10.49   VW is a German multinational automobile company. Founded in 1946, the company is headquartered in Wolfsburg, Germany. Volkswagen's signature cars include the Volkswagen Golf, Volkswagen Passat, and the iconic Volkswagen Beetle.

10.50   VW is managed by the Volkswagen Group, which also includes Audi, Bentley, Bugatti, Lamborghini, Porsche, and others. The Volkswagen Group is Europe's largest automobile manufacturer. It employs 592,500 people. In 2014, the Volkswagen Group sold more than 10 million vehicles. The Volkswagen Group sold 12.9 percent of the world's passenger cars that year. It was one of the largest automobile companies in the world, second in size (in 2014) only to Toyota.

The Volkswagen Group of America, a wholly owned subsidiary of the 10.51 Volkswagen Group, was founded in 1955. It is headquartered in Herndon, Virginia, and runs a manufacturing plant in Chattanooga, Tennessee. The Volkswagen Group of America employs 6,000 people. It aims to bring German engineering and design to an American audience, selling "attractive, safe, and eco-conscious" cars.

Much of VW's corporate identity relates to its German origins. German 10.52 automobile engineering is revered for its dependability and performance.

Facts of the case

VW sought to become the largest automobile company in the world, 10.53 surpassing Toyota. In order to achieve this goal, expanding its role in the United States was crucial. (The United States is the world's second largest car market; China is first.) VW's strategy focused on introducing Americans to its diesel-powered line of cars, which were already top-sellers in Europe.

Diesel engines are more fuel-efficient and produce fewer carbon diox- 10.54 ide emissions than gasoline engines. Their fuel-burning process, though, produces another emission: a number of oxides of nitrogen (NOx). Nitrous oxide emissions cause smog and can harm people who have sensitive lungs.

The United States has higher standards for NOx emissions than Europe: 10.55 which is to say that it permits *less* of these emissions. The United States limits NOx emissions to 0.07 grams per mile. Other car manufacturers that produce diesel-powered cars, such as Honda and Mazda, have found it difficult to meet this limit.

It is possible to control NOx emissions to meet the high U.S. standards. 10.56 The controls permitted by current technology, though, reduce the car's performance and fuel efficiency. Because VW takes pride in its reputation for high performance, these controls failed to offer a satisfactory way to limit the emissions. An emerging technology, selective catalytic reduction, uses ammonia to reduce NOx levels. Selective catalytic reduction reduces performance less than other options. It has the downside, though, of being expensive to implement.

10.57   In September 2015, the Environmental Protection Agency (EPA) announced that certain diesel-engine-equipped VW vehicles appeared engineered to trick the EPA's emissions tests. The VWs used a computer program to control NOx emissions; the EPA noticed that the cars used the program only under test conditions. Test conditions are highly regular and much more predictable than normal driving conditions. The program could detect when test conditions, as opposed to normal driving conditions, were present. Under normal driving conditions, the cars turned off the NOx-emissions-controlling program, producing better driving performance but NOx emissions that were 40 times the legal limit.

10.58   Nearly half a million cars were implicated in the United States. The EPA ordered a recall of these cars. VW later disclosed that there were 11 million vehicles that turned off NOx controls when not in testing conditions.

Sidebar Exercise

How would FUL evaluate VW's decision to use the defeat devices? Are you convinced by this evaluation? Why or why not?

Sidebar Exercise

How would ShareT evaluate VW's decision to use the defeat devices? Are you convinced by this evaluation? Why or why not?

What happened

10.59 VW's stock value decreased precipitously following the revelations. CEO Martin Winterkorn resigned. As of early 2016, many issues were still outstanding. The Department of Justice could fine VW $18 billion (its maximum fine is $37,500 per vehicle and 482,000 were sold). Class-action lawsuits are expected.

10.60   VW's reputation has suffered. Other carmakers, especially German manufacturers, are also threatened—under the expectation that if one company was cheating, others were likely to be cheating as well. In the

United States, the EPA checks car company's claims about their fuel efficiency. No such system exists in Europe, though. Car companies check their own cars and report their findings. The findings need not be verified by an external agency.

Historical significance

The VW case was a setback for reducing carbon-dioxide emissions from 10.61 automobiles. The ethics scandal focusing on Germany appeared to improve the U.S.'s (relative) ethical standing, which had been diminished following the debacles associated with the 2008 financial crises (some of which were discussed in Chapter 9).

Ethical significance: emissions

The ethical status of emissions is an active topic in contemporary business 10.62 ethics. In a seminal article about the ethics of emissions, ethicist Henry Shue argues that ethical questions about emissions are essentially questions about distributive justice. We must determine, first of all, a fair *allocation* of greenhouse gases. An allocation permits each person who wants to emit a certain amount that they are permitted to emit. This allocation prevents people from emitting too much.

Shue's argument about emissions is founded on the idea that emissions 10.63 involve trade-offs. Emitting has certain benefits for the person who emits. In the case of VW cars, emissions benefit the company by allowing it to pursue profits while producing high performance cars. Emitting benefits consumers by enabling them to purchase cars that drive and respond well at a lower price than cars that permitted the same level of performance but with lower emissions.

Government regulation is involved in establishing the level of emissions 10.64 that are permitted for each vehicle. As we saw in the VW case, different countries establish different emissions guidelines. The U.S. government permits less NOx emissions than European governments. One of the reasons that governments establish thresholds that automobiles must meet is to avoid the tragedy of the commons, as discussed in the Coca-Cola India case. If the government did not establish a standard for emissions, then all car companies would emit as much as possible. Eventually, though, the commons (in this case, the atmosphere) would be ruined.

Sidebar Exercise

Are U.S. standards for NOx emissions too high? Are European standards too low? Do some independent research to figure out the reasons for the respective U.S. and European emissions standards. What are the right standards for permitted emissions? Use an ethical theory to back up your claim.

References and Further Reading

Argenti, Paul. 2015. "The Biggest Culprit in VW's Emissions Scandal." *Fortune* (Oct. 13). http://fortune.com/2015/10/13/biggest-culprit-in-volkswagen-emissions-scandal/

Baron, Ethan. 2015. "Are MBAs to Blame for VW and Other Business Ethics Fiascos?" *Fortune* (Oct. 22). http://fortune.com/2015/10/22/mba-ethics-volkswagen/

Brenkert, George G. 1998. "Trust, Business and Business Ethics: An Introduction." *Business Ethics Quarterly*, 8(2): 195–203.

Bunge, Jacob. 2014. "Big Data Comes to the Farm, Sowing Mistrust." *The Wall Street Journal* (Feb. 25). http://www.wsj.com/articles/SB10001424052702304450904579369283869192124

Chaudhary, Archana. 2014. "Farmers Fight Coca-Cola as India's Groundwater Dries Up." *Bloomberg Businessweek* (Oct. 8). http://www.bloomberg.com/news/articles/2014-10-08/farmers-fight-coca-cola-as-india-s-groundwater-dries-up

Chrispeels, Maarten J. and Dina F. Mandoli. 2003. "Agricultural Ethics." *Plant Physiology*, 132(1): 4–9.

Genoways, Ted. 2015. "Corn Wars: The Farm-by-Farm Fight between China and the United States to Dominate the Global Food Supply." *The New Republic* (Aug. 16).

Graef, Christine. 2014. "Nebraska's Cowboys and Indians Unite Against Keystone XL Pipeline." *Mint Press News*. http://www.mintpressnews.com/nebraskas-cowboys-indians-unite-keystone-xl-pipeline/196821/print/

Hickins, Michael. 2014. "For Small Farmers, Big Data Adds Modern Problems to Ancient Ones." *The Wall Street Journal* (Feb. 25). http://blogs.wsj.com/cio/2014/02/25/for-small-farmers-big-data-adds-modern-problems-to-ancient-ones/

Hiler, Katie. 2014. "The Era of Big Ag Data Is Here: Can You Automate Farmers' Intuition?" *Modern Farmer* (Apr. 8).

Hills, Jonathan. 2005. "Coca-Cola in India: A Case Study." *CSR Asia: Business Solutions for Global Challenges* (Jun. 14). http://csr-asia.com/csr-asia-weekly-news-detail.php?id=4146

Hughes, Richard A. 2009–2010. "Pro-Justice Ethics, Water Scarcity, Human Rights." *Journal of Law and Religion*, 25(2): 521–540.

Husted, Bryan W. 1998. "The Ethical Limits of Trust in Business Relations." *Business Ethics Quarterly*, 8(2): 233–248.

Karnani, Aneel. 2014. "Corporate Social Responsibility Does Not Avert the Tragedy of the Commons – Case Study: Coca-Cola India." *University of Michigan Ross School of Business Working Paper* (February).

Lertzman, David A. and Harrie Vredenburg. 2005. "Indigenous Peoples, Resource Extraction and Sustainable Development: An Ethical Approach." *Journal of Business Ethics*, 56: 239–254.

Litman, Jessica. 2000. "Information Privacy/Information Property." *Stanford Law Review*, 52(5): 1283–1313.

McElroy, Michael B. 2013. "The Keystone XL Pipeline: Should the President Approve Construction?" *Harvard Magazine* (Nov.–Dec.).

Mufson, Steven. 2012. "Keystone XL Pipeline Raises Tribal Concerns." *The Washington Post* (Sept. 17). http://www.washingtonpost.com/business/economy/keystone-xl-pipel...cerns/2012/09/17/3d1ada3a-f097-11e1-adc6-87dfa8eff430_story.html

Sarathy, Ravi and Christopher J. Robertson. 2003. "Strategic and Ethical Considerations in Managing Digital Privacy." *Journal of Business Ethics*, 46(2): 111–126.

Shue, Henry. 1993. "Subsistence Emissions and Luxury Emissions." *Law and Policy*, 15(1): 39–60.

Singer, Peter. 2015. "Volkswagen and the Future of Honesty." *Project Syndicate* (Oct. 7). https://www.project-syndicate.org/commentary/volkswagen-emissions-business-ethics-by-peter-singer-2015-10

The Economist. 2014. "Digital Disruption on the Farm." (May 24). https://www.economist.com/news/business/21602757-managers-most-traditional-industries-distrust-promising-new-technology-digital

The Economist. 2015a. "A Scandal in the Motor Industry: Dirty Secrets." (Sept. 26). https://www.economist.com/news/leaders/21666226-volkswagens-falsification-pollution-tests-opens-door-very-different-car

The Economist 2015b. "The Volkswagen Scandal: A Mucky Business." (Sept. 26). https://www.economist.com/news/briefing/21667918-systematic-fraud-worlds-biggest-carmaker-threatens-engulf-entire-industry-and

11

BUSINESS ETHICS IN GLOBALIZATION

11.1 Business in the twenty-first century is global. Virtually all the firms we have examined in this book are multinational, in the sense that they do business around the world. In this chapter, we examine some of the ethical issues that arise from the multinational identities of business. These cases raise questions about: (1) how businesses should address ethical issues related to importing raw materials from foreign countries; (2) the extent to which American businesses may permissibly exploit less restrictive labor laws in foreign countries; (3) how companies with liberal values should handle the restrictions that repressive political regimes may place on their products; and (4) whether ethical businesses may permissibly do business with corrupt regimes in foreign countries, when doing so will benefit the businesses.

Obtaining Raw Materials: The GlaxoSmithKline Case

The Case

Most of the world's supply of legal opiates comes from poppies grown on the Australian island of Tasmania. The pharmaceutical companies that manufacture opiate-based prescription drugs question whether it is too risky to rely on a single region. They seek to develop genetically modified poppies and begin growing poppies on the Australian mainland and in other places.

This is Business Ethics: An Introduction, First Edition. Tobey Scharding.
© 2018 John Wiley & Sons, Inc. Published 2018 by John Wiley & Sons, Inc.

The Ethical Questions

How can businesses ethically manage risks associated with importing? What are businesses' obligations to their suppliers?

Obtaining raw materials ethically raises numerous problems. Ethical companies seek to collect efficiently the raw materials they need for their products, while preserving the environment, respecting the communities that produce the raw materials, and protecting the raw materials from illegal uses. In this case study, we examine how GlaxoSmithKline addressed ethical problems regarding its procurement of the opium it uses for its pain medications. 11.2

GlaxoSmithKline's corporate identity

GlaxoSmithKline is a British multinational healthcare company. Its business focuses on three areas: (1) pharmaceutical treatments for acute or chronic diseases; (2) pharmaceutical treatments for routine diseases and ailments; and (3) vaccines. Its corporate mission is to "improve people's health and well-being, ultimately helping them to live life to its fullest and contribute to the prosperity of their communities." GlaxoSmithKline is one of the world's largest healthcare companies. 11.3

Facts of the case

Poppies (*Papaver somniferum*) contain opium as a milky fluid in their seed pods. A variety of chemicals in opium have valuable pain-killing (analgesic) properties. These chemicals include morphine, codeine, thebaine, and oripavine. Pharmaceutical companies use poppies to create opiate painkillers like OxyContin, Roxicodone, and Percocet. All of those prescription painkillers are thebaine-based. Opium from poppies is also used to create heroin and other illegal narcotics. Heroin is morphine-based. 11.4

Poppy cultivation is illegal in most of the world due to the dangers of illegal narcotic opium. Pharmaceutical companies can grow the crop legally for their painkillers. They face a challenge, though, in deciding *where* to grow their opiate-producing poppies. First, the pharmaceutical production of opium requires a fairly dry climate. Although poppies can survive rainy weather, the rain dilutes the plants' opium. Pharmaceutical companies also seek fairly remote locations, so as to discourage uninformed pleasure seekers from 11.5

ingesting the plants. Raw opium bulbs can be fatal to human beings. Hard-to-reach fields also protect the poppies from theft by heroin manufacturers.

11.6   The United States currently obtains 80 percent of its legal supply of morphine from poppies grown in Turkey and India. Turkey and India were selected for legal poppy cultivation because of (1) their dry climates; and (2) their stable political systems. The United States trusted the Indian and Turkish governments' ability to monitor their poppy fields and protect them from heroin producers.

11.7   The vast majority of poppies used for illegal opiates are grown in Afghanistan: 90 percent in 2015. Approximately 780 square miles of Afghanistan farmland produce poppies exclusively. The United States has spent $8.4 billion trying to end illegal poppy cultivation in Afghanistan. It is difficult to eradicate poppy fields in this country, however, because the opium producers bribe the government to permit their illicit activities. Many farmers, moreover, are very poor: creating temptations to earn their living by the illegal trade.

11.8   Australia's fairly dry climate is also ideal for poppies. Like Turkey and India, Australia has a stable political regime that is trusted by the West. Tasmania, an island just south of the Australian mainland, has an especially desirable location because it is so isolated. The Glaxo Group, a precursor to GlaxoSmithKline, began growing poppies there in the 1960s. As of 2014, the island produced 85 percent of the world's supply of thebaine.

11.9   The poppy business is important for the island as well. In 2014, Tasmanian farmers earned $80 million in revenue from selling their poppies to pharmaceutical companies. Poppies comprised about 10 percent of the island's agricultural production. The were more lucrative at that time than any other Tasmanian farm sector, with the exception of dairy and beef.

11.10   Despite the success of the Tasmanian poppy fields for both GlaxoSmithKline and Tasmania, problems lurked. The company's main concern was maintaining an adequate supply of opiates while protecting its supply from heroin manufacturers. One way to assure an adequate supply was by creating stockpiles. A stockpile would allow the company to survive a downturn in poppy production in Tasmania due to inclement weather or other problems. In 2011, for example, an unusually rainy growing season greatly reduced productivity.

11.11   The stockpiles, though, would be vulnerable to theft by heroin producers. The heroin market is 400 percent bigger than the opiate prescription painkiller market. This creates great temptations to secure more poppies wherever possible. For this reason, the United Nations discourages pharmaceutical companies from maintaining stockpiles.

A second strategy by which GlaxoSmithKline could maintain an ade- 11.12 quate stock of poppies is via genetic engineering. Genetic engineering could help to reduce risk to poppy production by making poppies resistant to pests. Agricultural genetic engineering, which includes pharmaceutical agriculture, is currently banned in Australia, however.

A third strategy by which GlaxoSmithKline could assure the adequacy of its 11.13 poppy stock is by creating additional poppy fields in different locations. The danger here is securing those poppy fields from both heroin producers and pleasure-seeking scavengers. As noted above, ingesting raw poppies can be fatal.

Sidebar Exercise

What perspective do Rawls's ideas about distributive justice bring to the GlaxoSmithKline case?

Sidebar Exercise

How would StakeT evaluate the GlaxoSmithKline case? Are you convinced by this evaluation? Why or why not?

What happened

In March 2014, GlaxoSmithKline began growing poppies in several undis- 11.14 closed locations in mainland Australia. The company has specified only that the secret fields are in the vicinity of Melbourne. In March 2015, it sold its Tasmanian poppy fields and opiate production subsidiary to Sun Pharmaceuticals, an Indian multinational pharmaceutical company.

Sidebar Exercise

Think about other options that GlaxoSmithKline could have taken. For example, do a cost-benefit analysis of obtaining the poppies from Afghanistan instead of mainland Australia. What ethical issues would GlaxoSmithKline face in obtaining poppies from Afghanistan instead of Tasmania and mainland Australia?

Historical significance

11.15   Morphine and codeine used to be the primary opiate chemicals used in an analgesic context. In recent years, thebaine has become increasingly popular. The poppies used for thebaine are grown almost exclusively in Tasmania. OxiContin, Roxicodone, Percocet, and others have brought relief to many people suffering from great pain. Their sales have also brought large profits to pharmaceutical companies.

Ethical significance: raw materials

11.16   The GlaxoSmithKline case raises an interesting problem about protecting a raw material from illegal use. Even though it makes cultivating the poppies more difficult, the company takes extra measures to protect them from seizure by illegal heroin producers. Heroin use causes great harm to many communities around the world.

11.17   GlaxoSmithKline must also attend to other ethical issues in its poppy cultivation, including preserving its relationship with Tasmanian farmers. Tasmanian farmers depend on the poppy business for their livelihoods. If GlaxoSmithKline begins growing its poppies in alternative locations, Tasmanian farmers might be unable to earn enough to support themselves.

11.18   Finally, GlaxoSmithKline faces the familiar problem of whether to permit the use of genetically modified poppies in its pharmaceutical products. In this case, the problem is especially interesting, for the reason that the company and the farmers both want to genetically modify the poppies. They are impeded by the Australian government's ban on genetically modified agricultural products.

Child Labor: The Victoria's Secret Case

The Case

In 2011, Victoria's Secret was accused of fabricating its lingerie from cotton farmed by child laborers in Burkina Faso. According to an article published in *Bloomberg Businessweek*, the forced labor farms arose to capture benefits associated with Victoria's Secret's "fair-trade" program. Children were forced to withdraw from school, labor like animals, and suffer frequent beatings—often without adequate food to eat. Victoria's Secret claimed to know nothing of the child labor and states that the company opposes child labor.

The Ethical Questions

How much responsibility do businesses have for workers in foreign countries who labor on their behalf? What is ethically problematic about child labor? Is it ever permissible?

The production of cotton for people's clothing has a long, and often uneth- 11.19
ical, tradition. Fashions produced with cotton are beautiful and easy to care for: brightly colored, pattern-ready, washable. The fiber, though, is burdensome to grow and pick. Cotton picking was a common occupation among enslaved people in the antebellum South, for example. This case study focuses on a contemporary source of cotton: the West African nation of Burkina Faso. Unfortunately, there are parallels between Burkina Faso's cotton industry today and U.S. cotton production before the Civil War. In both countries, forced labor and child labor were used to grow and gather cotton. What is especially troubling about this case is that it was an ethical initiative, organized by the Fair-trade Foundation, that encouraged farmers to grow cotton. Companies paid more for Fair-trade cotton than for other local products. But Burkina Faso farmers were so poor that they did not have enough equipment and employees to produce the cotton. To capture the Fair-trade money, they turned to forced child labor to grow their cotton.

Victoria's Secret's corporate identity

The cotton in question was purchased by Victoria's Secret, the lingerie 11.20
retailer. Victoria's Secret is owned by Limited Brands, Inc., an American multinational corporation based in Columbus, Ohio. Victoria's Secret operates more than 1,000 stores in North America. It also sells lingerie through the internet and its mail-order catalogs. Some of its most popular products are a line of inexpensive cotton bras and panties.

Facts of the case

Victoria's Secret began purchasing cotton from Burkina Faso in 2007. The 11.21
company's goal in using fair-trade, organic cotton for its lingerie was to live up to certain ethical ideals. They hoped to benefit the women who farmed

cotton, to increase the use of sustainable raw materials, and to improve people's lives in Africa. Their slogan was that fair trade is "Good for women" and "Good for children" who depend on women.

11.22   So what exactly is *fair-trade* cotton? Fair trade is a certification provided by the Fair-trade Foundation. The National Federation of Burkina Cotton Producers manages Burkina Faso's organic and fair-trade cotton production. It works closely with Victoria's Secret to provide the cotton. Fair-trade certification assures consumers that the people who produced the goods were not exploited. One of the forms of exploitation that it prohibits is paying farmers too little for their produce. This means that companies pay farmers more for fair-trade products than for the other goods that farmers can grow.

11.23   The possibility of earning this greater pay encouraged subsistence farmers to begin growing fair-trade produce—whether or not the farmers have enough equipment and employees to produce the goods. In order to compensate for their lack of equipment and employee resources, some farmers have turned to unethical practices, such as forced labor and child labor, to grow fair-trade products.

11.24   The magazine, *Bloomberg Businessweek*, profiled one child worker in Burkina Faso. That child worker, Clarisse Kambire, a girl, was forced to labor for farmer Victorien Kamboule, according to the article. Victorien, an adult male, is Clarisse's cousin. Together, they farm a plot of land about 400 sq meters. They use neither machines nor farm animals. A plow costs about $150 in Burkina Faso, where 80 percent of the population lives for under 2 dollars a day. Victorien is too poor to afford those resources. He is so poor he cannot afford even herbicides and pesticides—so Clarisse weeds the entire crop, and removes pests from each plant, by hand.

11.25   Before the fair-trade program began in Burkina Faso, Victorien farmed millet. He began growing organic fair-trade cotton after observing that farmers who grew that commodity earned far more money than he did. In 2010, fair-trade farmers' profits were 70 percent higher than farmers growing genetically modified cotton.

11.26   Victorien acknowledges beating Clarisse when she does not work as hard as he wants her to. He says that he would be unable to farm the land without her help. Victorien removed Clarisse from school so that she could farm for him full-time.

11.27   Indeed, Burkina Faso's farmers struggle to produce fair-trade cotton. Victoria's Secret bought Burkina Faso's entire crop in 2010. Other buyers are interested but the crop has been shrinking: farmers are barely able to produce the 600 metric tons per year that has been guaranteed to Victoria's Secret.

Sidebar Exercise

How would feminist ethics evaluate the Victoria's Secret case? Raise an objection to this evaluation from the perspective of the DM. Which position do you prefer: that of feminist ethics or that of the DM? Explain the reason for your preference.

What happened

After the *Bloomberg Businessweek* article was published, the U.S. Department 11.28 of Homeland Security began an investigation of production conditions, including forced child labor, in Burkina Faso's organic and fair-trade cotton program. The Department of Homeland Security is responsible for enforcing the 1930 Smoot-Hawley Tariff Act, which prohibits the United States from importing products that involved forced labor. This law authorizes the Department to impose fines on delinquent companies and seize forbidden goods. Under the law, though, a company can avoid punishment for using forced labor so long as the forced labor had not given it a competitive advantage.

Victoria's Secret, through its parent company, Limited Brands Inc., com- 11.29 mented that it took the allegations very seriously "as we do not tolerate child labor." The parent company reported that its investigation revealed that Clarisse Kambire is a vegetable farmer and an adult. *Bloomberg Businessweek* responded that the birth certificate the company provided to substantiate its claims belonged to Clarisse's older sister, who had passed away. As of early 2016, it remains a contested issue.

Historical significance

The case demonstrates the ongoing difficulties in producing the raw mate- 11.30 rials that are needed for the products that people want to buy. Although people in the United States tend to think that we have made major moral progress since the days of slavery, cases like the Victoria's Secret one challenge that belief. American slaves no longer pick cotton—child slaves in Burkina Faso now do. The United States has abolished slavery in our own country but American consumers appear to continue to depend on forced labor in other countries.

Ethical significance: child labor

11.31   The Victoria's Secret case also challenges the extent to which the remedies for ethical problems in business can be effective. Fair-trade certification arose as a way to ensure that the people who produced raw materials in developing countries were fairly compensated for their labors. But the increased wages that it made available served as a temptation for farmers to produce fair-trade products, even when they lacked the resources that they needed to become fair-trade producers. This led them to other kinds of (apparently, highly) unethical business practices such as relying on child labor. The case speaks, in this sense, to the difficulty of eradicating unethical business practices in the developing world.

Different Cultures: The Yahoo! Case

The Case

While operating in China in the early 2000s, Yahoo! gave personal, incriminating information about its users to the Chinese government. The users were Chinese dissidents who had used Yahoo! email accounts to disseminate certain forms of illegal political speech. At the dissidents' trials, Yahoo! provided further information about the computers dissidents had used to disseminate the prohibited pro-democracy views. The dissidents were subsequently convicted and sentenced to 10 years in prison.

The Ethical Questions

When operating in a culture that has different laws and different ethical standards, is it ethical for a business to follow those laws and adopt those standards when they seriously differ from their own? What obligations do businesses have to uphold their own ethical standards?

11.32   There are many repressive political regimes around the world, which drastically limit their citizens' human rights. With more than 1.25 billion potential consumers as of the early 2000s, none of these political regimes was more lucrative than the People's Republic of China. Many Western multinational companies wished to sell their goods and services to Chinese citizens. But what if compliance with China's repressive political system were a condition of doing business there? In this case, Yahoo had to decide whether it should comply with the Chinese government's oppressive requests. On the one hand, doing business in China could help to liberalize the political system there. On the other, though, doing business in the way that China specified would require Yahoo to violate cherished ideals about political liberty, directly participating in an oppressive regime. Which consideration should win?

Yahoo's corporate identity

Yahoo is an American multinational internet services and technology company. It is best known for its internet search and email services. It runs a variety of other services related to news, finance, social media, videos, and advertising. 11.33

Yahoo was founded in 1994. It is headquartered in Sunnyvale, California. Its 2003 revenue was $1.6 billion; 2004 revenue was $3.6 billion. In 2004, it had 7,600 full-time employees. 11.34

Facts of the case

This case concerns the appeal, and the difficulty, of doing business in countries that have different forms of government and different cultures from the business's home culture. One of the most appealing—and most difficult—countries for American multinational businesses is China. First, the appeal of this country: 69 million people used online services in China in 2003, and 94 million in 2004, making it a lucrative market for internet service providers. 11.35

Second, the difficulty. Many outsiders regard the Chinese government as an oppressive political regime that actively violates the human rights of its citizens. In doing business in China, multinational companies must to some extent comply with the reigning political regime. The Chinese government, for example, forces internet providers to adhere to the country's strict censorship laws, including limiting the results for internet searches. These forms of censorship are in deep tension with Western ethics. 11.36

The Yahoo controversy arose in 2003–2004, when several Chinese dissidents used their Yahoo email accounts to discuss and transmit information about democracy, a prohibited topic in China. Yahoo provided Chinese 11.37

prosecutors with the dates and times when dissidents transmitted the illegal political materials. Yahoo even revealed the computers the dissidents had used. Chinese lawyers used this information to prosecute and imprison the Yahoo users.

11.38   Human rights activists subsequently argued that consumers should boycott Yahoo for their alleged attempt to increase their profitability by violating Chinese citizens' human rights. The activists also encouraged Yahoo shareholders to prevent Yahoo from further violating human rights.

Sidebar Exercise

How would FH evaluate Yahoo's decision? Are you convinced by this evaluation? Why or why not?

Sidebar Exercise

How would contract ethics evaluate Yahoo's decision? Are you convinced by this evaluation? Why or why not?

Sidebar Exercise

How would Mill's utilitarianism evaluate Yahoo's decision? Are you convinced by this evaluation? Why or why not?

What happened

11.39 Yahoo responded to the controversy in November 2007 with several policy changes. First, it joined a group of multinational internet service providers in constructing a code of conduct for technology companies operating in nations whose governments fail to support human rights.

11.40   It apologized to the dissidents and established a human rights fund to provide financial support for them and their families. Finally, Yahoo created a monitoring group to evaluate what human rights issues would likely arise in a new market before the company entered that market.

Historical significance

In one sense, this case is very specific to the early twenty-first century, as 11.41
multinational companies grapple with how to do business in the politically
repressive China. Another internet services and technology company,
Google, did not agree to comply with the Chinese government; Yahoo did.
In another sense, though, the case is more timeless. At least for the foresee-
able future, countries will have different forms of political organization
from one another. Some countries will be more developed, or more politically liberal, than others. When a more liberal company does business in a
more repressive country, it will have to decide whether to comply with the
repressive order. It will have to decide what kind of business it wants to be.

Ethical significance: repressive political regimes

The ethical issue in this case is repressive political regimes. A repressive 11.42
political regime fails to protect human rights that are widely recognized by
the international community. Widely recognized human rights include the
right to free speech and the right to freedom of conscience. When operating
in repressive political regimes, businesses can act unethically even when
complying with local laws.

Two arguments could be used to support businesses complying with the 11.43
government's repressive laws. First, noncompliance could put the employees
of the business at risk. If Yahoo had not complied with the Chinese government's investigation of its customers, the government might have prosecuted
Yahoo employees along with the dissidents. Second, complying with the law
ultimately helps to bring political progress to repressive countries. By maintaining good relations with the Chinese government, Yahoo guarantees that
it will be able to continue doing business there. In time, the company may be
able to share its liberal values more freely with its Chinese customers.

Poe, a business ethicist, argues that businesses may operate in countries 11.44
with repressive political regimes only (1) when they attempt to minimize
the harm to human rights that their compliance with the government's
repressive laws cause; and (2) when their business activities actively improve
the lives of people in that country. They have a responsibility to use their
"moral imaginations" to create as much good and do as little harm as possible. In the Yahoo case, for example, Poe (2009) suggests that Yahoo should
have done more to protect its customers' privacy: narrowly interpreting
legal requirements to disclose information, informing its customers about

what information would be retained and could be disclosed to authorities, or allowing customers send encrypted emails that would not reveal incriminating information.

Doing Business with Corrupt Regimes: The IKEA Case

The Case

In February 2010, IKEA fired two of its executives working in Russia, Per Kaufman and Stefan Gross, for engaging in corrupt business practices with suppliers to its St. Petersburg store. Kaufman and Gross paid bribes to an energy company to ensure that the store would have power. While such practices were widespread in Russia at that time, they explicitly opposed IKEA's corporate values.

The Ethical Question

Should businesses follow their own ethical cultures in countries that have different ethical cultures?

11.45   The IKEA case, like the Yahoo case, involves a clash of cultures. In the Yahoo case, we examined a conflict between a liberal company and a repressive government. The IKEA case explores a conflict between an ethical corporate culture and a corrupt political culture. Russian political culture is considered *corrupt* in the sense that it permits bribery. In the Yahoo case, the country asked the company to abide by its political values as a condition of doing business there. The IKEA case is somewhat more subtle. Rather than allowing the company to operate and letting the market decide whether it succeeded or failed, Russian government officials insisted that IKEA could not do business unless it paid them bribes. In this case, we explore what is unethical about bribery. We also observe how an ethical company dealt with the problem of doing business in a country in which bribery is part of business.

IKEA's corporate identity

11.46   IKEA is a Swedish multinational furniture manufacturer and retailer. It gained fame for selling low-priced furniture that customers assemble themselves. The simple, clean lines of its design style were matched by its clean style of business. IKEA has a reputation for upholding high ethical standards.

IKEA opened its first Russian store in 2000. By 2010, it was operating 14   11.47
stores in Russia across 11 cities. Its Russian operations comprised 5 percent
of its overall business and were growing at 20 percent per year. Its net profit
in 2010 was 2.7 billion EUR. Global sales were 23.1 billion EUR in 2010, up
7.7 percent from the previous year based largely on strong growth in China,
Portugal, and Russia.

Facts of the case

Transparency International's 2009 Bribe Payer Index includes Russia among   11.48
five countries in the world most susceptible to corrupt business practices,
along with China, Mexico, India, and Italy.

IKEA penetrated the Russian market quickly. Within ten years of its   11.49
initial entrance in 2000, it had built 14 of its huge storerooms and invested
US$4 billion in its Russian operations. IKEA used its connections with vari-
ous individuals, combined with effective networking, to succeed in the
Russian market. The well-connected individuals included Russian government officials, journalists, and suppliers. IKEA's connections helped it to
acquire permissions to build and run its stores in numerous Russian cities:
Moscow, St. Petersburg, Kazan, Yekaterinburg, Samara, Ufa, Nizhny
Novgorod, Novosibirsk, Rostov-on-Don, Krasnodar, and Omsk.

When IKEA encountered difficulties in its store operations, it relied on its   11.50
connections to solve the problems. One frequent issue in Russia is unreliable
electricity. To maintain a constant source of electric power, IKEA secured
generators to guarantee that its store operations would not be interrupted.

In 2010, a Russian IKEA executive was accused of accepting bribes from   11.51
the company from which IKEA bought its generators. The executive had
reciprocated by overpaying for the generators by around $200 million.

Also in 2010, IKEA terminated two other Russian executives, Per   11.52
Kaufman and Stefan Gross, for bribing a St. Petersburg electricity company.
The bribe was paid to guarantee that the company would not interrupt
power supply to IKEA stores.

What happened

IKEA had been a public critic of Russian corruption before entering the   11.53
Russian market. It had sworn to uphold its own Western business standards
and ethical principles in doing business in the country. In its actual operations, though, it was unable to manage its business connections effectively
while avoiding corruption.

11.54   IKEA decided to prioritize preserving its culture over pursuing increased growth. In 2011, it decided to slow its Russian development while it addressed concerns about bureaucracy and corruption. In 2012, incoming chief executive, Peter Agnefjäll, noted: "Every company needs something that glues it together. For some companies it is an organizational chart. For other companies such as IKEA, it's our culture."

Sidebar Exercise

How does Agnefjäll's claim about corporate culture versus the corporate "organizational chart" relate to Peter French's claim that the corporation's CID structure makes it a moral person? Do you think that Agnefjäll would consider IKEA to be a moral person, in French's sense? Offer one reason that Agnefjäll would consider IKEA a moral person in French's sense and one reason that he would *not* consider IKEA to be a moral person in this sense. Which reason is stronger? Discuss and support your preferred interpretation.

Historical significance

11.55   The IKEA case presents an interesting insight into the continuing detente between Russia and the West following the end of Cold War. It makes clear that relations between these countries are not totally normalized and that the transition to more normal relations is not without its bumps.

11.56   The Cold War was an era of hostility between Western, capitalist countries like Sweden and the United States, and Eastern, Communist countries. Chief among the Communist states was the Union of Soviet Socialist Republics (USSR), which governed Russia until its dissolution in 1991. After the end of the USSR, Russia experienced high unemployment and poverty. The economy has improved in recent years.

11.57   If IKEA avoids doing business in Russia to maintain its high ethical standards, it would harm its own profit-making interests. It would also, though, further isolate Russia from the rest of the world economy.

Ethical significance: bribery

11.58   One of the most interesting ethical issues in this case is the problem of bribery. Most Westerners intuitively condemn bribery as unethical. But it is worth considering in greater depth what is ethically wrong about bribery.

From a Russian perspective, bribery helps to get things done and main- 11.59
tains strong relationships of trust and loyalty between business partners.
For utilitarians, though, bribery makes goods and services more expensive
than they should be. It adds costs to every level of business: an inefficient
way of accomplishing business. A society that is free from corruption creates more goods and services than one that suffers from a corrupt culture.
That has significant ethical value, for utilitarians.

Sidebar Exercise

Evaluate bribery in the IKEA case from Kantian and virtue ethics
perspectives. What (if anything) do these ethical theories find problematic about bribery? Do you agree with their evaluations? Which
theory's evaluation do you prefer? Why?

The IKEA case is one in which different ethical perspectives truly clash with 11.60
one another. Does the disagreement in this case resemble the kinds of differences of opinion that occur between classmates in business ethics classes,
as they make different recommendations about what businesses should do?

Unlike business ethics class arguments, which are friendly, the IKEA 11.61
disagreement has a serious business consequence. If IKEA employees and
Russian government officials cannot reach accord about what ethical norms
are to govern their relationship, IKEA will be unable to extend its business
in Russia. Russia will be unable to benefit from the tax revenue levied on
IKEA's profits and Russian citizens will be unable to benefit from the utility
of IKEA's products. This situation draws out the importance of trying to
resolve ethical conflicts, which we explore more deeply in Chapter 12.

References and Further Reading

Antonova, Maria. 2010. "Ex-IKEA Boss Bares Russia's 'Chaotic Reality.'" *The
Moscow Times* (Mar. 25). http://www.themoscowtimes.com/business/article/
ex-ikea-boss-bares-russias-chaotic-reality/402494.html

Armstrong, Ashley. 2015. "Legal Highs: GSK Sells Off World's Biggest Opium
Poppy Field." *The Telegraph* (Mar. 4). http://www.telegraph.co.uk/finance/
newsbysector/pharmaceuticalsandchemicals/11449540/Legal-highs-GSK-
sells-off-worlds-biggest-opium-poppy-field.html

Asthana, S. N.. 1954. "The Cultivation of the Opium Poppy in India." *United Nations Office on Drugs and Crime.* https://www.unodc.org/unodc/en/data-and-analysis/bulletin/bulletin_1954-01-01_3_page002.html

Been, Fiona. 2014. "Tasmania Vows to Fight to Keep Poppy Monopoly as Other States Look to Cash In." *ABC News* (Feb. 21). http://www.abc.net.au/news/2014-02-22/tasmania-vows-to-fight-to-keep-poppy-monopoly/5273638

Bhasin, Kim. 2011. "Victoria's Secret Has a Big Problem to Deal with After Revelations of Forced Child Labor." *Business Insider* (Dec. 15). http://www.businessinsider.com/victorias-secret-pr-child-labor-west-africa-2011-12

Bradsher, Keith. 2014. "Shake-Up on Opium Island: Tasmania, Big Supplier to Drug Companies, Faces Changes." *The New York Times* (Jul. 19). http://www.nytimes.com/2014/07/20/business/international/tasmania-big-supplier-to-drug-companies-faces-changes.html?_r=0

Chuck, Elizabeth. 2015. "As Heroin Use Grows in U.S., Poppy Crops Thrive in Afghanistan." *NBC News* (Jul. 7). http://www.nbcnews.com/news/world/heroin-use-grows-u-s-poppy-crops-thrive-afghanistan-n388081

Kolk, Ans and Rob Van Tulder. 2002. "Child Labor and Multinational Conduct: A Comparison of International Business and Stakeholder Codes." *Journal of Business Ethics*, 36(3): 291–301.

Kolk, Ans and Rob Van Tulder. 2004. "Ethics in International Business: Multinational Approaches to Child Labor." *Journal of World Business*, 39: 49–60.

Kramer, Andrew E. 2009. "Ikea Tries to Build Public Case Against Russian Corruption." *The New York Times* (Sept. 11). http://www.nytimes.com/2009/09/12/business/global/12ikea.html?_r=0

Lenard, Brittney A. 2012. "Outsiders in an Inside Game: The Effects of the Traditional Soviet Economy of Favors on Foreigners Doing Business in Contemporary Russia." Pomona Senior Theses. Paper 67. http://scholarship.claremont.edu/pomona_theses/67

Milne, Richard. 2012. "Ikea: Against the Grain." *The Financial Times* (Nov. 13). http://www.ft.com/intl/cms/s/0/ae682db2-2cda-11e2-9211-00144feabdc0.html#axzz3pox3G7ev

Nikishenkov, Oleg. 2010. "Ikea Case Exposes Bribe Culture in Russia." *The Moscow News* (Feb. 23).

Poe, Stephen L. 2009. "Yahoo Goes to China: Lessons for Multinational Firms." *Southern Journal of Business and Ethics*, 1.

Simpson, Cam. 2012. "Victoria's Secret Revealed in Child Picking Burkina Faso Cotton." *Bloomberg Businessweek* (Dec. 15). http://www.bloomberg.com/news/articles/2011-12-15/victoria-s-secret-revealed-in-child-picking-burkina-faso-cotton

Simpson, Cam, *et al.* 2012. "Child Labor for Victoria's Secret Cotton Examined by U.S." *Bloomberg Businessweek* (Jan. 13). http://www.bloomberg.com/news/articles/2012-01-13/child-labor-for-fair-trade-cotton-probed-by-u-s-investigators

The China Post. 2011. "Sweden's Ikea Posts Higher 2010 Sales, Profits Due to China, Russia." (Jan. 15). http://www.chinapost.com.tw/business/europe/2011/01/15/287694/Swedens-Ikea.htm

Venezia, Gerald and Chiulien C. Venezia. 2010. "Yahoo! and the Chinese Dissidents: A Case Study of Trust, Values, and Clashing Cultures." *Journal of Business Case Studies*, 6(2).

Windle J. 2011. "Poppies for Medicine in Afghanistan: Lessons from India and Turkey." *Journal of Asian and African Studies*, 46(6): 663–677.

Xin, Katherine and Wang Haijie (2011). "HBR Case Study: Culture Clash in the Boardroom." *Harvard Business Review* (Sept.). https://hbr.org/2011/09/culture-clash-in-the-boardroom

Part IV
THE FUTURE OF BUSINESS ETHICS

12

PREDICTING AND PREVENTING FUTURE BUSINESS ETHICS SCANDALS

Some of the cases that we examined in the previous chapters involved clear 12.1 wrongdoing. With full knowledge that their decisions were unethical, companies deliberately acted unethically and, in some cases, tried to cover up their unethical actions. Many of those wrongly acting companies damaged their reputations, lost customers, and/or were punished under the law. In some cases, such as the Ford Pinto and the Lehman Brothers cases, federal law was changed so as to prevent other companies from making the unethical decisions those companies made.

Other cases that we examined, though, involved ethical *controversies* 12.2 rather than clear cases of wrongdoing. People disagree about what the company should have done but it wasn't obvious that what they did do was unethical. These kinds of business ethics cases are much more common than full-blown scandals. Controversies in business are, in fact, inevitable. Studying business ethics and becoming familiar with some of the biggest controversies of the past 50 years will not allow you to avoid completely ethical controversies. Rather, you now have tools to think more intelligently about the controversies that arise: to decide what kind of a person you wish to be and by what principles you wish to conduct your business life.

This final chapter has two main goals. First, we review the ethical work 12.3 that we have done throughout the book: using ethical theories to evaluate business ethics controversies. Now that we have a good sense of the resources that various ethical theories offer to evaluate business ethics controversies, we can think a little more deeply about our ethical theories. We saw that they offer different reasons for preferring one action to another.

This is Business Ethics: An Introduction, First Edition. Tobey Scharding.
© 2018 John Wiley & Sons, Inc. Published 2018 by John Wiley & Sons, Inc.

Sometimes, the recommendations conflict with one another. In this chapter, we consider how to address these kinds of conflicts when they arise in ethical business decision-making.

12.4   Second, we draw out some of the major patterns that we saw in our business ethics cases. The point of looking for patterns is to be more sensitive to ethical issues when they arise in our own lives. We can also use the patterns to generate a group of business-related values that we can use to think about what ethical standards we should require of businesses, and of ourselves, going forward.

Resolving Conflicts in Ethics

12.5 Let us begin with a relatively uncontroversial case of wrongdoing: Volkswagen (VW). In that case, VW executives intentionally committed fraud. They installed *defeat devices* in their vehicles that would turn off the technology that limited NOx emissions whenever the vehicles detected normal driving conditions. As a result of this decision, the vehicles emitted 40 times the permitted level of NOx emissions, harming both the environment and people who were in breathing distance of the fraud-committing vehicles.

12.6   This action seems straightforwardly to fail every ethical test we can use on it. Take Kantianism: VW's action obviously becomes self-defeating when universalized. If every car company constructed its emission-controlling technology to switch off whenever the technology detected normal driving conditions, the cars would not be able to trick the EPA that the car complied with environmental regulation standards. The EPA would know, rather, that all cars might be using defeat devices: so the EPA would be sure to check for this. Moreover, in sacrificing people's health to profit-making, VW failed to respect humanity as an end in itself.

12.7   Or, try contract theory. In order for an action to be ethical, according to contract theory, all parties must agree to the action (1) before its consequences of the action are felt; and (2) from the perspective of anyone who is affected by the action. In the thought experiment that contract theory uses to make ethical recommendations, everyone must agree on the action: VW executives earning profits, VW owners driving fraudulent and harmful cars, people living in the cities in which fraudulent VWs are driven— breathing in the excessive emissions. It seems unlikely that people in the latter two positions would agree to the defeat devices. Therefore, VW's action is unethical from the perspective of contract theory, as well.

Even utilitarianism seems well positioned to reject VW's decision. 12.8 Installing the fraud-creating program harmed consumers, harmed the community, and set up the VW executives for a great deal of harm once their fraud was discovered. Would the defeat devices maximize overall utility if the fraud had *not* been discovered? Even in that case, many people would have been harmed. The best outcome possible for VW, becoming the biggest car company in the world, seems insufficient to offset the harms that the defeat devices caused, from a utilitarian point of view.

Even if these ethical evaluations are conclusive, though, we know for a 12.9 fact that VW *did* design their cars deliberately to trick the NOx emissions tests. Does this suggest that companies need not include ethical evaluations in their decision-making processes? Consider whether it is acceptable for companies to decide, for example, "Ethics is fine, but it is not for me. I don't care about being ethical."

Although this might seem like a strange question to consider in the con- 12.10 text of a book about business ethics, it is an important one. From an ethical perspective, we need to take seriously people's decisions that they do not (or that they do) want to be ethical. This is because ethics is self-motivated. Its self-motivated nature plays a central role in what ethics is. Each person must decide for him- or herself what the right thing to do is. This is the point of ethics. Acting ethically is valuable because people hold themselves to the ethical standards upon which they have decided—even when it is difficult or costly for them to do so.

So, it is possible that some people could say, "I don't care about ethics." It 12.11 is unlikely, though, that this is a well-thought-out point of view. Ethical theories rely on aspects of rationality to claim that they are standards people should (or must) consider then rationally decide what to do. It is *possible*, then, for people to focus only on the issues immediately before them, such as succeeding in business or working for the largest car company in the world. But the decisions people have to make in order to succeed in business (or work for the largest car company in the world) implicate what kind of person they will be and what kind of world they will live in. Only a small-minded person, or perhaps one who had never been introduced to ethics, could ignore those issues. Both what kind of person one is and what kind of world one lives in are of deep importance. We examine them in the next two sections.

What kind of a person do you want to be?

12.12   As we saw in the Google case, one of the things that our actions (might) reveal are our *true characters*. Thinking about our actions and how they shape our characters *before* we act helps us to be sure that our actions, and our characters, are what we want them to be. Using ethical theories to think about our actions and our characters helps us to be sure that our actions and our characters are good. Remember that ethics is the study of goodness: what goodness is, how we can *be* good, and how we can act well.

Sidebar Exercise

Google decision-makers decided that they wanted the company to be inclusive, welcoming, and diverse. Which ethical theories (if any) could support these values?

12.13   Unlike science, which accepts or rejects scientific theories based on evidence that all scientists accept, there is no consensus view about which ethical theory you should follow. It's up to you as you think about what kind of life you want to lead. Some people never take the time to reflect on this important issue. One of the points of taking a business ethics class, though, is to do precisely this. Do such reflections distract us from more practical goals, such as being successful in business or working for the world's largest car company? Definitely not. On the contrary, our life goals can help to guide our actions: in the same way that some companies' cultures, like Google and IKEA, helped to guide them through the controversies they faced. As broached above, ethical theories offer insight into *rationality*: the cognitive abilities by which people make decisions about our lives. Reflecting on the various ethical theories, then, can help you to bring your decision-making processes into line with your values.

12.14   This is because different values are compatible with rationality and the main ethical theories express various rationally compatible values. Revisiting these theories to analyze the values they express can help you to start thinking about the important question of what you deeply value, what kind of a person you want to be, and what kind of a life you want to lead. We will consider Aristotle's virtue ethics, utilitarianism, Kantianism, contract theory, natural law theory, care ethics, and feminism.

First, Aristotle. People who have Aristotelian values are concerned about 12.15 moral perfection first and foremost. They always want to strive to be the very best people that they can be, in any situation. So, when they are making decisions at their jobs, they want those decisions to realize their company's aims better than any other choices.

Aristotelians are not narrow-minded in any sense. Even as they are 12.16 making decisions for their businesses, they pay attention to the decisions' other implications. In the VW case, for example, an Aristotelian would carefully think through all of the consequences of the decision to install defeat devices: not just that it would advance the aim of making VW the biggest car company in the world.

In this sense, it seems that Aristotelianism does a very good job of 12.17 answering the question "what kind of a person do I want to be?" The answer is that you are to be the very best person of which you are capable. The ethical theory also seems well suited to help companies avoid ethical problems. It urges them always to strive for the best possible solution, which includes all of the relevant considerations.

Aristotelianism does have some difficulties, however. In the first place, it 12.18 is a very demanding ethical theory. In making business decisions, though, deciding *quickly* is an important value. To make the very best decision requires time, as there are many details to be examined and included in the decision-making process. Another problem with using Aristotle to determine what kind of person you want to be is that people have different ideas about what excellence comprises in particular situations. There is no obvious way to decide between competing options in Aristotelianism. This ethical theory thus offers an important *ideal* for ethical decision-making. But we still have many reasons to turn to other theories.

Sidebar Exercise

Do you identify with or admire any aspects of Aristotelianism? Which ones and why? Do any of the cases we studied use Aristotelian values? Which ones and why? Would any of the cases have benefited from Aristotelian values? Which ones and why?

Utilitarianism offers more specific guidance. The values that it emphasizes 12.19 are happiness, efficiency, and maximization. People who are utilitarians want to do the most to increase happiness overall. Utilitarians in Bentham's tradition do not give a deep interpretation of what, in particular, people should do to increase happiness. Rather, they must discover what makes people happy and do more of that—whatever *that* happens to be. Utilitarians in Mill's tradition have more specific beliefs about what makes people happy. They consider some kinds of happiness to be more important than others. In particular, *higher* forms of happiness—like that brought about by intellectual activities—are more important than lower forms of happiness associated with physical activities.

12.20   Like Aristotelianism, utilitarianism is very demanding. Doing the right thing requires decision-makers to consider very carefully the effects that all possible actions will have on overall happiness. Decision-makers need to consider every little detail that can make people happy or unhappy. This is, again, time-consuming—and time is at a premium in business. In Bentham's interpretation of utilitarianism, moreover, the ethical theory does not lead to much character development. People are simply supposed to do what makes them happy, without thinking about whether the things that make them happy are good or worthwhile.

Sidebar Exercise

Does Mill's utilitarianism seem to support character development better than Bentham's? What kind of a character would Mill's utilitarianism encourage people to develop?

12.21   Kantianism also offers specific guidance about what kind of character people should try to develop. They should try to be fine, upstanding members of society. The most important thing, for this ethical theory, is that people respect humanity and avoid being hypocritical: always hold yourself to the same standard that you expect from other people.

12.22   Although these are important guidelines for character development, they may seem to leave out *personal* development. That is, Kantianism seems like all work, no play. As long as people do their duty, for Kantian ethics, it does not seem to matter much what kind of people they are or how much happiness they create for themselves or others.

12.23   So far, then, we have a few candidates for values that can inform characters. Aristotelians are perfectionists who strive for excellence. Utilitarians value happiness. People should be socially-minded and not put their own happiness first. Rather, they should think about how their decisions affect other people and try to create as much happiness as possible—even if that means that some people, including themselves might not be that happy. Kantians value being upstanding citizens who hold themselves to the same standards as those to which they hold other people. Kantians value logic and rational thought. They think that it is very important to reflect deeply and clearly about important matters.

What about natural law theory, contract theory, care ethics, and femi- 12.24 nism? Each of these ethical theories highlights additional values of ethical importance. Natural law theory focuses on the way that human beings are naturally—before they have affected their airs of cultural sophistication. It directs us to consider those things that are basic to human existence as being more important than what is superfluous. Its key value could be summarized as: basic is best. So, in the Walmart case, they might point out that Walmart employees' basic ability to support themselves and survive is more important than the Walton family enriching itself. Employees' basic subsistence might even be more important than Walmart consumers' convenience in making many purchases from the huge store.

Natural law theory provides excellent "rule-of-thumb" guidance. But 12.25 this guidance is rather general. Moreover, although considerations of what is natural for human beings are important, the fact is that most human beings today are far from their natural origins. And we need guidance about what kind of people we should be in our sophisticated cultural surroundings.

Contract theory appeals to the important value of consent. A person's 12.26 consent makes an action ethical; lack of consent makes the same action unethical. This viewpoint captures something deep about ethics. Like Aristotelianism and utilitarianism, though, it is very demanding. It is hard to imagine people who are harmed by an action agreeing to that action. But the world is full of difficult trade-offs and sometimes some parties will be harmed by an action. Our ethical values, and our ethical theories, must be able to address the possibility that it will be impossible to avoid harming every party that is affected by a decision.

Care ethics highlights key values neglected by other theories: the 12.27 importance of building and maintaining relationships with other people, the centrality of showing care to what is good in life. In business's competitive context, however, it may be difficult to know how to apply these values. And they leave many important questions unanswered, such as what is the right way to balance profit-making activities against cultivating relationships and showing care. One case that reflects this concern is the TransCanada case.

Sidebar Exercise

What other cases involve the importance of building and maintaining relationships? How do these cases involve this value? How important are relationships, ethically speaking?

12.28   Finally, feminist ethics focuses on the importance of empowering marginalized people. Centered on the value of equality, feminists work to extend equal care and concern to people who have been oppressed or excluded from society's opportunities. The Google case is a good example of a company acting with feminist values. In the Google case, the company's success and profit-making were already secure. Including more women and people of color in its workplaces was a goal to which it turned its attention once it was already extremely successful. Less prosperous companies, who are not already the leaders in their segment of the market, may be less able to attend to these important concerns.

Sidebar Exercise

What kind of people do their actions suggest that VW executives were trying to be? What kind of people do you think they *should* have tried to be?

What kind of world do you want to live in?

12.29   What kind of a person you want to be is not the only important ethical consideration involved in the decisions you make. Using ethical reasoning in decision-making also raises questions about what kind of world you want to live in. One of the things that ethics helps students to realize is how their decisions are connected to many things outside of themselves. Think back to our discussions about ethical norms in Chapter 4. The ethical norms according to which you make your decisions are the same ethical norms that other people use. The way you interpret the ethical norms can resonate with, and influence, other people's decision-making when you discuss important ethical issues with them. One of the reasons that philosophical conversations are so interesting, and so difficult, is that they engage norms that everyone uses. They might interpret those norms (and what they require) differently from one another, though.

Some of the most important ways that business decision-making implicates what kind of world you want to live in are as follows. Many business decisions have consequences for distributive justice: how wide are the economic inequalities in society and what entitles people to the share of social resources that they enjoy. Business decisions also impact the environment, including the availability of basic resources like water and how polluted the world is. Finally, business decisions can develop or harm their countries' relationships with foreign nations. 12.30

Let us begin with questions about distributive justice. Very many business decisions influence the extent of economic inequalities: how much executives and employees are paid, how much products cost, to whom products are marketed. The Walmart business model, for example, could have contributed to wide economic inequalities in society, in the sense that Walmart employees were paid a very low wage. On the other hand, though, Walmart provided many jobs for low-skilled workers. Those jobs might otherwise not have been available. So we need to be careful in thinking about how business decisions contribute to distributive justice. 12.31

On another aspect of economic inequalities, the decision of A.I.G. executives to trim their salaries to only one dollar following their bailout enforced the idea that compensation should track merit. Even though they could have demanded their full salaries, the executives decided to set an ethical example, instead. 12.32

Questions about the environment are similarly difficult, but also closely involved in many business decisions. Businesses use up natural resources. To act ethically, though, the businesses should consider how their uses of resources affect other people. Using groundwater in Rajasthan is good for Coca-Cola India. It allows it to create profits for itself. But Coca-Cola's use means that less water is available for the people who live in Rajasthan. If the company is using water ethically, it must carefully consider how to balance these interests. 12.33

The VW case presents a similar problem. VW's actions were clearly fraudulent and illegal. But perhaps U.S. NOx emissions standards are too high. Many people are willing to deal with some pollution. The question is how much. 12.34

Sidebar Exercise

What is your view of our relationship with the environment? Protecting it might mean limiting business innovations. What is the right thing to do? To what extent may business innovation be limited, in order to protect the environment?

12.35 Still other cases require us to think about relationships with foreign nations. Businesses can try to build a more global world, in which people share more values. But they have to decide if they want to try to extend liberal rights to people in countries where liberal rights are not currently respected. And, if they do want to try to extend liberal rights, they have to decide how to act ethically even if operating in the country that does not yet recognize liberal rights forces them to use that nation's values rather than their own.

Looking for and Understanding New Cases

12.36 Now that we have a firmer sense of what kind of people we want to be and what kind of world we want to live in—or, at least, how to think about these interesting and difficult questions—we can turn back to business. We begin by surveying the 20 cases we have covered, looking for patterns among the cases that can help us to be alert to ethical problems in our own lives. It is especially valuable to see patterns in the cases because the patterns help us to understand how recent cases, like the VW case, came about—and anticipate how future cases are likely to develop. We will analyze the kinds of ethical problems that businesses are most likely to experience. Next, we will generalize from these patterns to try to set forth some key values for business, again with the idea of offering guidance for future encounters.

Patterns of wrongdoing

12.37 We saw in our classic business ethics dilemmas that businesses can encounter ethical controversies when they fail to give enough consideration to the interests of their customers, employees, communities, and to the business itself. Let's take a look back at our cases to understand how the business ethics dilemmas relate to the company's failure to value these "stakeholder" interests. We will consider customers, employees, communities, and the business itself, in turn.

Customers   In the Pinto case, the ethical controversy arose because Ford   12.38
failed to give enough attention to its customers' interests. It failed to consider its customers' interests adequately in the sense that it sold a defective product that harmed, and in some instances killed, its customers. But Ford never warned its customers that these injuries were possible. We can also see this lack of enough regard in the Four Loko case. Four Loko might have shown inadequate concern for its customers' wellbeing when it failed to warn them about the dangerous effects of mixing alcohol and caffeine. The company also appeared to manipulate customers, especially young customers, through its advertising. In the Facebook case, furthermore, the company might have treated its customers unfairly by using their personal information to market to them.

There are many other cases that arose because of inadequate concern   12.39
for customers' interests. The Pfizer case, for example, focused on the company's efforts to sell its customers a high-priced prescription drug and to prevent them from purchasing the less expensive generic version. Abercrombie & Fitch might have mistreated potential customers by only marketing to people who met a certain fit, good-looking image. These two cases suggest that a company's advertisements are an especially good place to look when trying to determine whether companies demonstrate appropriate regard for their customers.

We also saw inadequate concern for customers' interests in a few other   12.40
cases. In the Countrywide case, for example, employees sold customers expensive loans when a lower-priced product might have been more suitable. They also may have sold customers loans that customers never would be able to pay, leading to customers losing their homes, along with their initial investments in those homes, and eventually to the 2008 financial collapse. The FieldScripts case also raised a concern about how businesses treat their employees. Similar to the Facebook case, it questioned whether businesses may use their customers data in ways that harm the customer, such as by selling the data to rivals who will use it to surpass the customers in business. This case also addressed the important issue of trust between the business and the customer.

In the Yahoo case, we saw a more troubling kind of disregard for the   12.41
interests of the customer. In that case, the company provided information

about the customer to the authorities (in this case, the Chinese government) that was used to incriminate and imprison the customer. In each of these cases, the business might have been able to avoid or mitigate the ethical controversy by taking more time to appreciate and respect their customers' interests in purchasing and using their goods and services.

Sidebar

The Pinto case resembled our early case study, the Case of the Substandard Notes. The earlier case ended with the warning: let the buyer beware. In both cases, the consumer has some responsibility. (In the earlier case, the *consumer* was the student who borrowed the other student's notes.) But the business has some responsibility, too. Figuring out how much responsibility to assign to each of them is an important part of developing your ethical reasoning.

12.42 *Employees* What about appropriate regard for the interests of their employees? In the Walmart case, the company forced employees to work very hard and paid them low wages. Although this was good for business, it was bad for the employees. Acting ethically does not necessarily require companies to pay employees the maximum possible wage and treat them as nicely as possible. It does, though, suggest that they should consider their employees' interests. A similar issue arose in the Amazon case. The Amazon employees did not complain that their wages were too low. They were overworked in a similar manner as the Walmart case, though. The Amazon case also brought out the important ethical idea that there is more to life than work. Some companies, though, do not appear to acknowledge the importance of life outside of work.

12.43   The Bechtel case, and perhaps the GlaxoSmithKline and Herbalife cases, raise questions about what companies owe their longtime employees and other people with whom they do business. GlaxoSmithKline decided whether to move its poppy fields, which would deprive Tasmanian poppy farmers of an important source of revenue. Herbalife continually recruited new salespeople, even though very few of these salespeople were able to earn a decent living by selling the Herbalife nutritional products. In the Google case, by contrast, we saw an employer taking extraordinary measures to increase the inclusiveness of their workplace culture. It is worth thinking about the differences in these companies' cultures.

Sidebar

The Walmart and Amazon cases resemble our early case study, the Case of the Overly Demanding Internship. In that case, a college student received a great work opportunity. The conditions of that work opportunity, though, might have been exploitative. Deciding how to balance the good of a work opportunity against the bad of exploitation is one of the skills we can develop in reflecting on these cases.

Communities   A number of companies in our case studies failed to dem- 12.44 onstrate concern for the interests of the community. Nomura might have fail to show adequate concern for other businesses and investors, in the sense that it engaged in insider trading. Insider trading provides non-public information to certain parties so that they, but not uninformed businesses and investors, can benefit from it. Coca-Cola India could have done more to benefit the community in which it was operating, at least according to some people in that community. TransCanada also experienced a conflict with the community that lived near the land through which it wished to build its oil pipeline. Did the company navigate that conflict appropriately? VW put its interest in becoming the world's biggest car company before the interests of the people living in the communities in which its NOx-emitting vehicles would travel.

Sidebar

The VW case resembled our early case study, the Case of the Fair Distribution of Chores. A college student found that her ambitious course load caused her to fall behind in fulfilling her obligations to her roommates. The students' efforts to succeed academically were impressive. It didn't seem fair, though, when she failed to do her part to maintain a nice apartment. In the same way, even ambitious companies need to do their part to maintain a pleasant world for us to live in. But how *much* are they required to do to keep our world habitable, as a matter of ethics? Try answering this question using Kantian ethics, utilitarianism, and virtue ethics. Do the answers provided by these ethical theories surprise you?

12.45 *The Business Itself*   Finally, some companies even failed to show regard for their own success as businesses in the future. We saw this especially in the cases about firms that went out of business: Enron and Lehman Brothers. Countrywide's and A.I.G's risky activities also nearly cost them their existence. All of the serious ethical scandals caused the businesses' stock prices to plunge. VW's deliberate deception, and the hefty fines that it might have to pay, might force it to declare bankruptcy as a result of its fraudulent business practices.

Sidebar

The VW case also resembled an early case study: the Case of the Too-Easy-to-Cheat Course. In that case, a college student deliberately cheated in a course when conditions permitted it. What the student did, and what VW did, were clearly unethical. They give us an opportunity to think about how people, and businesses, can try to fortify themselves to act ethically—even when there is a temptation to cheat.

Key values for business

12.46 When we think about business ethics, we should pay attention to these issues. How do companies' actions affect their customers, employees, communities, and the companies themselves? We want to ensure that businesses show appropriate regard for these crucial stakeholders. When stakeholders complain about businesses, we should listen carefully to those complaints. The mere fact that people are complaining does not mean that the company has acted wrongfully. It just signifies that we should pay attention to their claims and investigate further.

12.47   What other things should we look for? In deciding whether companies are acting appropriately in the future, we should go back to our values.

- *Excellence.* Is the business doing everything it can? Would people you admire act in the way that the company is acting?
- *Happiness.* Would different decisions create more overall happiness? Is the business failing to optimize?
- *Integrity.* Is the company holding itself to the appropriate standards?

- *Human nature.* Is the company respecting human nature and protecting basic human interests?
- *Consent.* Would all people affected by the company's decision agree with the decision, if they were given a choice?
- *Care.* Do the company's actions show appropriate respect for the importance of human relationships?
- *Feminism.* Is the company treating all people equally? Is it showing respect for every human being with whom it interacts?

Thinking about these questions as new business ethics questions emerge can help you to figure out when businesses are acting ethically. Monitoring businesses by reading the newspaper and discussing business activities with your friends and family will help to make these values part of your life. Thinking about the questions at work can make it more straightforward for businesses to include ethical concerns in their decision-making procedures.

But we should not hope for too much ease. Ethics is, by its very nature, 12.48 difficult. The questions it raises are deep and important. Answering them well can make the difference between having, and not having, a meaningful life that is of deep value to you: the person who is living your life.

Technology and the Future of Business Ethics

In addition to the values noted above, the cases bring out some other 12.49 important trends, which might play a role in business ethics controversies of the future. One of the most intriguing is the growing role of data in business. We will conclude the book with this topic.

We examined issues concerning ethical uses of data in the Amazon, 12.50 Facebook, and FieldScripts cases. In the latter two cases, we asked questions about who owns data: the person that the data is about or the company that tracks the data. In the Amazon case, we briefly discussed the way in which a technology company used data about its employees to monitor their performances, including making promotion and termination decisions. The Facebook and FieldScripts cases help to draw out how important data is and what a large role it is coming to play in twenty-first-century businesses and the businesses of the future. But the Amazon case might point to an even more significant way in which the widespread availability of data might affect business itself.

12.51   In Chapter 2, we surveyed the theory of the firm. We were interested both in why firms are structured the way they are and also in why firms exist in the first place. As we noted in that chapter, it would be less expensive for entrepreneurs to hire independent contractors to perform work for them as the work was needed. Concerns about finding those contractors in a timely way and assuring their loyalty to the firm ultimately motivated the creation of firms staffed with a large number of full-time employees, even though full-time employees are very expensive. Advances in data collection could address the two problems noted above: finding qualified contractors and assuring their loyalty to the firm.

12.52   In the 2010s, we have already seen some businesses move away from full-time employees and begin to use large numbers of independent contractors to perform work for them. Uber, the driving service, and Airbnb, the accommodations service, are key examples of large companies where numbers of full-time staff are greatly reduced due to the power of data science. Uber uses data to match drivers to people who are willing to pay for a ride. Airbnb uses data to match people with a place to stay to people who wish to rent a room. This form of business organization could become even more widespread as data collection and dissemination technologies improve, perhaps challenging the existence of large firms altogether.

Sidebar Exercise

How would the lack of big firms change what we have studied in this book? Should firms *try* to be smaller according to Kantian ethics, utilitarianism, virtue ethics, and other ethical theories?

INDEX

Abercrombie & Fitch, 162–166, 241
Ackman, Bill, 178–182, 188–189
action, 3–4, 9–12, 25, 35, 41–42,
    54–65, 68–74, 82, 89–90, 99,
    103, 124, 142–143, 157, 206,
    231–233, 237
alienation, 115–117
Altman, Matthew, 88–91
Amazon, 143–148, 242–245
American International Group
    (A.I.G.), 130–131
Aristotelian ethics, 70, 76, 235
Aristotle, 50–51, 67–76, 235

bailout, 130–133, 147, 174, 189, 239
Beauchamp, Tom, 152–155, 165
Bechtel Corporation, 121–126, 242
benefit, 19, 65, 97–99, 110–111, 147,
    207, 210, 215, 225, 243
Bentham, Jeremy, 50–57, 61, 67–68,
    76, 105
Blockbuster, 44–46, 156
Bowie, Norman, 66, 76
bribery, 222–225
British Petroleum (B.P.), 40–42, 50, 63,
    74–75, 77, 91

bureaucracy, 84, 88–90, 92, 133, 224
Burkina Faso, 226

capacity, 4–5, 73–77, 89, 116, 129, 153
capital, 15, 18, 173–174, 179, 181, 184
capitalism, 112, 115
categorical imperative, 62–63, 69
certainty, 54–55
chain of command, 84–85
child labor, 214–218, 226
China, 205, 208, 218, 219, 221, 223,
    226–227
choice, 16, 62, 72, 152–155, 164, 245
Civil Rights Act of 1964 (Title VII), 21,
    126, 128
Clean Air Act, 21
Clean Water Act, 21
Coase, Ronald, 31
Coca-Cola India, 190–193, 198,
    207–209, 239, 243
coercion, 152–153
collective responsibility, 89, 91
common world-ownership, 97
communism, 115
community, 9, 14, 18–19, 21, 23, 27–28,
    32, 40, 70, 78, 81, 146, 221, 233, 243

conclusion, 12, 29–30, 57
conscience, 4–5, 23, 50, 67. 77, 221
Consumer Product Safety Act, 20–21
contractors, 16, 246
contract theory, 51, 72–74, 108, 145,
    232–237
controversy, 12, 40, 132, 145, 151, 152,
    164, 168. 176, 219. 220, 241
corporate
    identity, 43, 80, 82, 83, 122, 131, 137,
        144, 150, 156, 159, 162, 168, 173,
        179, 184, 191, 194, 199, 204, 205,
        211, 215, 219, 222
    personhood, 77–80, 83, 92
    policy, 82
corporate internal decision-making
    structure, 80
corruption, 223–225
cost-benefit analysis, 18, 25–26, 33, 36,
    52, 85, 213
counter example, 106
countrywide financial, 168–171
credit-default swap (CDS), 131–132
customers, 14, 18–21, 23–5, 28, 35, 38,
    45, 74, 95, 131, 144, 149, 157–159,
    162–163, 168–169, 173, 221–222,
    231, 240–242

data privacy, 201–202
deductive argument, 29–30
Deepwater Horizon, 40–41
defeat device, 206, 232–233, 235
dependence effect, 149, 158, 161,
    165–166
derivative, 131
difference principle, 110–112
diffusion of responsibility, 88–89
discount rate, 25–26
discrimination, 21, 38–39, 121, 123,
    128, 136, 163–164
distributive justice, 95, 106–107, 111,
    207, 213, 239

diversity, 136, 138–140, 147–148, 164
division of labor, 93, 95, 112–117
Dominant Model, 18–19, 79, 106
due process, 127
duration, 54–56
duty, 61–63, 67, 72, 90, 236

emissions, 239
employees, 15–21, 23–24, 27–28, 32,
    38–39, 43, 45, 74, 80, 82, 85–90,
    93, 95–96, 111, 121–132, 135–141,
    143–147, 150, 159, 163–164, 168,
    184–186, 188, 201, 215, 216, 219,
    221, 225, 237, 239–242, 244–248
employment
    at-will, 121–122, 125
    just-cause, 136
end, 4, 35, 49, 56, 59, 63–66, 68, 71, 88,
    94, 106, 130, 164, 175, 192, 212,
    224, 225, 232
end in itself, 65, 232
Enron, 32, 42–46, 50, 63, 75, 83, 85, 91,
    145, 244
Epstein, Richard, 125, 128–130
Equal Pay Act of 1963, 21
equity, 15, 170, 172–173, 183
ethical
    question, 4, 55, 161, 172, 222
    standard, 5, 24, 71, 218, 222, 224,
        232–233
    theory, 10, 50, 56, 61–63, 73, 89–90,
        108, 114, 132, 155, 161, 203, 208,
        234–236
    value, 4, 49–51, 61, 77, 225, 237
ethics of care, 72, 74–75, 145, 185
event, 3, 11, 126
excellence, 70, 235–236, 244
exception, 62, 64–65, 125, 212
executive, 12, 15, 18, 24, 28, 32, 34–35,
    41, 74–75, 85–86, 95, 121,
    130–136, 140, 147–148, 160,
    185–186, 222–224, 232–233, 239

executive compensation, 121,
130–136, 148
extent, 5, 11, 21, 42, 54–56, 71, 77, 84,
90, 133, 149, 158, 160, 178, 183,
187, 194, 197, 210, 218–219,
239–240

Facebook, 138, 145, 146, 156–158, 166,
198, 241, 245
fair equality of opportunity, 110
Fair Labor Standards Act (FLSA), 39
fairness, 126, 128, 129
fair trade, 181, 216
Federal National Mortgage Association
("Fannie Mae"), 177
feminist ethics, 72, 75–76, 130, 160,
163, 171, 196, 217, 238
fiction theory, 79–81
FieldScripts, 198–203, 241, 245
First Nations, 197
food supply, 190, 198, 208
Ford Motor Company, 33, 36, 46, 78,
80, 125
Ford Pinto, 32–35, 46, 73, 78, 80,
82, 231
formula of humanity, 63, 65, 94, 153
formula of universal law, 63
Four Loko, 150–152, 158, 165–166, 241
Freeman, Edward R., 19–20, 22, 24–25,
27–28, 31, 79, 106
French, Peter, 78–85, 87, 90–91
Friedman, Milton, 22–25, 29–31, 70, 78
full-time workers, 16, 38

Galbraith, John Kenneth, 158, 161, 165
General Motors, 66
GlaxoSmithKline, 211–214, 242
global warming, 193, 198
Google, 136–141, 145–147, 162, 221,
234, 238, 242
guaranteed political rights, 126
Guz, John, 128

harm, 11, 20, 141, 205, 214, 221, 224,
233, 239, 241
hedonic calculus, 53–55, 59
hedonic utilitarianism, 60
Herbalife, 178–183, 188–189, 242
holism, 70–71
human rights, 209, 218–221
hypothetical agreement, 73

Iacocca, Lee, 34, 36, 46, 78, 80, 82, 85,
88–89, 95, 125
IKEA, 222–227, 234
impoverishment, 116–117
inclusion, 164
India, 44, 46, 185, 190–193, 196, 207–209,
212–213, 226–227, 239, 243
insider trading, 167, 184–189, 243
integrity, 70–71, 159
intensity, 54–56
intentionality, 78, 82, 87
interdependent, 16, 24, 83, 107,
113–114, 179–180, 202, 208, 246
intuition, 4, 13, 50, 94, 150,
199–200, 208
investment
banking, 173
funded, 177
long, 177
short, 177
unfunded, 177

Jackall, Robert, 83, 87
Jeffries, Mike, 162
judgment, 4, 54, 66, 69–71, 124, 151

Kantian ethics, 62–63, 65, 67–68,
73–74, 77, 82, 88–91, 94, 132–133,
139, 142, 236, 243, 246
Kant, Immanuel, 4, 13, 50, 61–63, 65,
67–68, 76, 88–89, 91
Keystone XL pipeline, 195–196,
208–209

labor
    alienation of, 116–117
    impoverishment of, 116
Lay, Ken, 42–44
legal aggregate theory, 80
Lehman Brothers, 131–132, 171–173,
    179, 181, 185, 189, 200, 231, 244
leverage ratio, 174–175
Lipitor, 158–161, 165
loan
    Alt-A, 170
    piggyback, 169
    prime, 168–170
    subprime, 168–171, 175
Lockean proviso, 106, 111
Locke, John, 96, 106

manipulation, 44, 45, 152–154, 158
mark-to-market accounting, 42–46, 50,
    67, 76
Marx, Karl, 112, 115
maxim, 63–66, 68, 142–143
McNamara, Robert, 36, 78, 85, 88–89, 95
mean, doctrine of the, 69
means, mere, 65–66, 68, 94, 197
Mill, John Stuart, 57–58, 61, 67–68, 76
Monsanto, 198–201
moral hazard, 174
Moriarty, Jeffrey, 134, 148
mortgage-backed security (MBS),
    131–132, 168, 171–173, 175
multi-level marketer (MLM), 179–180

National Labor Relations Act, 20
natural law theory, 51, 72–74, 136, 140,
    161, 234, 237
Nomura securities company, 184–189
norm, 10, 60–61, 64–65, 170

objection, 21, 22, 38, 40, 42, 45, 56, 57,
    67, 83, 87, 90–91, 101, 104–105,
    107, 111, 139, 151, 155, 161, 202,
    203, 217

Pershing Square Capital Management
    (PSCM), 179–180, 183
person
    artificial, 22–23
    legal, 81
    metaphysical, 82
    moral, 80, 81, 88, 90–91, 122, 183,
    191, 224
persuasion, 152–153
Pfizer, 159–161, 241
phronimos, 68
Phusion Projects, 150–151
pleasures
    higher, 57–59
    lower, 57–59
political economy, 92–95
Ponzi scheme, 180–181
predatory lending, 167, 171
premise, 29
principles of justice, 108–109
private property, 110–112
productivity, 112, 115–116
profit motive, 14–15
public policy, 126, 128
purity, 54–56
pyramid scheme, 178, 180–182

quantify, 53–54

rank and yank, 145–146
rational capacity, 62
Rawls, John, 96–107
raw materials, 210–211, 214, 216–218
redistribution, 172
remoteness, 54–56
repeatability, 54, 55
reporting system, 86
repressive political regimes, 210,
    218, 221
risk, 135, 167–168, 172–174, 176,
    178, 179, 182, 188, 195, 200,
    203, 213, 221
risk tolerance, 174

ritual deference, 86
role identity, 70
Russia, 222–227

Sac and Fox Tribe, 195
security, 17, 41–42, 217
self-ownership, 99–101, 143
sensitivity analysis, 26, 52
shareholder, 15, 18, 20, 25, 135, 187
shareholder theory, 18, 22
short
    selling, 167, 179, 182–183, 187
    squeeze, 182
Skilling, Jeff, 43–44
Smith, Adam, 112–117
social responsibility, 22, 31, 209
sole proprietor, 18
Solomon, Robert, 70
special purpose entities (SPEs), 42, 45
stakeholder theory, 49, 79, 106
state of nature, 96, 98, 102, 107, 111, 117
stock exchange, 15, 186
stockholder, 15, 45
suppliers, 14, 18–19, 23, 28, 66, 195,
    211, 222–223
sustainability, 28, 201
synthetic collateralized debt obligation
    (synthetic CDO), 176–177, 179
systemic risk, 176

targeted advertising, 156–158
theory of the firm, 14, 16
thought experiment, 109, 193, 232
too big to fail, 174
trade secrets, 16, 34
tragedy of the commons, the, 190–191,
    193, 207, 209
Trail of Tears, 196
TransCanada, 194–196, 238, 243
trust in business, 203, 209

unconscious bias, 139, 141–143, 147
universal law, 63–64
utilitarianism, 53–57, 59, 61–63, 65,
    67–68, 71, 73–74, 76–77, 90, 114,
    132, 197, 233–237, 243, 246
    act, 59–61
    Bentham's, 52–53, 59–61, 123, 160
    Mill's, 57, 59–61, 73, 140, 201,
        220, 236
    rule, 59–63, 169
utility, 51–53, 56–57, 59–63, 69,
    128–129, 134, 225, 233

Victoria's Secret, 214–218, 226
virtue, 17, 51–52, 67–73, 76–77, 90,
    100, 103, 124, 132–133, 142,
    159, 175, 181, 185, 202, 225,
    234, 243, 246
virtue ethics, 68–69, 71, 73, 77, 90, 124,
    132, 133, 142, 175, 181, 185, 202,
    225, 234, 243, 246
Volkswagen (VW), 203–208, 232–233,
    235, 238–240, 243–244

Walmart, 32, 38–40, 46, 50, 63, 74, 77,
    85, 90–91, 95–96, 110–11, 144,
    237, 239, 242–243
Walton family, 38, 111, 237
Walton, Sam, 38
water shortage, 191, 193, 198
Werhane, Patricia, 125–129, 148,
    187, 189
Williamson, Oliver E., 17, 31
work-life balance, 121, 143–144,
    146, 148
wrong, 3–6, 11–13, 21, 26, 33–34,
    41–42, 49–50, 79, 126–127,
    172, 224

Yahoo, 138, 218–222, 226–227, 241